Religion, Secularization and Political Thought

The increasing secularization of political thought between the mid-seventeenth and mid-nineteenth centuries has often been noted, but rarely described in detail. The contributors to this volume consider the significance of the relationship between religious beliefs, dogma and secular ideas in British political philosophy from Thomas Hobbes to J.S. Mill.

During this period, Britain experienced the advance of natural science, the spread of education and other social improvements, and reforms in the political realm. These changes forced religion to account for itself and to justify its existence, both as a social institution and as a collection of fundamental articles of belief about the world and its operations. The intellectual endeavours that fuelled this predicament, and the consequent maelstrom of disputation, engaged some of the most influential figures in the British political tradition. The essays in this collection highlight a selection of these writers, and examine their ideas with reference to other writers of the age. The volume as a whole conveys the crucial importance of the association between religion, secularization and political thought.

The Editor

James E. Crimmins is Assistant Professor of Political Theory and International Politics, Huron College, University of Western Ontario.

RELIGION, SECULARIZATION AND POLITICAL THOUGHT
THOMAS HOBBES TO J. S. MILL

Edited by James E. Crimmins

Routledge
London and New York

First published 1989 by Routledge
11 New Fetter Lane, London EC4P 4EE

Simultaneously published in the USA and Canada
by Routledge
a division of Routledge, Chapman and Hall, Inc.
29 West 35th Street, New York, NY 10001

©1990 James E. Crimmins

Typeset by LaserScript Limited, Mitcham, Surrey
Printed and bound in Great Britain by
Biddles Ltd, Guildford and King's Lynn

British Library Cataloguing in Publication Data

Religion, secularization and political thought: Thomas Hobbes to J.S. Mill.
  1. Great Britain. Religion. Political aspects
  I. Crimmins, James E. (James Edward), *1953– .*
  291. 1' 77' 0941

ISBN 0-415-02653-9

Library of Congress Cataloging-in-Publication Data

Religion, secularization, and political thought: Thomas Hobbes to J.S. Mill /
  edited by James E. Crimmins.
     p. cm.
    Collection of essays, the result of a series of seminars held at Huron
    College during the academic year 1987–1988.
  Bibliography: p.
  Includes index.
  Contents: The religious and the secular in the work of Thomas Hobbes /
  S.A. State — John Locke, Socinian or natural law theorist? / David
  Wootton — The religious, the secular, and the worldly / Roger L. Emerson
  — Science and secularization in Hume, Smith, and Bentham / Douglas G.
  Long — Edmund Burke and John Wesley / Frederick Dreyer — Religion,
  utility, and politics / James E. Crimmins — From God to man? / T.R.
  Sansom — J.S. Mill and the religion of humanity / Richard Vernon.
    ISBN 0-415-02653-9
    1. Religion—History. 2. Secularism—History. 3. Political
  science—Great Britain—History. I. Crimmins, James E., 1953– .
  II. Huron College.
  BL50.R4616 1989
  320'.01—dc 19

                                           89-5910
                                            CIP

Contents

List of Contributors

Acknowledgements

Introduction
James E. Crimmins   1

1 The religious and the secular in the work of Thomas Hobbes
   S. A. State   17

2 John Locke: Socinian or natural law theorist?
   David Wootton   39

3 The religious, the secular and the worldly: Scotland 1680–1800
   Roger L. Emerson   68

4 Science and secularization in Hume, Smith and Bentham
   Douglas G. Long   90

5 Edmund Burke and John Wesley: the legacy of Locke
   Frederick Dreyer   111

6 Religion, utility and politics: Bentham versus Paley
   James E. Crimmins   130

7 From God to man? F. D. Maurice and changing ideas of God
   and man
   T. R. Sansom   153

8 J. S. Mill and the religion of humanity
   Richard Vernon   167

Bibliography   183

Index   196

Contributors

James E. Crimmins is an Assistant Professor in the Department of History and Political Science at Huron College, where he teaches Political Theory. He is the author of articles on the moral and political thought of eighteenth-century England, is currently editing Bentham's *Church-of-Englandism* for *The Collected Works of Jeremy Bentham*, and his book on *Secular Utilitarianism* is to be published by Clarendon Press, Oxford. Dr Crimmins is the 1989–90 recipient of the American Society for Eighteenth Century Studies Fellowship.

Frederick Dreyer is Professor of History at the University of Western Ontario. He specializes in the history of modern Britain and has published articles on the thought of John Wesley and Edmund Burke. His publications include *Burke's Politics: A Study in Whig Orthodoxy* (Wilfrid Laurier Press, 1979).

Roger L. Emerson is Professor of History at the University of Western Ontario and a former editor of *Man and Nature/L'Homme et la Nature*, the journal of the Canadian Society for Eighteenth Century Studies. He has published widely on eighteenth-century life and thought in the journals of his discipline, including a three-part history of 'The Philosophical Society of Edinburgh' (1737–83) in the *British Journal for the History of Science*.

Douglas G. Long is an Associate Professor of Political Science at the University of Western Ontario, where he teaches Political Theory and the History of Political Thought. He is the author of *Bentham on Liberty* (Toronto University Press, 1977), has written a number of articles on the English utilitarian Jeremy Bentham, and is currently editing several volumes of early manuscripts for *The Collected Works of Jeremy Bentham*.

Robert Sansom is an Associate Professor of Political Science at the University of Western Ontario. His teaching and research interests centre on nineteenth- and twentieth-century Political Thought.

Contributors

Stephen State has taught Political Theory and the History of Political Thought in the Department of Political Science at the University of Western Ontario. At present he has a two-year leave from teaching financed by the Social Sciences and Humanities Research Council of Canada. He has published articles and reviews in various journals in the United Kingdom and North America, and is now working on a new translation of Hobbes's *Ecclesiastical History*.

Richard Vernon is Professor of Political Science at the University of Western Ontario, where he teaches Political Theory. His publications include *Commitment and Change: Georges Sorel and the Idea of Revolution* (University of Toronto Press, 1978), and *Citizenship and Order: Studies in French Political Thought* (University of Toronto Press, 1986). He is currently working on the development of liberal political thought.

David Wootton taught the History of Political Thought in the Department of Political Science at the University of Western Ontario from 1987–89. He now occupies the Lansdowne Chair in the Humanities at the University of Victoria. He has published articles on religion and political thought, edited and introduced *Divine Right and Democracy* (Penguin, 1986), and is the author of *Paolo Sarpi: Between Renaissance and Enlightenment* (Cambridge University Press, 1983).

Acknowledgements

It is one of the happy coincidences of my period of study and lecturing at the University of Western Ontario and Huron College that among my colleagues I should find so many who shared my interest in the vexed question of the affiliation between religious beliefs and dogma and political thought. A seminar series seemed the way to quarry effectively this mine of sacredness and secularity. This was duly arranged at Huron College, the founding institution of the University of Western Ontario and a testimony to its Anglican roots, during the academic year 1987–88. The result is the collection the reader now holds.

I would like to thank those colleagues (not all of whom are represented by the following essays) from whom I received encouragement and advice, and to Huron College for providing the appropriate setting for us to explore the subject-matter of this anthology. Finally, I would like to take this opportunity to express my warmest gratitude to Johanne Lapensée-Crimmins for her patience and support over the past few years during which I have sought to bring to fruition this and other projects.

J.E.C.
Huron College
University of Western Ontario

Introduction

James E. Crimmins

For long the potent, often dangerous mix of religion and politics was thought to be a thing of the past. The existence of counter-examples – places like Ulster and Cyprus, where sectarian and national identities coincide clothing nationalist struggles in religious garb – did little to dispel this myth. They were either ignored or dismissed as archaic exceptions. It is only in recent years that we have come to question this view of the relationship between religion and politics. The reappearance of dogmatic authoritarian religions – fundamentalist, literalist and doctrinaire Christianity in the USA; Muslim clericalism in the Middle East and Asia; the reassertion of orthodox authority by the Catholic Papal hierarchy; and the rise of nationalistic religious Judaism – is in large part, no doubt, responsible for this dramatic change of perception. Religious zealots are now seen as having definite political objectives: the de-secularization of constitutions, the creation of theocracies, the occupation of unredeemed territories promised by God. But this does not mean that the battle between the religious and the secular is now suddenly a one-sided fight.[1] What it does reveal, however, is that the balance between the religious and the secular is in perpetual, occasionally erratic flux and is as much an issue today as ever. In the period covered by the essays in this anthology, the advance of natural science, the spread of education and other social improvements, together with reforms in the political realm, worked to put religion upon the defensive. In the latter part of the eighteenth and early nineteenth centuries, religion was forced to account for itself and to justify its existence, both as a social institution and as a collection of fundamental articles of belief about the world and its operations. The intellectual endeavours which fuelled this predicament and the consequent maelstrom of disputation, engaged some of the profoundest and most influential figures in the British political tradition. The present collection highlights but a selection of these writers, indicating facets of their thought of special interest and illuminating their ideas *vis-à-vis* the ideas of other writers of the age. It is on the writings of Hobbes, Locke,

Hume, Smith and other Scots, Wesley, Burke, Paley, Bentham, Maurice, and J. S. Mill that the following essays focus.

An inherent problem with collections such as this is that invariably the critic will say, 'But why is X omitted?' One might reasonably have expected something on the third Earl of Shaftesbury, the English deists (Tindal, Toland, Trenchard, Gordon and Collins), the dissenters (Paine, Priestley, Godwin), Coleridge perhaps, and so on. The political ramifications of the religious beliefs defended and denied by these writers were obviously of consequence in the age in question, and there is much still to be considered in this regard.[2] The following essays do not aim to cover every religious–political thinker of note, but rather to convey in a selection of cases the importance of the association between religious beliefs and dogma and developments in the area of secular ideas, principally but not solely political in nature.

In approaching this issue, interpretive problems necessarily conjoin with the chronology of events and the development of ideas. The term 'secular', for example, has a long history and a variety of meanings. As early as the late thirteenth century it was used to describe members of the clergy who eschewed monastic seclusion in favour of 'living in the world' – a member of the 'secular clergy' as opposed to the 'monastic clergy'. One could also employ the term at that time to distinguish 'secular courts' – courts of law – from 'ecclesiastical courts'. To 'secularize' something was to make it secular, to convert it from ecclesiastical to civil possession or use, or to dissociate something from religious or spiritual concerns and transform it to material or temporal purposes.[3] By the mid-seventeenth century it was a term in common usage, generally employed to indicate those things, buildings or people belonging to the world and its affairs, not to the church and spiritual affairs. In this sense the term gradually evolved with a negative connotation, meaning non-ecclesiastical, non-religious or non-sacred. But the term could still be used in a neutral, descriptive sense with regard to profane literature, history, art or music (and by extension writers and artists); that is, with regard to creative work not concerned with or devoted to the service of religion. When applied to education in England in the eighteenth and early nineteenth centuries however, the opponents of secularization were quick to perceive a sinister intent. As well they might. It became a compelling argument, for example, during the 'Schools for All' dispute that education, if it was to be provided at the public expense, should be purely secular. But here we have arrived at a meaning decidedly different from the one with which we started.

A degree of clarification is possible if we reduce the nature of the relationship between the religious and the secular to two essentially different categories. The first and most obvious correlation lays emphasis on the essential antagonism that exists between the two; here religion is gradually dispensed with, both as a source for explanations about the world, its creation and operations, and as a basis for morality. Owen Chadwick invoked this meaning of the term when he employed it to allude to the tendency in humankind to do without religion,[4] and Alasdair MacIntyre had the same thing in mind in his brilliant Riddell Memorial Lectures when he defined 'secularization' as 'the transition from beliefs and activities and institutions presupposing beliefs of a traditional Christian kind to beliefs and activities and institutions of an atheistic kind'.[5] Arnold Loen takes this to its logical conclusion when he refers us to that 'historical process by which the world is de-divinized', de-divinized, he means, 'as far as human consciousness is concerned'.[6] On this view of the matter the key development affecting ideas in both the religious and secular realms was the progress made in natural philosophy. But as intellectually significant as the development of the 'new science' undoubtedly was, it would be misleading to trace all the various meanings of the 'secular' and its relations with the 'religious' to that phenomenon. Questions of morality, utility, psychology, and politics inevitably intrude upon the matter.

The second form of the association between the religious and the secular defines a world in which religion responds to the changing conditions of life and thought and remains an integral and vital part of social and intellectual activity. Chadwick, again, draws our attention to the nature of this relationship when he refers to the Reformation as entailing 'a baptism of the secular' – a time when Christianity came to embody tenets demanding action not merely contemplation.[7] No longer enjoined simply to quit the world with the ledger of the soul balanced, increasingly the urge was to change it. This became a prominent part of Protestantism as it fragmented and took new forms in the early modern period of the British political tradition. Religion was summoned to play a role in the temporal world in a way it had not hitherto.

From Hobbes forward British philosophers developed ideas about the relationship between the religious and the secular which conform to one or other of these two basic categories, though a mixture of the two occasionally produced a very different perspective – most evidently the case, for example, in J. S. Mill's advocacy of a 'religion of humanity', a type of secular humanism.

Whatever the form of the association however, it is clear that to say what is secular about an idea or a thinker it is incumbent on us to say where the idea or the thinker stands in relation to some fact or feature pertaining to religion. This is not to say that there are no problems with saying what constitutes 'religion', but the only understanding of the term relevant at any one moment is how the writer or writers being considered themselves understood the tenets, rituals and institutions of religion. It is in this definitional sense that the religious and the secular go hand in hand. What the essayists in this collection collectively demonstrate is not only the importance of religion to an understanding of other social and political currents, but also the manner in which it was intellectually appraised, dissected and, with certain notable exceptions, forced to give way to concerns and paradigms of belief alien to its own temporal and transcendental heritage. In order to understand the relationship between religion and ideas in the period in question, therefore, we need to pay close attention to the particular thinkers whose work constitutes the principal threads of its intellectual life.

One of the central issues in the relationship between the religious and the secular, a question raised in our own day by George Grant, is 'Does public morality rest on the widespread practice of piety?'[8] It was this question, and related questions to do with the role of institutions in maintaining social order, which most exercised the minds of moralists in the early modern period and in the age that followed. The Renaissance inherited from classical culture the view that religion had a vital role to play – if a demeaning one in the eyes of the church – in the maintenance of social and political order. The consensus in early modern Britain was that piety was necessary to the public good, hence the presence of statutes which excluded unbelievers, atheists and an assortment of heretics from political office. But already the questioning of this assumption had begun. Bayle in the seventeen thcentury, followed by Hume and Bentham to name only the most influential, set in train an inexorable critique which was to become part of the consciousness of large numbers of their fellow citizens. A social morality without God was one of the age's most feared and, for a select group of critical moralists, one of its most vaunted projects. This was inconceivable in any previous age. What it amounted to was the possibility of a secular society, a society of people in which the fear of God was not crucial for the maintenance of social order; rather the public good was to be based on socially useful passions which could be inculcated regardless of the practice of piety.

Until quite recently it was usual to depict Hobbes as the theorist who occupies precisely that point in the tradition of English political thought where the 'religious' is transformed into the 'secular'. What is Hobbes's Leviathan other than a mortal God? Just as fear of God gives force to the law of nature, so fear of the sovereign binds the subject to obedience to civil laws. In other words, Hobbes sought a secular equivalent for God as a foundation for social order. But, as Stephen State explains, the theological framework of this analysis is at no point discarded. None the less, it is here that so many of Hobbes's contemporaries, even if they approved of other features of his work, found him unacceptable. This ambivalence is understandable given the subtle complexities of Hobbes's work.

State detects and describes three possible alignments of the religious and the secular in Hobbes's thought. First, there are occasions when they appear to coexist in a happy relationship. In the eighteenth century, bishop Warburton and Edmund Burke found much support for their respective attempts to buttress the 'alliance' of church and state. In Hobbes's day, supporters of this arrangement held to the dictum 'render unto Caesar what is Caesar's and unto God what is God's'. But Hobbes provided a far more controversial panoply of reasons to maintain the association, not the least of which is the priority he gave to political obedience. This was the political dimension he prescribed for Anglicanism, and it is in this sense that the religious and the secular – in terms of church and state – are brought together in his thought. For Hobbes, Caesar must have a place in the church. Second, State draws our attention to the separation of reason and divine revelation in Hobbes's thought, where reason (the secular) is employed to achieve conclusions concerning theological matters without the help of revelation (the religious). Hobbes affirms their separation in the sense that revelation is a matter of authoritative pronouncement through the office of the sovereign and not a matter for public debate. Occasionally however, Hobbes ignores this affirmation. This is most obviously the case when he sets about revising theology and doctrine with insights derived from what he takes to be a more 'scientific' position than the scholastic metaphysics he eschewed. It is also evident when he interprets Scripture in a 'rational' way, and when he grants to God a pivotal position in his theistic version of natural law. In the final analysis, the so-called rational argument of the first part of *Leviathan* is inescapably linked to the belief in an omnipotent God. Hence – and this is the third of State's alignments – there are aspects of Hobbes's thought that involve an overlapping of the religious and the secular where neither one is excluded. Hobbes's discussions of the divine law of reason and his use of reason as an instrument of scriptural exegesis, and to clarify theology and doctrine, are all aspects of his thought that involve reason and revelation working, as it were, in tandem. Clearly, State does not subscribe to the view that Hobbes was an atheist who merely dressed up his subversive thoughts in religious attire in order to make them palatable to his countrymen. Rather he was a philosopher acutely sensitive to the interdependency of secular and religious ideas.

It was not Hobbes but Pierre Bayle who argued that a society of atheists could be law-abiding and even virtuous. Not that atheism should be tolerated. Religion, Bayle maintained, played a valuable, if not logically necessary, role in upholding social order.[9] Nevertheless, from this point on, the claim rehearsed in John Locke's *Letter Concerning Toleration*, that atheists could not be trusted, could no longer be logically sustained, as Locke well knew. Even so, Locke's writings on human nature, civil society and government have always depended for an important measure of their explanatory and justificatory power upon his basic assumptions about the nature of God. A consideration of God's attributes and purposes was indispensable to his accounts of law, reason, property and power: in short, of man, society and politics. More specifically, Locke's political theory only makes sense on the assumption that men in the state of nature have secure knowledge of the divine law and that they are motivated to act by fear of divine justice. On this basis they construct a political order for the specific purpose of protecting their God-given rights, and they retain the liberty to alter that order whenever those rights require defending.

Be that as it may, it is apparent from David Wootton's discussion that on the subject of religious beliefs Locke's place in the history of political thought is an ambivalent one. For example, deists in both England and France felt greatly indebted to the arguments of the *Essay Concerning Human Understanding*, and yet Locke himself in his later writings laid great stress on the importance of revealed religion. But what is at issue in Wootton's interpretation is not that Locke's readers read him in decidedly different ways (though this is also true); rather the problem is that Locke seems to have contented himself with believing different things when dealing with different problems. His epistemology was designed to overturn the claim of conscience to infallibility: men's consciences were no better than the rules they judged by, and these varied from time to time and place to place. The effect of this strategy was to undermine the possibility of a reliable moral philosophy based on natural law. Locke's political theory, on the other hand, was designed to justify the rights of the people against their rulers. But here his thought depended upon a principle of equality which could only be grounded in natural law. Finally, his theology was based upon the recognition that it was to Christ that we owed the promise of eternal life (contemporaries suspected Locke of Socinianism). And this worked to undermine the very idea of natural rights which could be recognized by all men solely by natural reason. Wootton's Locke, therefore, is far more complex than the Locke of the standard history of ideas literature, a man locked (if the pun can be excused) in a futile struggle to harmonize essentially incompatible epistemological, theological and moral ideas, each of which is honestly arrived at and coherent within the terms of its own logic.

Roger Emerson moves the focus of the collection to the North Britons to discuss the shift in the thinking of eighteenth-century Scots away from the old biblically-based theology to a philosophical outlook that encompassed, in primitive form, most of the social sciences. The driving force behind this development was empiricism and its 'scientific' methods, made manifest in the increasing worldliness of Scottish intellectuals during this period. But Emerson denies that they were secular – if by that is meant a deliberate distancing from the claims of religion – and supports this claim by showing that 'secular' does not adequately describe their outlook and concerns.

Science has often been set against religion and depicted as one of the principal agents of the retreat of traditional religion in the west: a process of 'desacralization' or, to use Weber's terminology, 'disenchantment'.[10] From the seventeenth century forward, it is argued, the sacred and mystical gradually gave way to a view of the world as a self-contained causal nexus shorn of providence.[11] Now it is true that during the period covered by these essays man and nature increasingly became the object of rational–causal explanation. Yet matters were never quite so straightforward as the conventional juxtaposition of science and religion would seem to imply. Not all natural philosophers were out to strip the world of its mystery; a good many (Samuel Clarke and William Wollaston, for instance) were out to establish the exact opposite and others, like William Paley, simply borrowed the epistemological apparatus of natural philosophy to further bulwark the truths of religion. That the two need not be contradictory is Emerson's point: the increasing worldliness of Scots thinkers, with the notable exception of Hume, did not necessarily mean a forsaking of traditional beliefs, but rather heralded an accommodation between the two. Christianity, he argues, had a new place in the Scottish world of learning; the increasing worldliness of the learned did not yet mean that they lived in a secular world. Their world was still religious, but in a rational way.

Despite the efforts of Shaftesbury, Francis Hutcheson and others to elaborate a theory which made the internal conscience of man and not fear of God the final arbiter of morality, it is only with David Hume, it is said, that a conscious effort was mounted to develop a purely secular moral philosophy. For the first time in the British political tradition, the view that only those who feared God should be trusted was explicitly attacked and rejected. Yet here again the framework of analysis which sets science and religion at odds with each other has its limitations.

Douglas Long focuses upon Hume's conception of a 'science' of human nature resting upon 'experimental' foundations, as symptomatic of an important shift away from explanations of man, society and politics resting on theological premises to more secular modes of theorizing. Tracing the patterns of employment of the term 'science' (together with related phrases) through selected writings of Hume, Smith and Bentham, Long tests the hypothesis that the centrality of this concept in the thought of eighteenth-century social theorists was a cause and a symptom of a more general secularization of their views. But important differences are brought to light between Bentham and the Scots.

In Hume and Smith, religious scepticism accompanies epistemological scepticism, and is associated with a view of the nature,
development and purposes of 'science' which reflects the inability of
humankind to be certain of the nature of the 'external' material world.
For Bentham, on the other hand, a simplistic materialist metaphysic, a
distaste for the subtleties of epistemological scepticism, and an
unmatched enthusiasm for empirical science were united with a militant
atheism. In Hume and Smith, philosophy, religion and science are all
seen as attempts to allay man's inevitable uncertainty about things
natural and divine. This was exactly what Bentham refused to accept;
what Hume and Smith doubted Bentham categorically denied (I shall
say more about Bentham presently). On the other hand, what Locke had
attempted to explain by recourse to theological conceptions of nature,
reason and right, Hume and Smith analysed more experimentally by
relying on concepts such as history and habit, interest and utility. The
use they made of these ideas reflected their scepticism and was a
harbinger of the special position they subsequently were taken to occupy
as political thinkers, poised between Whig and Tory, retroactively
claimed as ancestors by both liberals and conservatives.

Traditionally, no such quandary is to be found among the
commentators on Burke's unsystematic philosophy; here, it is claimed,
Christianity and 'conservatism' stand in a seemingly necessary
relationship to each other. Frederick Dreyer challenges this view by
pointing up the Whig origins of Burke's thought. Clearly, Burke's
defence of church and state, being 'one and the same thing, being
different integral parts of the same whole',[12] carries the authentic mark
of 'conservatism' in the age in question. But, according to Dreyer, the
foundations of his thought owe more to his reading of the radical Locke
than is commonly credited. For example, in Burke and in the sermons
and pronouncements of John Wesley, J. C. D. Clark detects an erudite
rejection of the individualist values and assumptions that are the
hallmarks of Locke's political thought.[13] For Clark the central
orthodoxy of the eighteenth century was prescribed by the Caroline
divines; this orthodoxy was at bottom patriarchal and anti-individualist
in its assumptions. If Locke's individualism found any audience in the
age, therefore, it was only as a minority preference. Burke and Wesley
both testify against the 'quick triumph of Lockeian empiricism and the
swift demise of the divine right of kings'.[14]

On Dreyer's alternative account however, Burke and Wesley were
both significantly indebted to Locke. It is precisely in their thought,
Dreyer argues, that we can find the Lockeian identity of the times most
powerfully asserting itself. For example, both men accept the validity of
Lockeian empiricism. When Wesley insists upon experience as a
necessary manifestation of faith, he in fact assumes an epistemology

that derives from Locke's *Essay*. And when Burke asserts experience against reason in his debate with Price over the French Revolution, it is again Locke's epistemology that is being assumed. On the basis of Locke's theory of knowledge, Burke can dismiss reason as an authority in political matters. On the same assumption, Wesley can urge the Christian to seek the evidence of his conversion in the experience of his heart. Similarly, both men accept the validity of Lockeian contract-ualism, evident in Wesley's theory of the church and in Burke's theory of the state. In both theories it is consent that validates the authority that governs men in their public associations. The Methodist society was for Wesley nothing more than a club, and as a club it could claim no authority independently of the consent of its members. In his management of the Methodist society, Wesley figured not as a priest but as a steward. Here religion is 'privatized', and this in part, was the goal of Wesley's Methodism.[15] As Dreyer explains, in Wesley's conception the Methodists were a society held together on a Lockeian contractual basis and whose rules reached only as far as its subscribers. Burke's state is also a club deriving its existence from the consent of its members. His criticism of the French Revolution, ultimately, is that it lacks a proper basis in the consent of the French people. The new regime is condemned as a usurpation that governs in defiance of contract. Once promises are made they must be kept. In both cases an intimate association exists between secular and religious ideas, and in both cases practical institutional consequences result.

As I have already suggested, it was with a rancour unsurpassed by any other critical moralist of the day that Bentham sought to destroy this alliance between religious beliefs and secular ideas. Indeed, if we think of secularization for the moment in the first of the senses I outlined above – as the tendency in mankind to do without religion – it might justifiably be argued that a greater intellectual force for secularization than Bentham did not exist in late eighteenth- and early nineteenth-century Britain. In Bentham's utilitarian ethics, influenced primarily by the work of the continental philosophers, the great secular project of the age reached its purest form: a doctrine of morality based solely on a regard for the well-being of humankind in the present life, to the exclusion of all considerations drawn from belief in God or in a future state.

In the thought of his near contemporary William Paley, Bentham perceived a recognizable and formidable opponent. Paley, along with many other churchmen of the age, sought to revive the flagging spirit of the church by adapting Christianity and its official practice to the changing needs of the times. Following the French Revolution when the expropriation of the goods of the church became part of the official policy of the new republic, it was thought to be but a short step to the point where secularization became the name of a programme aimed at the totality of life and experience, and subsequently assumed the status of an 'ism'.[16] The perception is that at the end of this process stands the entirely secular society. It is this perception which informs the contrast between the thought of Paley and that of Bentham, two contemporaneous advocates of utility as the criterion of action and policy; the one determined to halt secularization, the other to promote it. In contrasting their respective systems, it becomes clear that profound differences lurk behind superficial similarities. So much so that it is fair to say that in Paley and Bentham we have the quintessential exponents of the two competing versions of the doctrine of utility bequeathed to the nineteenth century. If, in the hands of Paley, utility (with few exceptions) could be used as the philosophical justification for the *status quo*, in Bentham it became the instrument of unmitigated religious and political radicalism, calling not only for the separation of church and state, but also for the reconstruction of society, free from the inhibiting psychological constraints of Christian theology. The reason why one ought to proceed with such and such an action, obey this or that institution, or seek improvement in one area of social life or another, is the same in all cases: the maximization of happiness and the reduction of pain. God has no place in this scheme of things; he is neither feared nor held up as the final cause of existence.

Not that Bentham's (or Hume's) views received immediate applause in Britain. Not surprisingly, it was in many respects an up-hill fight. The Anglican school of bishop Warburton (John Brown, Edmund Law, William Paley *et al.*), the Scottish adherents of the Kirk, the 'moral sense' disciples of Shaftesbury and Hutcheson, the supporters of Wesley and of Nonconformist sects, and the redoubtable Burke – all, in their various ways, contrived to retain the religious dimension in their explanations of social order. For many apologists of Christianity the strongest argument for religion remained the apparently incontestable truth of a future life and the necessity of the sanctions this entailed for society. Little had changed by the opening decades of the new century, when hell-fire preaching Evangelicalism came into its own. But by then the social problems caused in part by the Industrial Revolution combined with the growing admiration for reason and science had profoundly affected both religious institutions and religious beliefs.

Owenism marked a sharp departure from previous forms of radicalism. For Robert Owen and many, though not all, of his followers, God's intentions in creating the world no longer entered essentially into the question of how it should be managed, or what duties the poor were owed by the rich. This meant that the adherents of Owenite socialism could not invoke images of a divinely-intended, original, positive community of goods, but had to find a completely new basis upon which to argue in favour of such a property system.[17] The stronger this trend away from religion became, the more socialism came to be perceived simply as 'an alternative form of wealth production, . . . more just, more egalitarian, but otherwise more a part of the existing world than any future millenium'.[18] This trend of thought led the Owenites to distance themselves from some early, religious models of co-operative communities. In 1840 the Owenite *New Moral World*, referring to the efforts of the Shakers and others, commented that 'the benefits of co-operation display themselves not in consequence, but in spite of, the religious tenets of those societies . . . : their communities merely prove that co-operation works, which is why we cite them'.[19] In the wake of the disappointment over the failure of model communities in the first quarter of the nineteenth century, the debate about the relative merits and disadvantages of community of property came to focus on the nationalization of the land.[20] In the process, the idea of the peculiar status of landed property was gradually secularized until the argument that God's creation sanctioned this had been replaced by a secularized Lockeian view that labour provided the sole legitimate title to property. The conclusion socialists drew from this was that only the products of the land and not the soil itself could be privately owned. The moral implications of this line of thought did not stop here, but served to further the process of secularization by undermining faith in the notion of providential order, the consequence being that moral obligation came to be grounded in strictly utilitarian considerations, the sanctions for which lacked the special persuasiveness which those of religion provided.

T. R. Sansom focuses on certain aspects of these changes by drawing our attention to the much neglected work of F. D. Maurice. Here secularization is viewed in terms of the adaptation of Christianity to the task of relieving hardship, and Maurice's philanthropy is contrasted with the general line taken by those Evangelicals who equated poverty with sin, thereby distancing themselves from the various attempts to devise schemes for social improvement. In Maurice's thought the moral imperative to alleviate the hardships of social life became part and parcel of man's duty to God.

The collection is completed by Richard Vernon's insightful interpretation of the place of religion within the political thought of J. S. Mill. When Mill wrote his essays on religion around the middle of the century, he found it impossible simply to argue its tenets away. With a profound sense of the place of religion in the history of the Christian world, and an unmatched understanding of the subtleties of human nature, Mill, perhaps more than any other major thinker in the British political tradition, was conscious of both the failings of traditional dogma and its benefits as a binding agent in society. Out of this awareness he developed a 'religion of humanity' and an extraordinarily sophisticated model of the community, in which individuality is tempered only by the need for social cooperation. It is in this way, Mill thought, that societies could best advance, intellectually and morally, as a progressive and social whole.

In Vernon's discussion of the communitarian character of Mill's thought, the traditional understanding of religion is left behind and the term 'secularization' assumes a less familiar character than hitherto. In one sense, the secularization of religion means the conformity of religion with the world, with the 'religious' sect focusing its attention not on the supernatural or the next life but on concerns which characterize the temporal society it inhabits. F. D. Maurice's version of Christianity in which the devotion to God encompasses the devotion to humanitarian concerns is a religion of this type. A more recent manifestation of the same thing is the 'liberation theology' currently employed by some South and Central American Catholics, which provides a spiritual basis for organizations whose occupation is entirely given over to social and economic improvement. In this case the religious is forced into secular clothes. But the secularization of religion Vernon has in mind in the case of Mill involves a reverse trans-formation: here the secular takes on a religious form. The consequence of the transposition of beliefs and patterns of behaviour from the 'religious' to the 'secular' spheres of social life Larry Shiner tells us, would be 'a totally anthropologized religion' and a society which had assumed all the functions once associated with religion.[21] The 'religion of humanity' first advocated by Auguste Comte and later taken up by Mill – a social ethic in which sentiments are directed to one's fellow men and not to a Being beyond the physical world – is of just such a character. In its most developed form, 'secular humanism', as it has come to be termed, holds that it is possible to lead a good life and contribute significantly to human culture and social justice without a belief in theistic religion or hope of personal reward.[22]

It is not unusual today to find theorists of 'religion' employing the term, following Durkheim, to refer to a 'system of belief (whether true or false) which binds together the life of individuals and gives to those lives whatever consistency of purpose they may have'.[23] Under this rubric, liberal humanists and Marxists count as religious people, and, indeed, all persons, in so far as they adhere to a consistent set of principles, are religious. As an instance of this, George Grant offers 'the religion of democracy', the virtues of which young people in liberal democracies are expected to accept on faith.[24] Grant comments further that the fact that in the USA, where the separation of church and state is entrenched in the Constitution, those liberals who most object to any teaching about the deity in schools 'are generally most insistent that the virtues of democracy be taught, should make us aware that what is at issue is not religion in general, but the content of the religion to be taught'.[25]

The issue was vividly brought to view by the 1987 Alabama Supreme Court ruling that for all intents and purposes 'secular humanism' was a religion and, since it constituted a violation of the First Amendment, should not be allowed in the state's classrooms. The distinction between the religious and the secular was rejected, it seemed.[26] The plaintiffs argued that 'secular humanism', a belief system with few 'acknowledged' adherents, is a religion, albeit a 'Godless' one that elevates transient human values and advocates the view that humans can handle their own affairs without divine intervention. They also contended that this 'religion' had made significant inroads into the textbooks approved for use in the Alabama public schools. Referring to a previous Supreme Court ruling, US District Judge W. Brevard Hand ruled

> that teaching religious tenets in such a way as to promote or encourage a religion violates the religion clauses (of the Constitution). This prohibition is not implicated by mere coincidence of ideas with religious tenets. Rather, there must be a systematic, whether explicit or implicit, promotion of a belief system as a whole. The facts showed that the state of Alabama has on its state textbook list certain volumes that are being used by school systems in this state, which engage in such promotions.[27]

Remarkably, Judge Hand then proceeded to order seventeen social studies textbooks, nine history books and six home-economics texts stricken from the approved list. Forty-four books were subsequently banned in the state of Alabama for promoting 'secular humanism'.[28] Evidently the transformation of liberalism into a secular faith does not necessarily fulfil the moral purpose of its advocates, and may even produce precisely the opposite result.

This is not to suggest that 'secular humanism' is an entirely alien standpoint in the context of the essays in this collection, or that Mill's views were necessarily at odds with the discourse of earlier thinkers. To the central place afforded religion in moral and political thought in the age before him Mill undoubtedly added a unique synthesis of the religious and secular. But to a significant degree the propositions of this synthesis were features of Britain's intellectual climate throughout the epoch covered by the essays here. As we have seen, secular trends – looking forward to a new age in which experimental philosophy was to provide the key to understanding and to moral progress – were clearly evident. The consequence of the development of new ideas about man, nature, society and government during this period was to provide an incessant challenge to the belief systems upon which the *ancien régime*, in its various religious and political shapes, was founded. When the religious and political blocks of the *ancien régime* came toppling down in the upheaval of 1828–30, it was the consequence of a long and gradual 'secular' intrusion which had its birth in the Reformation and the advancement of physical science. But this is not to doubt the fact that in theological terms the Anglican intelligentsia fought a hard-pressed and convincing battle against the infidels who sought to weaken the foundations of established religion. On the contrary, well into the nineteenth century, religion had a hand in nearly every major social and political question of the age and specifically religious matters were generally deemed to take priority over purely secular issues, thus providing a compelling testament to the enduring value of religion. All the while, the relationship between religious beliefs, dogma and institutions on the one hand and secular ideas and concerns on the other developed in a multitude of forms: from the attempts of Hobbes and Locke to wed the two together, in the realms of both political theory and theological discourse, to the non-theological, critical morality of Hume; and from the 'alliance' of the religious and secular, championed in their different ways by Warburton, Burke, Wesley and Paley, to the virulent religious radicalism of Bentham. Viewing this history of the relationship between the religious and the secular, it is apparent that Mill's affinity with the discourse of his intellectual forebears is a substantial one.

Collectively then, what the authors in this collection illustrate is not a world in which the secular increasingly overwhelms the religious, but rather an age marked by a tension between the two, explicit or in the background, which propelled the effort to understand, to explain, and to develop new ideas and models. In short, the following essays provide samples of how particular thinkers or groups of thinkers contended with one of the most pressing issues of the modern period of the history of ideas in Britain.

Notes

1 In the USSR, the much vaunted socialist desecularization of the constitution may well be illusory. 'Glasnost' has brought with it a certain tolerance of religious practices, it is true, but at the time of writing reforms have yet to be translated into law and without new laws the recent liberalization rests on uncertain foundations.

2 On Shaftesbury and the English deists see C. Robbins, *The Eighteenth Century Commonwealthmen*, Cambridge, Mass., Harvard University Press, 1961; R. L. Emerson, 'Latitudinarianism and the English deists', and D. Berman 'Deism, immortality and the art of theological lying', both in J. A.

Leo Lemay (ed.), *Deism, Masonry and the Enlightenment: Essays Honoring Alfred Owen Aldridge*, Newark, University of Delaware Press, Newark, 1987, pp. 19–48, 61–78 respectively. On the dissenters see I. Kramnick, 'Religion and radicalism: English political theory in the age of revolution', *Political Theory*, 1977, vol. 5, no. 4, pp. 505–34.

3 Occasionally, 'laicize' is a term used to mean essentially the same process: to deprive a person or thing of its clerical character or remove it from clerical control.

4 O. Chadwick, *The Secularization of the European Mind in the Nineteenth Century*, Cambridge, Cambridge University Press, 1975, p. 17. A. Quinton appears to follow suit, see *The Politics of Imperfection: The Religious and Secular Traditions of Conservative Thought in England from Hooker to Oakeshott*, London, Faber and Faber, 1978, p. 14.

5 A. MacIntyre, *Secularization and Moral Change*, London, London University Press, 1967, p. 8.

6 A. E. Loen, *Secularization: Science without God?*, London, SCM Press, 1967, pp. 7, 8. Though Loen patiently reveals the elusiveness of 'secularization' as descriptive nomenclature, his analysis presumes this definition as the root meaning of the term.

7 Chadwick, *The Secularization of the European Mind*, p. 8.

8 G. Grant, *Technology and Empire: Perspectives on North America*, Toronto, House of Anssi, 1969, p. 50. The idea that religion is the foundation of social order has as long a history as almost any idea one can think of, a point well illustrated by D. Wootton, 'The fear of God in early modern political theory', *Historical Papers 1983/Communications Historiques*, Canadian Historical Association, pp. 56–80. I have benefited greatly from Wootton's historiography in this paper.

9 Wootton, 'The fear of God in early modern political theory', p. 76.

10 L. Shiner, 'The meanings of secularization', in J. F. Childress and D. B. Harned (eds), *Secularization and the Protestant Prospect*, Philadelphia, Westminster Press, 1970, p. 35; and M. Weber, 'Science as a vocation', in *From Max Weber, Essays in Sociology*, ed. and trans. H. H. Gerth and c. W. Mills, Oxford, Oxford University Press, 1946, p. 139.

11 Peter Gay gives vibrant expression to the conventional association between science or natural philosophy and secularization in *The Enlightenment: An Interpretation*, 2 vols, London, Norton, 1977, vol. 2, ch. 3.

12 E. Burke, 'Speech on a motion made in the House of Commons by the Right Hon. C. J. Fox, May 11, 1792, for leave to bring in a bill to repeal and alter certain acts respecting religious opinions, upon occasion of a petition of the Unitarian Society', *The Works of the Right Honourable Edmund Burke*, 12 vols, London, 1887, vol. 7, p. 43.

13 J. C. D. Clark, *English Society 1688–1832: Ideology, Social Structure and Political Practice During the Ancien Régime*, Cambridge, Cambridge University Press, 1985, pp. 4, 50, 56–8.

14 ibid., pp. 44, 57–8, 81, 152, 227, 237, 258, 279.

15 The culmination of secularization in this sense would be a religion of a purely inward character influencing neither institutions nor corporate action and a society in which religion made no appearance beyond the boundaries

of the religious group.

16 Shiner draws our attention to G. J. Holyoake's organization to promote 'secularism'. See Shiner, 'The meanings of secularization', p. 31.

17 G. Claeys, *Machinery, Money and the Millenium: From Moral Economy to Socialism, 1815–1860*, Princeton, NJ, Princeton University Press, 1987, p. 33.

18 According to one Owenite paper, 'Socialism, in a few words, is a system which secures in the best manner the most efficacious production, with the just distribution of wealth. It has nothing to do with religious opinions. It may be carried out by religionists or anti-religionists – by Christians or Heathens.' *Star in the East*, 1840, no. 176 (25 January), p. 153. See Claeys, *Machinery, Money and the Millenium*, p. 152.

19 *New Moral World*, 1840, vol. 7, no. 81 (9 May), p. 1288, quoted by Claeys, *Machinery, Money and the Millenium*, p. 153.

20 For the background to this see ibid., ch. 6.

21 As an example Shiner suggests the 'spirit of capitalism' as a secularization of the Calvinist ethic, Shiner, 'The meanings of secularization', p. 39.

22 In the late 1970s in the United States, it became the vogue to view 'secular humanism' as a religion. See J. H. Whitehead and J. Conlan, 'The establishment of the religion of secular humanism and its first amendment implications', *Texas Tech Law Review*, 1978–9, vol. 10, no. 1, pp. 1-66. The ideals of modern American 'secular humanism' are set out by P. Kurtz in 'A secular humanist declaration', first published in *Free Enquiry*, Winter 1980, and reproduced in Kurtz, *In Defense of Secular Humanism*, New York, Prometheus Books, 1983, ch. 2, pp. 14–24.

23 Grant, *Technology and Empire*, p. 46.

24 ibid., p. 49. Along similar lines Robert Bellah refers us to the American 'civil religion'. The most important ceremonial event in this religion is the inauguration of the president, through which the religious legitimation of the highest political office in the land is reaffirmed. It would be difficult to think of a self-confessed atheist becoming president, would it not? R. H. Bellah, 'Civil religion in America', in Childress and Harned (eds), *Secularization and the Protestant Prospect*, pp. 93–116.

25 Grant, *Technology and Empire*, p. 49.

26 The case had been brought by fundamentalist groups (600 Alabama parents and a teacher) concerned that the separation of church and state had made the teaching of religion of whatever kind unacceptable in the classroom. By arguing that teachers were teaching a religion of a secular kind they hoped to force the teaching of traditional Christianity.

27 Cited by W. Raspberry, 'Humanism banned', in *Manchester Guardian Weekly*, 29 March 1987.

28 ibid., p. 18: are advocates of vegetarianism, humanism, environmentalism and transcendental meditation also to be deemed members of a religion in accordance with this ruling? The question could not be lightly dismissed. Fortunately, the Alabama decision was overturned by an Atlanta federal appeals court (26 August 1987). Had it been allowed to stand the ramifications for high school curriculum development would have been catastrophic.

Chapter one

The religious and the secular in the work of Thomas Hobbes

S. A. State

Were we to visualize, in the manner of mathematical set theory, the 'religious' and the 'secular' as potentially overlapping circles on a two-dimensional plane, the number of possible arrangements of those circles might be quite large. They could, however, be reduced to three general patterns: perfectly coextensive (with one subsuming the other), perfectly distinct, or overlapping in various ways. In the case of the religious and the secular as they appear in the work of Thomas Hobbes, a plausible argument could be advanced for all three possibilities depending upon which aspect of Hobbes's thought is chosen for consideration and upon what is specified as 'religious' and 'secular'.

Church and state

If we restate the distinction between religious and secular as a distinction between church and state then the two circles come very close to merging -- at least in the context of those states where an official religion has been so declared by the civil sovereign. The word 'church' has, in Hobbes's view, various significations ranging from the building itself to the universal multitude of Christians 'how far soever they be dispersed'. This clarification of terminology is important to Hobbes and he wants to insist that there is only one pertinent sense in which it may be said that a church has the power to command and be obeyed. A church in this pertinent sense would be one which is united in the person of a sovereign, 'at whose command they ought to assemble and without whose authority they ought not to assemble'.[1] Hobbes affirms that it follows from this definition that a church is equivalent to a civil commonwealth composed of Christians. This 'political' definition serves to limit the kind of churches that may properly be said to be authoritative and in Hobbes's view it renders spurious the conventional distinctions between the 'Christian' and the man; the sword of justice and the shield of faith; the spiritual and the temporal; and, finally,

Thomas Hobbes

between church and state. The distinctions are spurious in the sense that the antitheses which they suggest will disappear with a combination of semantic clarification and scriptural exegesis.

This political definition of the concept of church creates some problems for Hobbes's account. For one thing the possibility of several authorized churches at the discretion of the sovereign within a single commonwealth (which he at one point suggests)[2] is difficult though not impossible to square with the equation of church and commonwealth. Presumably this problem is overcome by substituting one of the other definitions of 'church', all the while recalling that the sovereign retains authority even if he delegates some of his powers. A further problem concerns non-Christian religions within the Christian Commonwealth. It is not clear what 'authority' Jewish or Moslem 'churches' would have over their members. It seems that they are tolerated but it is not clear in what sense they could undertake any acts in a corporate capacity since they are not united in the person of sovereign.[3] Moreover, the lack of authority in Christian churches in non-Christian countries is in part a contingency of Christian sacred history: Christ was a fisher of men not a commander, hence there was no kingdom on earth and no authority in the strict sense of the word. Other sacred histories need not take account of the New Testament. For this reason, Locke's argument in *A Letter Concerning Toleration* is more generally useful. A church for him is any voluntary association of people practising a religion and they may in their corporate capacity enforce rules upon their members as long as those rules are not repugnant to civil society and as long as the enforcement of those rules entails nothing more drastic than excommunication.[4]

At any rate, the medieval distinction between *regnum* and *sacerdotum* which was manifested in John of Salisbury's doctrine of the two swords – spiritual and temporal – has no place in Hobbes's scheme. Indeed, merely to suggest the possibility of a contemporary spiritual *authority* distinct from temporal authority is, in his view, to distract people from their proper obligations. This does not mean, however, that the two cities of Augustinian description have collapsed into one; rather, it means that Jerusalem will only replace Athens at the coming of the Messiah. Until the time of their more permanent citizenship, people are advised to keep their hands clean, to have faith and to obey their sovereign on religious concerns. After Hobbes, John Locke would see his deference to prescribed doctrine as a good way to encourage hypocrisy; but, before him, Richard Hooker saw it the way Hobbes did, as an antidote of humility in the face of a religious zeal that threatened to undermine all social life.[5]

The Protestant invocation of that familiar passage from Rom. 13, 'Grant unto Caesar the things that are Caesar's', would only be acceptable to Hobbes with the understanding that Caesar might acquire authority in religious matters as God's lieutenant on earth, which is not, one suspects, what Zwingli or Calvin had in mind in mentioning the passage. Indeed when Hobbes alludes to the passage in *Leviathan* he ignores any possibility that the obligation to Caesar might be only partial in scope.[6] Nevertheless, it is important to realize that although the sovereign may of necessity provide an authoritative interpretation of religious matters he does not therefore present a necessarily correct interpretation. No particular church nor any particular man is infallible.[7] Religion remains a matter of private belief. Despite Hobbes's disparaging remarks about the conscience he should be more widely recognized as a proponent of religious toleration. In the context of the question of what to do if one's civil sovereign should forbid belief, Hobbes responds, 'that such forbidding is of no effect; because belief and unbelief never follow men's commands. Faith is a gift of God, which man can neither give, nor take away by promise of rewards, or menaces of torture'.[8] Citizens are discouraged not from believing what they will but from contradicting authorized religion and thus embroiling the commonwealth in civil war. By the same token sovereigns are discouraged from probing into the private beliefs of their citizens; such probing would be more than a plausible concern for public safety could ever require.[9] Furthermore, although the sovereign is presented as God's lieutenant, Hobbes is not thereby pushing a version of gnosticism. The state of nature may sound a lot like Hell but Leviathan is decidedly not a heaven come down to earth and is designed more to prevent that sectarian nonsense about the Revolution of the Saints which was not uncommon in Hobbes's day and which has reappeared with such surprising force in our own times.

Revelation and Reason

If the distinction between the religious and the secular can be understood in terms of the relationship between church and state, it may also be understood in terms of another distinction, that of faith and reason or, related to it, revelation and reason. And here the two circles with which we began can be given a new alignment even if it is not immediately clear what the nature of that alignment should be. The strongest case for separating the circles comes from Hobbes himself in recognition of the limits of a naturalistic or rational theology. In *Leviathan* and elsewhere Hobbes dabbles with arguments which attempt to achieve conclusions concerning theological matters without the help of divine revelation. Medieval Europe witnessed a variety of such attempts by, among others, Anselm, Roger Bacon and Raymond Lull.[10] Some of the results of these attempts seem, in retrospect, not even incorrect but absurdly misconceived as they purport to demonstrate by purely rational means very specific, contingent details of Christian doctrine. Hobbes by contrast recognizes the limits to the kind of 'religious' knowledge that can be predicated upon the reflections of a 'secular' reason.

He does, however, venture two arguments designed to demonstrate the existence of God.[11] One is an argument of causal regression to a first mover, 'so that', in his words, 'it is impossible to make any profound inquiry into natural causes, without being inclined thereby to believe there is one God eternal; though they cannot have any idea of him in their mind, answerable to his nature'.[12] The other is sometimes labelled the argument from design where Hobbes contends that 'by the visible things in this world and their admirable order a man may conceive there is a cause of them which men call God'.[13] If a philosophically-based God and a philosophically-based religion were possible then the religious sphere might be erased completely or at least subsumed under the sphere of secular reason. But Hobbes does not conceal the difficulties that arise in an attempt to provide a naturalistic or purely rational foundation to matters of religious significance, and he later concedes the inadequacy of reason in providing unambiguous knowledge of God and the origin of the world. In *de Corpore* he points out that reason is unable to determine whether the universe is finite or infinite and the argument of causal regression would leave undecided the issue of whether the first mover was 'eternally immoveable' or 'eternally moved'.[14]

One piece of advice that Hobbes gives here is that matters of religious significance should be left for the pronouncements of 'those that are lawfully authorized to order the worship of God'.[15] Another piece of advice he gives is that on matters that may plausibly come within the compass of philosophy one yields to natural reason whereas on matters pertaining to religion one yields to revelation:

> The Scripture was written to show unto men the Kingdom of God, and to prepare their minds to become his obedient subjects; leaving the world and the philosophy thereof, to the disputation of men, for the exercising of their natural reason.[16]

Both pieces of advice would serve to push the religious and the secular well apart. Religion is a matter of faith not secular reason; religion is a matter of authoritative determination not of scientific disputation. As it happens, Hobbes does not follow his own advice and his inconsistency here opens up the possibility for the third kind of relationship between the religious and the secular, that of overlap or interaction.

Overlapping spheres

There are at least three significant aspects of Hobbes's work where the religious and the secular overlap, especially as these are understood in the sense of a relationship between matters of faith or revelation on the one hand and reason or science or philosophy on the other.

The first aspect arises in Hobbes's discussion of divine natural law or, as it is sometimes called (by Hobbes and others), the divine law of reason. Since this topic promises to wed matters divine with matters rational almost by definition, Hobbes's discussion – assuming we can make sense of it and assuming Hobbes's sincerity – is bound to be instructive. The second area of overlap arises where reason, understood here primarily as conceptual analysis, is put to work as an instrument of scriptural exegesis. In this role, reason generates the semantic criteria which facilitate the understanding of the political message of divine revelation. Reason helps to clarify the nature and limits of ecclesiastical authority and the relationship between church and state. Finally, reason, understood more in the sense of science or philosophy, has a major role in the clarification of what are ostensibly matters of faith: theology and doctrine. Despite the fact that he is sceptical of having any real knowledge of God and despite the fact that in his view religious doctrine should be a matter of authoritative pronouncement, Hobbes has quite a lot to say about both.

The divine law of reason

With regard to Hobbes's treatment of natural law some commentators have suggested that the role he gives to God is insufficiently important to warrant considering his enterprise a proper instance of theistic natural law theory at all.[17] Others contend that Hobbes does employ propositions which would be considered proper instances of natural law theorizing but that these are not seriously intended. To use Gierke's analogy, Hobbes's use of the natural law idiom is 'like a ship under false colours';[18] he presents a traditional exoteric doctrine in order to conceal a novel, esoteric doctrine. Thus, whether Hobbes is insufficiently traditional (by leaving out that 'old tyme religion') or disingenuously traditional, the entire question of considering the interplay of the religious and secular in the context of a theory of natural law would be pointless. In contrast, the contention here is that whether or not God has a sufficiently large role in Hobbes's theory the billing that God receives is not critical in determining the entry requirements to the tradition of theistic natural law. Moreover, the suggestion that Hobbes is passing off his new-fangled ideas in old boxes is less than convincing when we examine what he actually says about his natural law theorizing. In three of his major political tracts he explicitly advertises to the reader both the novelty and soundness of his natural law argument compared to those that went before. It seems hard to swallow that brazen and self-serving publicity might be seriously entertained as a form of concealment.

Hobbes's stated intentions with regard to his enterprise of natural law theorizing are made clear in his treatise on *Human Nature*.[19] In the first sentence of the chapter he points out that his 'present scope' is the 'true and perspicuous application of the elements of laws natural and politic'. His subsequent account of how he perceives his enterprise *vis-à-vis* the earlier tradition is tinged with sarcasm but is not the less interesting for that. He suggests that the predicament of natural law theorizing is such that all previous writers have without exception generated only doubt and controversy. Since it is in the nature of true knowledge to avoid doubt and controversy, it must follow, he continues, that no previous writer can have given us any true knowledge on the subject of Natural Law. He concedes that in his exposition to follow on the same subject he himself may be unable to eliminate all controversy and doubt. But he hastens to add that this will not be the result of any failure of his argument. Rather, it will result from the anticipated inability of others to give sufficient attention to his arguments. In other words both Hobbes and previous Natural Law theorists may produce controversy, but the controversy produced by earlier treatments of Natural Law resulted from internal problems in those arguments. By contrast, the controversy produced by Hobbes's treatment will result from problems in the readers of his argument.

Hobbes's readers may not all have been as amused in reading this as Hobbes probably was in writing it but it certainly seems an odd way to go about concealing his departure from earlier versions of Natural Law theory (even if it does involve a schoolboy error in logic). Much the same point is made in the dedication of this work to the Earl of Newcastle. Hobbes complains that previous writers of 'justice and policy' have failed to establish a grounding which is free of bias:

> And from hence it cometh that they do all invade each other and themselves with contradictions. To reduce this doctrine to the rules and infallibility of reason, there is no way but, first, put such principles down for a foundation, as passion, not mistrusting, may not seek to displace, and afterwards to build thereon the truth of cases in the law of nature (which hitherto have been built in the air) by degrees, till the whole have been inexpugnable.[20]

Similarly, in the epistle dedicatory to *De Cive*, Hobbes laments the errors and deficiencies of earlier moral theory, particularly the absence of a proper method. Instead of the immortal peace that would result from a sound theoretical framework there is a situation such 'that the knowledge of the law of nature should lose its growth not advancing a whit beyond its ancient stature'.[21] Again, in *Leviathan*, Hobbes contrasts his own position which breaks new ground by being structured on a solid foundation with earlier positions, particularly those of the Greeks which, in his view, were biased and subjective.[22] The satisfaction he expresses at the novel argument he considers himself to have advanced in that work is explained as follows:

> I ground the civil rights of sovereigns and both the duty and liberty of subjects, upon the known natural inclinations of mankind, and upon the articles of the law of nature; of which no man that pretends but reason enough to govern his private family, ought to be ignorant.[23]

Hobbes's natural law argument may be illogical or otherwise untenable and he may be mistaken about the tradition of natural law theorizing which preceded him,[24] but he is straightforward about his attempt to revise and in his view improve natural law theory.

What about the role of God in the theory? In Parts One and Two of *Leviathan*, Hobbes presents us with a series of reflections on the nature of man and the human condition which is self-consciously abstracted from positive revelation. His account incorporates a discussion of natural theology but at this stage (i.e. in terms of the so-called rational argument) the treatment of God is neither extensive nor significant. As we know, Hobbes suggests that living without civil society, human beings would find themselves in a state of war, a state which would be 'solitary, poor, nasty, brutish and short'. The motivation to escape this natural condition arises in the passions, the fear of death and the desire for felicity. The instrument of escape is provided by reason – the scout of the passions – which generates a set of rules designed to achieve that which is a necessary condition for escape: peace. For the most part, people disagree about the objects to which they will attach the labels 'good' and 'evil'. However, virtually everyone concedes that peace is good because, properly considered, it is a necessary requirement for any and every version of the good life. These rules that reason suggests include justice, gratitude, modesty, equity and mercy or, as they may more generally be called, moral virtues.

Here we confront a problem. Hobbes tells us that human beings are motivated to seek peace as the condition of their conservation. But are they obliged to do so and if they are obliged (whatever that may mean in the context of Hobbes's argument) is there any connection between such an obligation and God? Some would contend that the structure of Hobbes's argument at this juncture is such as to require removal from the category of theories deemed to be moral theories because people are only obliged to do what they are motivated to do.[25] Moreover, the obligations they have might be called rational obligations or prudential obligations but are hardly moral obligations; they seem conditional upon the desire to pursue felicity and avoid death and might be compared more to doctors' orders than to laws of nature which are properly and fully obligatory.[26]

Hobbes might be said, without too much anachronism, to be aware of some of these problems (even if unaware of the Kantian terminology in which they are sometimes expressed).[27] The perspective of reason only provides a set of *instrumental* goods: a set of 'theorems concerning what conduceth to [conservation and defence]'. Rational theorems only become laws and hence properly obligatory (not merely advice which can be accepted or rejected at will) if they are *considered* as 'delivered in the word of God, that by right commandeth all things'.[28] This obligation to God as a commander of natural laws, incidentally, is called by Hobbes a natural obligation. His right to command and our duty to obey arises from God's irresistible power rather than from the voluntary transferral of right which is the source of artificial obligations among men. This, after all, is the God of the Book of Job whose actions are not to be queried by proud men. This natural obligation is, in a manner of speaking, unnatural to the natural condition of man because men are naturally equal.

There is a further issue that must be addressed here. God may, in Hobbes's argument, transform rational theorems into natural law obligations but is this enough of a divine role to warrant depicting Hobbes's argument as a case of *theistic* natural law? This question raises a prior one: what role need God have in an argument for that argument to meet the entry requirements of theistic natural law? An examination of the tradition of theistic natural law would show considerable variety in the role attributed to God as compared to that attributed to reason. One example may serve to illustrate this point. The Spanish Jesuit, Francisco Suarez, who has been called the last of the Schoolmen, presents a theistic natural law argument in the course of which he reproduces the argument of other theorists for purposes of criticism. He isolates a group of people whose arguments proceed at a rational level without any necessary, continuing participation of God; indeed, the authors Suarez isolates contend that the rational theorems of natural law would have the same legal character 'even if God did not exist'.[29] Not everyone went so far but certainly a great many of those who made use of the idiom of natural law were prepared to concede that God could delegate considerable responsibility to reason and nature. In fact, many theorists specifically noted that natural law was meant to apply to those not favoured by positive revelation. The 'light of the natural reason', that conceptual metaphor that Locke found so absurd, was thought to be universally available to mankind who were therefore morally obliged even if unaware of the source of the obligation.[30] Since in Hobbes's view there are no proper natural laws without God, his natural law theory is even more God-centred than some.

Yet, having said that, it would be unwise to overstate the clarity of the connection between the sphere of the divine and the sphere of the rational in Hobbes's theory of natural law. As has been pointed out,[31] Hobbes does not bother to demonstrate to his readers the precise sense in which the 'theorems' of reason might be considered as the word of God in the critical passage in *Leviathan* where he tells his readers that the laws of nature he has elaborated are indeed properly laws.[32] There would seem to be at least two different ways of understanding Hobbes here. We might take him to mean that the rational theorems in question may literally be found in the Bible. The problem here is that Hobbes does not systematically articulate the parallels between Scripture and reason. If rational theorems only become properly obligatory through appearing in Scripture then surely, a critic may contend, Hobbes ought to show us where these theorems do appear. What Hobbes does say is that, in a general way, Scripture connects God with reason even if it does not reproduce the enumeration of the laws of nature presented in Chapters 14 and 15 of *Leviathan*. He says,

> There are also places of the Scripture, where, by the *word of God*, is signified such words as are consonant to reason and equity, . . . The *word of God*, is then also to be taken for the dictates of reason and equity, when the same is said in the Scriptures to be written in man's heart; as *Psalm* xxxvi. 31; *Jer.* xxi. 33; *Deut.* xxx. 11, 14, and many other like places.[33]

A second approach to this problem proceeds with a different sense of what Hobbes means by the 'word of God' and hence a different sense of what is involved in the connection between God and reason. Hobbes elsewhere in *Leviathan* tells us that the 'word' of God understood as a clearly promulgated command may be construed in three different ways: sensible, prophetic and rational. The sensible word of God arises when God talks to particular people. Here, as in the case of Abraham, God's commands are directly promulgated. By contrast, the prophetic word of God is a command of God believed to be such indirectly through the mediation of some 'man to whom by the operation of miracles, he procureth credit with the rest'.[34] Concerning the first, not much of a general nature can be said because God's sensible word is a matter of contingent particularity. The contemporary possibility of the prophetic word of God is, in Hobbes's view, greatly reduced because miracles are so rare; as well, one must be on guard against false prophets whose secret desire is to rule, 'which is a thing, that all men naturally desire, and is therefore worthy to be suspected of ambition and imposture'.[35]

The rational word of God is that which is declared in the 'dictates of natural reason' and it is this sense of the word of God which gives rise to the natural kingdom of God. This non-metaphorical kingdom is constituted by those subjects 'that *believe* there is a God that governeth the world, and hath given precepts, and propounded rewards, and punishments to mankind, ... all the rest, are to be understood as enemies'.[36] Without belief in a God who actively governs the world there would be no natural kingdom; without a kingdom there would be no natural laws and hence no commands. Perhaps it is faith that perfects reason after all. At any rate it seems clear that the religious and the secular understood here as God and reason are intimately connected in Hobbes's treatment of natural law. Neither is subsumed by or reduced to the other; both are necessary and neither is sufficient.

Reason and scriptural exegesis

A similar interdependence of the religious and secular may be observed if we turn to consider the way in which Hobbes approaches scriptural interpretation. The use of Scripture in the first two parts of *Leviathan* is largely decorative in the sense that the primary focus of these parts is that of reason. We have suggested that in important respects the perspective of reason is given some assistance by the divine. Yet, for the most part what is presented is a conscious attempt at a rational argument. In speaking of the first two parts, Hobbes tells us that its argument rests on 'principles of nature': 'from the nature of men, known to us by experience, and from definitions of such words as are essential to all political reasoning, universally agreed on'.[37] Those references to Scripture which do appear are not fundamental to the argument although a belief in a governing God may be.

Part Three of *Leviathan* breaks new ground in this respect since its focus is not politics in general but, specifically, Christian politics. For that reason the discourse is grounded not only on principles of nature (the natural word of God) but also on Scripture. Importantly, the principles of nature are not discarded when approaching the prophetic word of God:

> we are not to renounce our senses, and experience; nor, that which is the undoubted word of God, our natural reason. For they are the

talents which he hath put into our hands to negotiate, till the coming again of our blessed Saviour; and therefore not to be folded up in the napkin of an implicit faith, but employed in the purchase of justice, peace, and true religion.[38]

One of the problems in depending upon Scripture is that Scripture does not fully explain itself. Reason is useful here in the sense that it provides the proper semantic criteria to enable readers to understand Scripture. Scripture does not come with a glossary of terms or a conceptual primer and people are apt to go astray in eliciting the correct message from the potentially confusing array of stories. Reason can also be of assistance in the problem of authenticity. We have no knowledge that what we take for Scripture is indeed the word of God. One indication of its authenticity is its congruence with the rational principles of natural law.[39] To the extent that the content of what we take to be the prophetic word of God corresponds with what we take to be the rational word of God, we are encouraged to accept the authenticity of the former. However, it should be noted that Hobbes also maintains that the credibility of his version of natural law principles is enhanced by congruence with Scripture.[40]

Authenticity, however, is not for Hobbes such a pressing concern. If one is blessed with a personal revelation indicating the genuine works of Holy Writ then one should, of course, follow that revelation. Otherwise, our determination of works as being genuinely holy is a function of private belief. However, any work taken to be divine is only *authoritatively* so through the office of the sovereign.[41] Some critics have seen in this an underhanded way of removing the authority of Scripture because in the end it is the sovereign who controls what citizens may accept as the divine word. But this charge is misleading. First of all, Hobbes contends that people may believe what they will; they must defer publicly to sovereign-authorized doctrine in the interests of that peace which God commands through both divine natural law and divine positive law. Deference to authoritative doctrine and to authoritative enumeration of the works of Scripture was certainly not uncommon in the English Reformation.

What was more of a problem for Hobbes was the way in which he employed reason as a guide to scriptural interpretation. Published in 1651, *Leviathan* is distinctive among Hobbes's political works in that it contains a much more extensive analysis of revealed doctrine. Hobbes considered that at the time there was no official religion. It was therefore permissible and indeed desirable to offer 'to the consideration of those that are yet in deliberation . . . some new doctrines' in the interest of peace.[42] Had the religious issue been settled at the time of publication, Hobbes would not merely have been presumptuous in speaking out but his action could be construed as treasonous in terms of the very argument he puts forward. The implied consent to a sovereign by acquisition must be understood to include consent to that sovereign's control of religious doctrine. And it may not be too much of a digression to note that, in spite of all that is said about Hobbes's timidity, his forthright discussion of these matters strikes one, given the circumstances, as courageous. He was certainly correct to predict that, 'that which perhaps may most offend, are certain texts of Holy Scripture, alleged by me to other purpose than ordinarily they use to be by others'.[43]

Be that as it may, Hobbes sets out in Part Three of *Leviathan* to provide a coherent scriptural exegesis informed in large measure by the conceptual insights he develops in the first two parts of the book. In this way the various parts of *Leviathan* form a necessarily integrated whole just as the religious and the secular (if we can refer to reason as something 'secular') overlap and indeed interact in a fruitful way. One important example of this interaction occurs in Hobbes's reading of the biblical story of Abraham. This story is interesting because, first of all, it involves a covenant and covenants are important generally in Hobbes's political theory.[44] An understanding of this concept, as depicted in the first half of *Leviathan*, is therefore essential to understanding the story of Abraham. It is important in another sense as well since among Hobbes's contemporaries some were apt to extract from the story public policy implications which could have what for Hobbes would be disastrous results. If subjects felt that they could dispense with their present political obligations in favour of following someone who claimed to speak with God then the commonwealth would be in trouble. This was an interpretation that Hobbes very much wanted to undermine.

Chapter 40 of *Leviathan* contains Hobbes's discussion of Abraham and it is worth looking at it in some detail.[45] Curiously, although I have just suggested that the concept of contract is important to this story, it is not the contract between God and Abraham which is the focus of Hobbes's attention in analysing this story. Hobbes's focus is rather on some related issues which will ensure that readers come to the correct conclusion about the political message that the story reveals. The title of the chapter is 'Of the rights of the kingdom of God, in Abraham, Moses, the High-Priests, and the Kings of Judah', and Hobbes points out that Abraham was first in the kingdom of God by covenant. But, importantly, it was not this covenant that created the obligation of Abraham and his seed to God. As rational men, 'to the moral law, they were already obliged, and needed not have been contracted withal, by promise of the land of Canaan'. This is not something that Scripture tells us. Rather, it is something that Hobbes has previously told us in the first two parts of *Leviathan*: there exists a natural kingdom of God constituted by all rational people who believe in a God who issues commands via natural laws. This emphasis is significant in that it resists the distinction between a kingdom of God and a secular kingdom. Sovereign right is a divine right whether it arises directly according to a peculiar covenant or indirectly through natural principles. Abraham's covenant with God constituted a peculiar kingdom and for our purposes it is interesting to note that the word 'kingdom' is not expressly used in this context in *Genesis*. Knowledge of what is entailed in the concept of kingdom (which is what Hobbes purports to provide) allows the reader to appreciate the kingdom which, textually, is only implied: 'And though the name of *King* be not yet given to God, nor of *kingdom* to Abraham and his seed; yet the thing is the same; namely, an institution by pact, of God's peculiar sovereignty over the seed of Abraham'.[46]

Another significant point that Hobbes makes regarding this covenant is that it involved only God and Abraham. The family and seed of Abraham were not a party to the covenant,

> otherwise than as their wills, which make the essence of all covenants, were before the contract involved in the will of Abraham; who was therefore supposed to have had a lawful power, to make them perform all that he covenanted for them.[47]

It was not the covenant with God that created the obligation on the part of Abraham's family and seed; they were already obliged since Abraham was not merely a father but also a civil sovereign. *Genesis* Chapter 18 does not make this point quite as clearly as *Leviathan* Chapter 20. By knowing what is involved in the concept of 'civil sovereign', readers of Scripture will know that they should obey their sovereign's revelation unless they have had one of their own. Yet, given the possibility of pretending a private revelation to counter the sovereign, the sovereign is within his rights to 'punish any man that shall oppose his private spirit against the laws: for he hath the same place in the commonwealth, that Abraham had in his own family'.[48] Similarly, Hobbes concludes that 'as none but Abraham in his family, so none but the sovereign in a Christian commonwealth, can take notice of what is, or what is not the word of God'.[49] Although this point has already been made in the first half of *Leviathan* it is doubtlessly reassuring for Hobbes to find it confirmed (with the help of some conceptual analysis) in the story of Abraham.

It would be inaccurate, however, to see the employment of Scripture here merely as corroboration of what people should understand anyway on the basis of reason. The inclusion of control over religious matters within the right of the sovereign is something that is established in the first half of *Leviathan*; in other words, it is a function of politics in general. But the differentiae of a distinctively Christian commonwealth are a function of what the sovereign (in conjunction with whatever ministers he may choose and whatever advice he may accept) establishes as authoritative doctrine by means of an authorized reading of authorized holy texts. What Hobbes is doing here is making the task of interpretation easier for the Christian sovereign and this is done primarily by bringing conceptual analysis to bear upon the language of what are believed to be holy texts.

What Hobbes wishes to do is to circumscribe very carefully the semantic scope of the concept of 'kingdom'. And, he wishes to show that Scripture complies with the proper understanding of the concept as depicted in the first half of *Leviathan*. Were we unclear about what was entailed in the concept of 'kingdom' or were we to misconstrue the proper sense of the kingdom of God in the Bible we might go astray in trying to conform to the requirements of God's kingdom. Properly understood as a real (albeit special or peculiar) kingdom based upon consent it can also be understood to have ended, Hobbes contends, at the time of Saul.[50] The fact that it lasted provided further demonstration that sovereign right should include both ecclesiastical and civil power. The fact that it ended (until the Messiah comes) should help to remove the pretext of arguing the kingdom of God against the kingdom of the civil sovereign. Our appreciation of these facts is brought about in part by the sphere of reason.

Hobbes's analysis of the New Testament proceeds in a similar vein to his analysis of the five books of Moses. As in the earlier work he concludes that the civil sovereign ought to be in control of both ecclesiastical and civil affairs. And, as with the analysis of the earlier material, it is reason understood as conceptual analysis which is put to work in order to extract a coherent message from the potentially ambiguous holy words. The overriding concern is to clarify the sense in which Christ may be properly said to be a 'king' and to exercise authority over his kingdom. This was an important contemporary concern because citizens of earthly sovereigns might be tempted to give priority to the kingdom of Christ over their temporal monarchs. Similarly, there were those who claimed spiritual authority over Hobbes's contemporaries as lawful successors to Christ's apostles.

Hobbes is able to undermine such claims by resorting to 'definitions of such words as are essential to all political reasoning, universally agreed on'.[51] If the reader of Scripture needs to be reminded of these definitions he can turn to the first half of *Leviathan*. There he will find what is entailed in the concept of 'kingdom'; what is the nature of sovereign authority; and what is the distinction between command and counsel. Armed with these concepts and distinctions the reader of Scripture will appreciate that Christ's kingdom was not meant to be of this world but of the world to come. Christ is depicted as someone who advised and counselled rather than commanded or issued laws. It is command and law which suggest the concept of kingdom and the exercise of sovereign authority. Speaking of Christ's office Hobbes notes that one part of it was,

> by teaching, and by working of miracles, to persuade and prepare men to live so, as to be worthy of the immortality believers were to enjoy, at such time as he should come in majesty to take possession of his Father's kingdom. And therefore it is, that the time of his preaching is often by himself called the *regeneration*; which is not properly a kingdom, and thereby a warrant to deny obedience to the magistrates that then were.[52]

Strictly speaking Christ had no authority while on earth; the basis of his authority in the kingdom to come, in Hobbes's view, is the practice of baptism which Hobbes considers a covenant for the next world.[53] Once again, it is reason understood as conceptual analysis which aids in Biblical exegesis. If, in the case of natural law, it is God that comes to the rescue of reason to transform its conclusions into proper laws, in the case of scriptural analysis it is reason that repays the debt and allows God to express himself intelligibly.

Theology and the 'new science'

Another aspect of the interaction of reason and revelation in Hobbes's treatment of religious matters comes in his discussion of specific doctrinal points. In this context the concept of reason is linked to what Hobbes took to be the 'new science'. For him the new science was circumscribed exclusively by reference to matter in motion: 'the variations of fancies or (which is the same thing) of the phenomena of nature have all of them one universal efficient cause, namely, the variety of motion'.[54] The notion of substance is semantically equivalent to the notion of body. 'Accidents' and 'qualities' are words that designate different kinds of motions; universals are general terms that indicate the presence of a perceived similarity among different particulars. According to Hobbes the central problem with the old Aristotelian-Scholastic metaphysics is that it generated philosophical confusion by speaking about the secondary qualities of things as if they were distinct and separable from the matter in motion of which they are in fact constituted. A noumenal realm of abstract essences is thus improperly granted ontological status and the result is absurd speech about things which form no part of the universe.

It should be emphasized that Hobbes himself regards his philosophical-scientific clarification as a contribution to religious illumination. Referring to the introduction of Aristotle's philosophy into Christian doctrine he remarks,

> From that time, instead of the worship of God, there entered a thing called 'school-divinity' walking on one foot firmly, which is Holy Scripture, but halted on the other rotten foot, which the Apostle Paul called 'vain' and might have called 'pernicious philosophy'; for it hath raised an infinite number of controversies in the Christian world concerning religion, and from these controversies, wars.[55]

The renunciation of philosophy as the fruit of hubris is common enough in Reformation literature but Hobbes is prepared to renounce only 'pernicious philosophy'. The doctrinal points of Scripture require a primer in order that they be properly understood and Hobbes assumes that most of his contemporaries do not understand it properly for which reason, 'we are yet in the dark . . . The enemy has been here in the night of our natural ignorance, and sown the tares of spiritual errors'.[56]

Hobbes's contemporaries were not disposed to accept his reading of their spiritual errors. A religion imbued not with Scholastic metaphysics but with corporeality and structured according to Hobbes's *philosophia prima* was one of the issues that caused concern among Arminian theologians of the Anglican church. John Bramhall, the once bishop of Derry with whom Hobbes carried on an extensive debate, argued that by taking away all incorporeal substance Hobbes had taken away God as well.[57] Hobbes considered incorporeal spirit and incorporeal body to be 'insignificant sounds . . . coined by schoolmen and puzzled philosophers' resulting from the joining together of 'two names whose significations are contradictory and inconsistent'.[58] Strictly speaking, 'spirit' is a kind of body even if in common speech the name of body is reserved for such things 'that have some degree of opacity'. Whereas in strict terms it would be absurd to speak of incorporeal spirit, Hobbes would be prepared to admit such a term as a 'name of mere honour' which 'may . . . with more piety be attributed to God himself in whom we consider not what attribute expresseth best his nature which is incomprehensible; but what expresseth best our desire to honour Him'.[59]

In much the same way that the conceptual clarification of political terms in the first two parts of *Leviathan* contributes to the evaluation and understanding of the otherwise potentially ambiguous political message of Scripture, so does Hobbes's mechanical-corporeal ontology contribute to the generation of semantic criteria that structure the propositions of theology and facilitate the extraction and clarification of doctrinal points from Scripture. Hobbes's corporeal treatment of spirit and God is related to a wide ranging critique of demonology. Conventional religious practice and language, which encouraged belief in the existence of demons, witchcraft and spiritual (i.e. non-corporeal) phenomena, were predicated upon conceptual confusion: 'it was hard for men to conceive of those images in the fancy and in the sense, otherwise, than as things really without us'.[60] The Scholastic-Aristotelian explanation of vision, in Hobbes's view, was to argue that sight occurred when a visible object gave off a 'visible species' which was then received by the eye.[61] If one saw a demon or a ghost, these things must really exist because their existence would, presumably, be required to transmit the visible species. For Hobbes, sight and indeed all sensual perceptions are caused by motions set up by the external material world. Internally, the heart and brain respond with a counter pressure or outwardly directed endeavour, 'which endeavour, because outward, seemeth to be some matter without'.[62] Sensible, perceived qualities are motions in the objects which produce them; in us they are motions as well since 'motion produceth nothing but motion'.[63] It is the appearance of this motion in us that Hobbes calls 'fancy' and it is the same waking as dreaming. Dreaming occurs when the internal motions, that generates fancy and that are normally produced by the external world pressing inward, are caused instead by 'distemper of some of the inward parts of the body'.[64] Visions and apparitions can similarly be caused by motions set up internally. Once we appreciate this we are able to separate the phenomenal realm given in the fancy from the external world and we are not therefore committed to the real existence of ghosts and demons.[65] It was the inability of pagan philosophers (and those Christian theologians who followed them) to appreciate the nature of vision that generated so much absurdity:

> From this ignorance of how to distinguish dreams, and other strong fancies, from vision and sense, did arise the greatest part of the religion of the Gentiles in time past, that worshipped satyrs, fawns, nymphs and the like; and now-a-days the opinion that rude people have of fairies, ghosts and goblins and of the power of witches.[66]

Since for Hobbes the universe should be spolen of as a corporeal plenum operating mechanically (as a sceptic Hobbes claims we cannot know what the universe is like since it wasn't made by man), he cannot accept the conventional understanding of demon or spirit. Nor can he accept intuitive or non-mechanical modes of operation, particularly inspiration or infusion in so far as these terms are understood to signal non-mechanical processes involving non-material entities. Hobbes contends therefore, on grounds of consistent and plausible semantics, that the phrase 'divine inspiration' or 'divine infusion', when found in Scripture, should be construed metaphorically; this is because 'the proper use of the word infused, in speaking of the graces of God is an abuse of it; for those graces are virtues not bodies to be carried hither and thither to be poured into men as into barrels'.[67] Hobbesian semantics, rooted as they are in assumptions of corporeal mechanism, act as a guide for the appreciation of holy texts. When we confront the word 'infused' in Scripture we should understand that it cannot mean the imparting of a separable divine essence. When it is said of God that he inspires into man the breath of life we should take it to mean an imparting of vital motion. And where it is written that all Scripture is given by inspiration from God, we should understand it to mean that God 'inclined [literally moved] . . . the mind of those writers to write that which should be useful, in teaching, reproving, correcting and instructing men in the way of righteous living'.[68]

There are in fact various doctrinal issues that Hobbes confronts with his tools of rational discourse. He concedes that some of the words that Scripture uses are distinctive to it and here exegesis must extract the meaning of those words from the text.[69] Yet even when he is engaged in ostensibly textual analysis, Hobbes makes use of extra-textual considerations. Space does not permit a full discussion here of all of these issues which would include the trinity, baptism, communion, the afterlife, the human soul, predestination and free will. His brief discussion of angels may suffice as a characteristic example. Hobbes tells us that he initially took the word 'angel' to entail the creation of some apparition in the fancy of many by the operation of God through secondary material causes. But, he changed his mind on this because

> the many places of the New Testament, and our Saviour's own words, and in such texts, wherein is no suspicion of corruption of the Scripture, have extorted from my feeble reason, an acknowledge-ment and belief, that there be also angels substantial, and permanent. But to believe they be in no place, that is to say nothing, as they, though indirectly, say, that will have them incorporeal, cannot by Scripture be evinced.[70]

We are still entitled to speak of angels but we need to add a bit of flesh (or at least corporeal matter) to our conception of them. In general our understanding of the concepts of Scripture needs to be purged of the 'empty bottles of Gentilism, which the doctors of the Roman Church either by negligence or ambition, have filled up again with the new wine of Christianity that will not fail in time to break them'.[71]

Conclusion

In conclusion it is safe, if cowardly, to assert that the relationship between the religious and secular in Hobbes's work is not straightforward nor uncomplicated. Understood as a relation between church and state, the two come together in some situations: perhaps those situations of most concern to Hobbes's English contemporaries. Their union is the result of a semantic point: a clarification of what is entailed in the concept of authority. To issue commands binding upon others and to have religious 'authority' a church must, according to Hobbesian semantics, be united in the person of a sovereign. Religion can have no claim to authority *jure divino* which does not arise in this way. Those Anglicans, Puritans and Catholics who thought otherwise were misinformed about the semantic entailment of important political concepts.

If we understand the religious and the secular more generally as the interaction of faith and reason, the relationship becomes more complicated. In the context of the theistic natural law argument (and at the very least this is the way Hobbes referred to what he was doing), faith assists reason in the transformation of rational theorems into laws of nature. What might otherwise be hypothetical imperatives to those desiring their preservation become the commands of an all-powerful God to whom we are therefore *naturally* obliged.

Reason is similarly useful to faith in the sense that conceptual analysis is a necessary ingredient of scriptural exegesis. Faith needs to be instructed by the principles of universal rational discourse in order that the potentially ambiguous political message and doctrinal substance of Scripture should not be misconstrued. In particular, we need to understand what is properly entailed in the kingdom of God so as not to fall prey to the charlatans and hucksters of false gods and false kingdoms. As well, we need to purge religion of the absurd metaphysics inserted by Scholastic philosophers and replace it with the common sense of corporeal mechanics. In this way faith and reason – the religious and the secular – can get on very well together in the view of Thomas Hobbes.

Notes

1 T. Hobbes, *Leviathan*, ed. M. Oakeshott, London and New York, Collier-Macmillan, 1962, p. 340.
2 ibid., p. 499. Admittedly, this passage may be read as encouraging not the proliferation of churches but the toleration of individual consciences.
3 For a discussion of Hobbes's treatment of toleration see A. Ryan, 'Hobbes, toleration and the inner life', in D. Miller and L. Siedentrop (eds), *The Nature of Political Theory*, Oxford, Oxford University Press, 1983, p. 197.

4 J. Locke, *A Letter Concerning Toleration*, ed. J. Tully, Indianapolis, Hackett, 1983, pp. 28–32.

5 See, for example, R. Hooker, *The Works of that Learned and Judicious Divine Mr. Richard Hooker with an Account of his Life and Death by Isaac Walton*, 3 vols, ed. J. Keble (revised Church and Paget), 7th edn, Oxford, Clarendon Press, 1889, vol. 1, p. 151.

6 Hobbes, *Leviathan*, pp. 355, 363.

7 ibid., p. 427.

8 ibid., pp. 363–4.

9 ibid., pp. 399, 491.

10 For a brief discussion of these matters see E. Gilson, *Reason and Revelation in the Middles Ages*, New York, Scribner and Sons, 1952, pp. 29–31.

11 For a good discussion of this and other issues of Hobbesian natural theology see R. Hepburn, 'Hobbes on the knowledge of God', in M. Cranston and R. Peters (eds), *Hobbes and Rousseau*, New York, Anchor-Doubleday, 1972, p. 85.

12 Hobbes, *Leviathan*, p. 85.

13 ibid. K.C. Brown contends that the argument from design is more important to Hobbes but it is not clear why this is thought to be so, see his 'Hobbes's grounds for belief in a deity', *Philosophy*, 1962, vol. 37, p. 336.

14 T. Hobbes, *The English Works of Thomas Hobbes*, ed. W. Molesworth, 11 vols, London, John Bohn, 1889, vol. 1, pp. 411–13.

15 ibid., vol. 1, p. 412.

16 Hobbes, *Leviathan*, p. 67. See also Hobbes, *English Works*, vol. 2, p. 305.

17 See, for example, F. McNeilly, *The Anatomy of Leviathan*, London, Macmillan, 1968, p. 211.

18 O. von Gierke, *Natural Law and the Theory of Society*, Cambridge, Cambridge University Press, 1927, p. 97. Michael Oakeshott's elegant expression is 'artful equivocation', see his *Rationalism in Politics*, London, Methuen, 1962, p. 283.

19 Hobbes, *English Works*, vol. 4, p. 1.

20 ibid., p. xiii.

21 ibid., vol. 2, p. vi.

22 Hobbes, *Leviathan*, p. 481.

23 ibid., p. 509.

24 Richard Tuck has suggested plausible debts to Selden about which Hobbes is less than forthcoming in his *Natural Rights Theories: Their Origin and Development*, Cambridge, Cambridge University Press, 1979, p. 83.

25 See J. Plamenatz, 'Mr. Warrender's Hobbes', *Political Studies*, 1957, vol. 5, p. 297.

26 See, for example, J. Watkins, *Hobbes's System of Ideas*, 2nd edn, London, Hutchinson, 1965, p. 83.

27 Whether Hobbes's theory is a moral theory raises a point that cannot be explored here.

28 Hobbes, *Leviathan*, p. 124.

29 F. Suarez, *Selections from Three Works*, ed. J. B. Scott, Classics of International Law, vol. 20, Oxford, Clarendon Press, 1927, p. 188.

30 See, for example, Hooker, *Works*, vol. 1, p. 227. Hobbes makes a similar

point, 'mildly' inconsistent, alas, with the interpretation here advanced, Hobbes, *English Works*, vol. 4, pp. 284–5.

31 This point is important to Gauthier whose formal definition of Hobbes's law of nature omits reference to God as a commander. D. Gauthier, *The Logic of Leviathan*, Oxford, Clarendon Press, 1969, pp. 36–9.

32 Hobbes, *Leviathan*, p. 124.

33 ibid., p. 307.

34 ibid., p. 262.

35 ibid., p. 315.

36 ibid., p. 262 (my emphasis).

37 ibid., p. 271.

38 ibid.

39 ibid., p. 284.

40 ibid., p. 249. An incorrect interpretation of Scripture coupled with a faulty natural law principle could produce, it would seem, mutually reinforcing errors.

41 ibid., p. 284.

42 ibid., p. 509.

43 Dedication to Francis Godolphin, ibid., p. 5.

44 For a different view see R. Halliday, T. Kenyon, and A. Reeve, 'Hobbes's belief in God', *Political Studies*, 1983, vol. 31, p. 418.

45 See also Hobbes, *Leviathan*, ch. 35, for a discussion of 'The kingdom of God' and its various senses in Scripture.

46 ibid., p. 298.

47 ibid., p. 342.

48 ibid., p. 343.

49 ibid.

50 ibid., pp. 300–1.

51 ibid., p. 271.

52 ibid., p. 354.

53 ibid., p. 353.

54 Hobbes, *English Works*, vol. 7, p. 83.

55 ibid., vol. 1, pp. x–xi.

56 ibid., p. 438.

57 ibid., vol. 4, p. 305. See S. Mintz, *The Hunting of Leviathan*, Cambridge, Cambridge University Press, 1962, p. 67.

58 Hobbes, *Leviathan*, p. 39.

59 ibid., p. 483.

60 ibid., p. 460.

61 ibid., p. 22.

62 ibid., p. 21.

63 ibid., pp. 21–2.

64 ibid., p. 25.

65 This issue was a point of contention between Hobbes and Descartes with Hobbes insisting, unconvincingly, that one could distinguish between dreaming and wakefulness. See ibid., p. 25.

66 ibid., p. 26.

67 ibid., p. 296.

68 ibid., p. 295.
69 ibid., p. 286.
70 ibid., pp. 294–5.
71 ibid., p. 477.

Chapter two

John Locke: Socinian or natural law theorist?

David Wootton

This essay brings together a number of arguments, each one of them open to dispute, in order to suggest a new picture of the place of religion in Locke's moral and political philosophy. Since the space available to me is limited I will not rehearse at length the arguments or evidence that others have presented elsewhere. For the full case I want to make to be true, each of the following arguments would have to be true. Not only

(i) Locke's religious position from 1695 (the date of the publication of *The Reasonableness of Christianity*) was close to that of Socinianism (this has been argued by others, so that my concern will be rather to define Socinianism than to show that Locke became one);[1] but also

(ii) Locke's religious and philosophical position before he published the *Two Treatises* in 1689, and perhaps even before he wrote them in around 1681, had (and was known by Locke to have) Socinian elements.[2] From these it follows that

(iii) the claims that Locke made for a deductive science of morality in the *Essay Concerning Human Understanding* were known by him to be deeply problematic and perhaps false; and that

(iv) Locke had no good grounds for confidence in the natural law position adopted in the *Two Treatises*.

One might therefore characterize the *Two Treatises* as a work directed at solving a practical political problem, not at honestly tackling the central problems of political philosophy, and the *Essay* as failing to show what Locke claimed it showed: that if there were many things we could not know, we could nevertheless discover through natural reason everything we needed to know for the proper conduct of our lives on earth. It also follows (although, as we will see, Locke may not have seen the full logic of his position until 1695, or even later) that

(v) those who attacked the *Essay* as a philosophy constructed to support Socinianism were not simply reading into the text views that Locke had only come to later, in *The Reasonableness*, but were giving an accurate account of the implications of the argument, implications that Locke is likely to have been aware of from the beginning.[3]

My argument turns on problems regarding the dating of changes in Locke's religious and philosophical views. I will not be denying that Locke's position changed significantly between 1689 and 1695, and even more between 1681 and 1704, but I will be stressing certain elements of continuity, elements which subvert conventional interpretations of the *Essay* and the *Treatises*, and in doing so I will be claiming that Locke's thought is a great deal less coherent than has been claimed.[4] This argument does not only affect our understanding of Locke's relationship to his own work. The *Two Treatises* are often treated as the foundation of modern political thought, and of modern liberalism in particular.[5] If the intellectual assumptions they rested on were unsatisfactory in Locke's own view, this is a valuable pointer as to why contemporary liberal theories often seem incoherent and ill-founded.

The contemporary testimony

Historians of political theory and of philosophy have a tendency to dismiss accusations levied by polemical pygmies against great philosophers. Few turn to Hobbes's opponents to learn about Hobbes, or Locke's opponents to learn about Locke. This is a mistake, as I hope to show in this section.

Hobbism

In 1689 John Locke published his *Essay Concerning Human Understanding*. This was a book he had been working on since 1671 and which had occupied him during two periods of political exile. Amongst its first readers was James Tyrrell, who had been present at the discussions on morality and religion in which Locke's *Essay* had originated, who had been Locke's collaborator in the past, and who had been entrusted with a copy of an early draft of the *Essay*.[6]

Tyrrell would seem an ideal commentator to tell us what was important about the *Essay*. What we learn from him comes as a surprise. He had read the work, he told Locke, and discussed it with some acquaintances in Oxford. They had pointed out to him (and clearly he had been persuaded by their arguments) that the discussion of morality at the end of the book led straight to Hobbism. Locke had identified three laws governing moral action: the law of philosophy or (for he boldly equated the two) the law of opinion, which varied from society to society and which carried sanctions of praise and blame; the law of the state, which also varied and which carried sanctions of corporal punishment; and the divine law, which depended on an historical revelation. This left no universally binding moral law, and left man, outside any particular state or religion, free to pursue his own naked interest: in short, Hobbism.[7]

The charge of Hobbism was a serious one. In the 1670s, to Hobbes's personal alarm, there had been repeated attempts in Parliament to make Hobbism punishable by death. In any case, no work against which the accusation of Hobbism could be tellingly made could hope to have anything but a marginal existence in intellectual life. Locke's response to the accusation – from which his friendship with Tyrrell never recovered – was one of indignation, anger, and perhaps panic. His initial defence was internally contradictory. On the one hand he said he had meant by the 'divine law' the law of nature as well as the revealed law of God; Tyrrell replied that this usage was unprecedented and his meaning therefore incomprehensible. On the other hand he said he had been talking not about the true law of God, but about the particular divine laws that happen to be respected in different societies. This meant admitting that he had not identified a universally applicable moral law. Locke's initial response to Tyrrell's objection was to rephrase the passage in question, so that it referred to both natural law and any and every divine law, but when the substance of Tyrrell's objection was repeated in print by Lowde, Locke further replied at length in the preface to the second edition of the *Essay*.[8]

Locke's indignation in face of Tyrrell's attack was comprehensible, for a similar argument had appeared in the draft of the *Essay* which Tyrrell had read.[9] Tyrrell insisted that he would have advised Locke of the dangerous implications of the wording he had finally adopted, but it is not clear that the original phrasing could not have given rise to the same objections.

Locke was entitled to protest that he had been misunderstood, but behind the misunderstanding lay a central problem: Locke's failure to explain how we could establish the content of natural law. Since his *Essays on the Law of Nature* of 1663 Locke had attacked the idea of any innate knowledge of right and wrong.[10] Men had no infallible conscience; no automatic sense of guilt to guide and punish them. Since that date he had been under an intellectual obligation to show how one could come by knowledge of a moral code that was not subjective and relative. This was an intellectual debt that he had not paid, either in the drafts of 1671 or in the *Essay* of 1689. Tyrrell urged that he address himself to the problem as a matter of urgency, offering him as models Samuel Parker and Cumberland, whose account of natural law Tyrrell was soon to translate. Locke's new friend Molyneux (whose tactful praise of the *Essay* was in such sharp distinction to Tyrrell's criticism) repeatedly urged him to deal with the problem. The same request came from Catherine Trotter, in a spirited reply to Lowde.[11] Locke promised to address himself to these concerns, but none of his numerous revisions to the *Essay* dealt with the problem.

The charge of Hobbism against Locke was levied not only by Tyrrell, but by another privileged commentator. The third Earl of Shaftesbury, whose education Locke had supervised and who was a personal friend, was to repeat the accusation. His objection was not only to the fact that Locke denied any innate sense of right and wrong, but also to the fact that Locke identified the good and the bad with pleasure and pain, and moral good and bad with the pleasures and pains attached to obedience to or infraction of a law.[12] In Shaftesbury's view this made morality entirely a question of self-interest, and destroyed any idea of things that were good and bad in themselves, making morality entirely relative to the arbitrary commands of society, the sovereign, or of God. Where Hobbes had made his sovereign a 'mortal God', Locke had made his God a Hobbist sovereign, whose commands were to be obeyed out of fear of pain and hope of pleasure.

What was the real relationship between Hobbes and Locke? The main trend of scholarship since Laslett's edition of the *Two Treatises* has been to argue that Locke had no reason to pay attention to Hobbes; that the *Two Treatises* were directed against Filmer not Hobbes; that the defence of absolutism to be found in the early *Two Tracts* or the attack on the idea that the only obligation was to pursue self-interest in the *Essays on the Law of Nature* arose not from Locke's trying to come to grips with Hobbes but from his reading authors such as Samuel Parker.[13] Cox's view, that the *Two Treatises* embody an esoteric Hobbism, has received no support from historians of ideas.[14] It is only now that Richard Tuck has written an essay on 'Hobbes and Locke', showing how close their views on toleration were between 1667 and 1673 and thus defending Aubrey's assumption that Locke would have approved of what Hobbes was writing during that period, that the question of Hobbes and Locke seems likely to be reopened.[15]

For the moment, let us ask whether Tyrrell and his friends were justified in expressing alarm. Did Locke believe in a law of nature that could be known by every reasonable man and that was binding on all men, at all times, in all places? Certainly he had done when he wrote the *Essays on the Law of Nature*, for this is one of their central claims. Equally clearly he really did not by the end of his life, for in the posthumous *A Paraphrase and Notes on the Epistles of St Paul* he maintained that there was no clearly established moral law aside from the revealed law; the Jews before Moses, the Gentiles until the crucifixion had been 'laws unto themselves' (a phrase similar to ones he had used elsewhere about atheists) because they had been governed by no known, absolute moral law.[16]

If the charge of Hobbism, thus narrowly interpreted, was unjustified in 1690, it was valid by 1705. But was it really invalid in 1690? Locke's claim was that the morality studied and taught by moral philosophers through the ages had been one whose only sanction was public opinion; no absolute moral law had been identified by unaided human reason. As for the revealed law, it evidently varied from society to society, interpreter to interpreter. Everyone was agreed that a law was only a law if it was promulgated; and yet the clear message of the *Essay* was that no law of nature had been promulgated, despite Locke's occasional insistence that it was easy for us to know what our duties were. Instead of a known law of nature, man's behaviour was in fact governed by a happy artifice of divine providence. By and large what was pleasurable and painful corresponded with what was morally right and wrong; in particular what was necessary for the survival of society was almost everywhere the same and corresponded closely to the commandments of the revealed law.[17] Thus, in practice, worldly self-interest and the quest for collective security substituted for a known moral law, and this was an adequate substitution, for, as James Tully and Ian Harris have shown with regard to the *Second Treatise*, Locke believed that the law of nature could be summed up in the obligation to ensure that mankind multiplied and prospered on earth.[18]

In his *De Iure Belli et Pacis*, a work carefully studied by Locke, Grotius had denied that the law of nature was identical to individual self-interest; but he had recognized that it was closely similar to the collective interests of mankind, so that even atheists, who had no knowledge of an absolute moral law or a system of eternal rewards and punishments, would, Grotius argued, have to recognize that the law of nature had *some* force.[19] Locke never seems to have mentioned this much-commented upon passage, but there is no doubt that by the end of his life he thought that most men, through history, had been in the position of Grotius's atheists.

Socinianism

In 1695 Locke published *The Reasonableness of Christianity*. Immediately, accusations of Socinianism were levied against the work, which was banned by the Grand Jury of Middlesex in 1697. By 1698 Socinianism was covered by the new blasphemy act which provided for penalties that were modest compared to those envisaged under the

Commonwealth and actually enforced in Scotland, but that were still not negligible: they included the loss of any government office upon a first conviction.[20] Locke's main critic was John Edwards who argued that *The Reasonableness* was entirely silent on the doctrine of the Trinity; it attacked original sin and said nothing about the atonement; it reduced (as Socinians did) the Gospel message to a simple, rational creed, and identified it with the single principle – that Jesus is the Christ – that Hobbes had singled out in *Leviathan*; it emphasized the Gospels alone and paid virtually no attention to the Old Testament and the Epistles. In short, it was Socinian, and a work that was not an antidote, as Locke claimed, against unbelief, but a dangerous ally to *Christianity not Mysterious*, written by Toland, a former friend of Locke's who claimed to be arguing from Lockean principles, and who employed them to undermine orthodox Christianity.[21]

Edwards's attack upon *The Reasonableness* led to a whole series of new attacks upon the *Essay*. Read in the light of *The Reasonableness*, it could be argued, the *Essay* seemed to be nothing so much as a work of Socinian philosophy. Stillingfleet complained that Locke's account of substance amounted to an attack upon the doctrine of the Trinity. Burnet protested that Locke's claim that the soul might be material and his account of identity were attacks upon the belief that the soul was immortal and that the same body would be resurrected after death. Leibniz, in a work published posthumously, set out to defend the doctrine of the immortality of the soul against Locke, an undertaking that he believed involved attacking each and every aspect of Locke's philosophy, from his denial of innate ideas and his insistence that the soul did not think continuously to his account of mathematical reasoning. Even Locke's friend Molyneux was somewhat surprised at the account of moral responsibility that Locke gave in the first edition of the *Essay*, in discussing liberty and necessity; by making all sins proceed from defects of understanding Locke had seemed to leave no scope for a theory of human depravity, or (one could add) for original sin, atonement, and predestination.[22]

In discussing Locke and Hobbism it did not seem necessary to identify the central doctrines of Hobbes's system. I want to proceed here again by accepting the definition of Socinianism assumed by Locke's opponents – in this case, particularly, the definition of Burnet and Leibniz – but it is worth pausing to show that this is a sensible definition, and it will be necessary later to ask whether Locke was a full-blooded Socinian, as Edwards suspected.

For my purposes, Socinianism can be identified with the 1609 text of the Racovian Catechism, rather than the teachings of Socinus.[23] As we shall see in a moment, Socinian thought changed and evolved (there are even two versions of the Catechism) and I think we are urgently in need of a study of Locke in the context of changing Socinian views. But the fundamental issues did not change.

Socinianism is regularly presented primarily in terms of those doctrines of orthodox Christianity that it denied. Such an account is likely to go somewhat as follows. Socinianism denied the Trinity (nowhere mentioned in the Bible), and with it the pre-existence of Christ before the virgin birth. It denied original sin and predestination, for these doctrines seemed to deny moral responsibility and make God the author of man's downfall. In insisting on moral responsibility it necessarily rejected the atonement (the doctrine that Christ died as a sacrifice for our sins), and its insistence on God's justice was incompatible with the doctrine of the eternal punishment for the wicked. Indeed it claimed that the punishment for sin was annihilation.

By the late seventeenth century Socinianism could be freely taught nowhere, but it was widely believed that there were many secret Socinians. Its illegality presents us with the same class of problem that we encounter in studying the history of atheism, for we must expect Socinian convictions were sometimes presented indirectly or incompletely. A key difference though is that we do have at our disposal a significant Socinian literature.

Let us try, for a moment, to summarize Socinianism from a Socinian point of view. Such an approach immediately brings to light the fact that Socinianism did not consist merely in a set of theological doctrines, but that it depended upon a view of the capacities of human reason, and that it therefore bore directly on the problems of the *Essay* as well as on those of *The Reasonableness*. What Socinianism fundamentally did was shift the focus of Christianity from the crucifixion to the resurrection. Christ was not God made man, nor did he die as a sacrifice for our sins and to wipe out the consequences of Adam's sin. He was a messenger from God, but his death was proof of his fundamental identification with humanity. The important fact is, a Socinian would say, that he rose again. What makes this so important? But for Christ's resurrection we would have no certainty of life after death. The punishment for Adam's sin was that man became mortal. To Moses and the Jewish people God offered a new covenant: obedience to the law would lead to prosperity in this world. The Mosaic law was too demanding, the rewards promised too slight. What Christ offered was immortality, and with it God's grace, which would make obedience to the law easy, and which would also make sin, in those who both believed and sought to obey, forgivable.

This offer was made to all men. It marked a new moment in history, for until then the Gentiles had had no divinely-appointed law to follow, and no rational grounds for adopting a moral code based on anything other than worldly self-interest and prudence. Now, for the first time, all men had a divinely-appointed moral law, with accompanying rewards and sanctions, to obey. With Christ's resurrection a true standard of right and wrong, justice and injustice was for the first time given to the world. The Bible, especially the New Testament, provided the record of God's commands to man, commands that primarily concerned fulfilment of a moral law, and that rested upon the fact of Christ's resurrection.

Socinianism thus hinged upon the claim that natural reason could not establish the immortality of the soul or the content of the law of nature; hence the necessity of Christ's teaching and of the resurrection.[24] From this central claim, Socinians proceeded to develop varying conclusions. Some, particularly in the early seventeenth century and including Socinus himself, concluded that Biblical morality forbad oaths and military service, and made it unacceptable for a Christian to be a magistrate. Others, especially in the late seventeenth century, sought to harmonize Christian virtue and natural virtue. Crell, for example, sought to maintain a fundamental continuity between Aristotelian doctrines and Christian teaching, encouraging the Christian to practise the same political virtues (although with better reasons and stronger motives) as a pagan philosopher. Przypkowski sought to integrate Grotius's conception of natural law into the Socinian tradition, while recognizing that only a Socinian would be able to have a full grasp of the character of natural law.[25] Such authors insisted that the state existed to serve worldly purposes; the Church must be quite separate from the state and must benefit from toleration. For the state to concern itself with salvation was improper, for the state was a natural institution with no interest in spiritual matters. For Christians to be intolerant towards each other was equally mistaken, for the Gospel message could only be conveyed through words, not blows.

Socinianism thus had, for our purposes, a core doctrine: that immortality was a supernatural gift, which correlated with a core problem: that of the relationship between the spiritual and the secular. Enemies of Socinianism did not always see it this way, with the result that they accused of Socinianism many who did not hold this doctrine. The accusation of Socinianism was particularly levied against those who, like the Socinians, said that there were only a few fundamental doctrines necessary for salvation, that the Bible must be read in the light of reason, that the message of the Gospel was largely concerned with moral conduct and was liable to be severely misconceived by those who taught the servitude of the will. Latitudinarians, in particular, were therefore the butt of accusations of Socinianism, and indeed many who defended a latitudinarian creed – men like Grotius and Limborch – had amicable relations with Socinians.

Socinianism is thus a term with many definitions: negative ones, which stress its rejection of orthodox Protestantism; broad ones which extend it to include latitudinarians and Arminians; but with, for our purposes, one core definition that defines it in its own terms.

We are now better able to assess the accusation of Socinianism directed against Locke. The scholarly responses to this accusation fall into two main groups. One group believes the accusation to be a reasonably accurate labelling of Locke's views. The other believes that Locke was a latitudinarian, and falsely accused.[26]

At once it should be apparent that Edwards's accusations have a certain plausibility. Crucially, in *The Reasonableness*, Locke presented the crux of Christianity as being the promise of immortality and the clarification of men's moral obligations, obligations that no one had fully understood before Christ came. Edwards's accusations only gained in strength when Locke refused to declare that he believed in the doctrine of the Trinity (his private papers suggest strongly that he did not, and that he had made a close study of the contemporary debate on Trinitarianism). Nevertheless, he denied that he had read any Socinian books, and insisted that he was no Socinian, but merely an honest Christian.

Is it possible that Locke was merely a latitudinarian? Compare *The Reasonableness of Christianity* with Chillingworth's *The Religion of Protestants*, the founding text of English latitudinarianism:[27] Chillingworth insists on the Apostle's creed, where Locke does not. And he specifically approves doctrines that Locke passes over in silence: the immortality of the soul, the atonement, the Trinity. Of course like Locke he insists that there are only a few fundamental truths, that Christianity is a religion of moral action, that it is fully described in the New Testament. Nevertheless, the differences are as important as the similarities.

A closer comparison can be made between Locke's *The Reasonableness* and Grotius's *De Veritate*.[28] Grotius, who is writing a book ostensibly aimed at Jews, Muslims and pagans, minimizes the implications of the doctrine of the Trinity and, like Locke, makes no mention of original sin and the atonement. Nevertheless, his book is sharply distinct from Socinianism in that it presents the immortality of the soul as a truth of natural reason, merely confirmed by Christianity. Grotius stresses the resurrection, but it is because he sees the promise of the resurrection of the body (the same body that one has had in life) as fundamentally new in the Christian message. Elsewhere, of course, Grotius entered into a polemic with Crell in which he defended the doctrine (which he obviously felt to be too abstruse for a work such as *De Veritate*) that Christ died as a sacrifice for our sins.

Another work provides an even more interesting comparison: Limborch's *Theologia Christiana*.[29] Locke discovered in Limborch a man who held similar theological views to his own when they met in

1683; he wrote the *Letter Concerning Toleration* to him, and continued to correspond with him as a theologian to whom he could express himself frankly.[30] At first sight the *Theologia Christiana* is an orthodox work: the Trinity and the atonement are, for example, defended in it, and Limborch criticized Locke's *The Reasonableness* for failing to discuss Christ's role as a sacrifice for our sins.[31] However, Limborch presents a strong attack on predestination, in the course of which he minimises the impact of original sin. The *Doctrina Christianae* was therefore a work much approved by English Latitudinarians, and was translated into English under their patronage. If Limborch was Locke's preferred theologian, is this not strong evidence in favour of a latitudinarian reading of Locke?

It would be, were not Limborch in one respect exceptional. He is keen to stress the limits of natural reason when it comes to a knowledge of immortality. Natural man might well reason that the soul was in some sense immortal, but could scarcely know whether he would be properly conscious after death (one might even suspect that Limborch's treatment of this question betrays his conversations with Locke and implies prior knowledge of the argument of the *Essay*). Moses and the Jews were given only the most uncertain and obscure promises of a life after death. As a consequence, natural law receives from Limborch only the most cursory treatment. For it is only with the resurrection that men obtain secure knowledge of a real afterlife, accompanied by the reunification of body and soul and making possible a real system of rewards and punishments. Only then do they have an adequate motive to obey the moral law. In this key respect Limborch's argument may be described as semi-Socinian, and it is relevant to note that Limborch as a Remonstrant was in communion with Socinians.

The first point to be made then is that Locke's *The Reasonableness* does come uncommonly close to Socinianism. The second is that Locke's defences of *The Reasonableness* were based on a lie: he owned numerous Socinian works, had obviously read them, and had been influenced by them. To claim that they were arguing not as the members of a sect but as honest Christians was a standard ploy (though something more than a ploy, for it reflected a commitment to open debate and honest argument) of Unitarian propagandists, some of whom were amongst Locke's friends and associates. Some have therefore felt it right to conclude that Locke was to all intents and purposes a Socinian.

This is, I think, less than the whole truth. By the end of his life Locke certainly held some views that no orthodox Socinian would have defended. He not only believed that there would be hell fire for the wicked – though it would be limited in duration and followed by annihilation – but he believed in the pre-existence of Christ before his birth and he believed that immortality had been promised the Jews in the

Old Testament.[32] He was not only hostile to distinctions between clergy and laity, but he rejected both the ceremony of ordination and the doctrine of the priesthood of all believers to insist that Christ was the last priest.[33] Nevertheless, Locke's *A Paraphrase* shows that he accepted the essential core doctrine of Socinianism: that before Christ's coming mankind as a whole had no reason to believe that there was a law of right and wrong, enforced by other-worldly punishments, for they had no reason to expect a life after death.

The accusation of Socinianism, particularly as formulated by Burnet and Leibniz, thus joins hands with the accusation of Hobbism as formulated by Tyrrell's associates: it is an accusation of moral relativism, based on the claim (a claim that is certainly accurate for Locke towards the end of his life) that Locke believed that men in general could not be expected to identify the content of the natural law through reason, or to acknowledge, without the assistance of revelation, the existence of a divine economy of rewards and punishments, without which (given Locke's hedonism) no Lockean natural law could function.

As with the accusation of Hobbism we are obliged to recognize that the accusation of Socinianism casts light on the *Essay*; Locke had undermined existing proofs of the immortality of the soul, as any Socinian philosopher would need to. Moreover, Burnet and Leibniz were right to see that what often looks to us like technical philosophy had in fact devastating consequences for natural theology. If the soul could sleep, then mere survival after death was no guarantee of a real immortality. If the same soul could exist in a different body, and thereby potentially become a different person, then reincarnation was a genuine alternative to the Christian idea of immortality. If the body had nothing to do with identity then the Socinians were justified in arguing that the resurrection of the dead might see the resurrection of new spiritual bodies in place of men's existing mortal bodies, a belief that Locke's private papers show he shared with them.

Nor does it seem plausible to imagine that Locke can have been blind to the theological implications of his work, for every seventeenth-century philosopher had cause to imagine an orthodox theologian reading his work even as he wrote. In a suspiciously offhand remark in the *Essay*, Locke says that a friend, having read what he had written, had suggested he should read Herbert's *De Veritate* if he wanted to identify some doctrines that were accepted by all men; but Locke protests in reply that the ideas of immortality, of heaven and hell, are far from being universally inscribed upon the hearts of men. The remark is suspicious because Locke preserved its studied casualness over two decades, from draft B to the final text.[34] In fact what Locke had done in the *Essay* was leave only one of Herbert's principles of natural theology as being evidently demonstrable by reason: the principle that God existed. Herbert's principles were, he declared, 'clear truths, and such as, if rightly explained, a rational creature can hardly avoid giving his assent to', but only one of them did he seek to rightly explain to a rational reader.

Reconstructing Locke's thought

We have now seen that *The Reasonableness*, and indeed the *Essay*, appeared to undermine the idea of a universal natural law, and that by the end of his life Locke had effectively given up the idea. At first sight we might seem to have here a simple evolution, from the natural law doctrines of the *Essays on the Law of Nature* and the *Two Treatises* to the revealed law of *The Reasonableness* and *A Paraphrase*. But the *Essay* and the *Two Treatises* were published within months of each other, and the composition of the *Essay* began long before the composition of the *Two Treatises*. If the *Essay* casts in doubt the fundamental prerequisites that Locke insisted any theory of natural law must meet, can Locke have really believed in that law as expounded in the *Two Treatises*? Should we follow Leibniz and Burnet in being sceptical of Locke's claim in the *Essay* that he believed that reason could provide an adequate account of men's duties? Is the true foundation of the natural rights argument of the *Two Treatises* not natural reason but Socinian theology? The first step to resolving these problems is to try to reconstruct the internal logic and evolution of Locke's thought on the question of natural law.

Proofs of natural law

Natural law, by Locke's definition, depended on a promulgated law, a scheme of rewards and punishments, and an afterlife in which this scheme could be implemented. Tyrrell's advice to Locke in 1690 was that he should imitate Cumberland and Parker in his approach to the problem. Let us look first at the implications of this advice.

Grotius, Cumberland and Parker all adopted a common and simple strategy for solving the problem of proving an afterlife and a system of rewards and punishments.[35] God was just, they said, and since in this world the wicked flourished and good suffered, it was clear that there must be a next world in which justice would be done. They thus argued from one of God's acknowledged attributes in order to establish the validity of a system of natural law.

Now it is clear that there was a time when Locke was willing to argue in this way. In a note on natural law in 1678, for example, Locke portrayed God as a father, concerned to punish and reward his children for their own good.[36] Knowing God's character men could foresee how he would behave towards them. The precondition of such an argument, however, was a proof that God was good; as Burnet pointed out, no such proof appears in the *Essay*, and Locke surely did not need Bayle or Hume to show him that it was hard to prove God's goodness from experience, since experience suggested there was no consistent moral pattern to his activities. Locke's view was that our knowledge of God's nature came largely from reflection on our own attributes, but this too would scarcely provide reliable evidence of an unquestionable goodness or sense of justice.

Locke made no attempt to follow Tyrrell's recommendation and, apart from a brief passage in the *Essay* where he claims that it should in principle be possible to formulate an argument of this sort,[37] I can find no trace of him arguing from God's justice to a system of rewards and punishments after 1678. Clearly, he felt this road was closed, in practice if not in principle. Thus in a note entitled 'Ethica' of 1692 Locke presents it not as a view he is committed to, but as one that others ('he that will deny' that one can reconcile morality and secular hedonism: a view we will discuss below) are obliged to put forward. Cumberland had presented other-worldly rewards and punishments as supplementing rewards and punishments in this world to create a double motivation for morality. In 'Ethica', Locke is exploring the possibility of arguing in terms of worldly happiness alone, a procedure that would have been quite unnecessary had he been content to proceed by 'laying a necessity on God's justice by his rewards and punishments to make the good the gainers, the wicked losers'.[38]

Locke may well have realized that the ethical hedonism he had been committed to since 1676 made it very difficult to argue from God's attributes in this way.[39] As we have seen, Locke in the *Essay* held that the good was the pleasurable; the morally good was that which was seen to have pleasure attached to it by reference to some law offering rewards and sanctions of a sort that could be understood by a rational agent. God can scarcely be held to be subject to any law of this sort, and therefore he certainly cannot be said to be morally good or bad in the sense that we can be. This makes it almost impossible to establish the existence of a moral law by arguing from God's attributes, unless we can show that God is good, not in himself, but in his relationship to us: something that it is difficult to do unless one can show that the moral and the pleasurable do indeed coincide, or unless one can demonstrate independently the truth of revelation or the existence of a life after death.

It is hard to date the exact moment when Locke abandoned the strategy of demonstrating the existence of natural law on the basis of God's attributes. We do know, however, that in 1682 he abandoned the other main line of proof for the immortality of the soul, and by implication for other-worldly rewards and punishments, a proof which had been most systematically developed by Descartes. Descartes's argument was a double one: that an immaterial substance must be immortal, and that it was the essence of the soul to reason, so that the soul could never be deprived of consciousness or thought. Consequently, the survival of the soul meant the survival of the individual's identity. Locke's attack was directed at the second claim: if the soul was indestructible, might its material not simply be used to construct a new individual?[40] Survival of the soul was perfectly compatible with the sleep of the dead or with metempsychosis. The immortality of the individual thus could not be demonstrated from any supposed characteristics of the soul. In 1683 Locke developed a similar point in a note on identity, and it was in terms of the problem of identity rather than the problem of immortality that the issue was raised in the second edition of the *Essay*.[41] But the first edition had already made clear Locke's hostility to standard proofs of the immortality of the soul, which depended on its immateriality, by arguing that the soul might in fact be material.[42]

The argument from probability

It seems likely, then, that by 1682 Locke's hopes of demonstrating the moral attributes of God, or of proving immortality, had faded. How then was he to justify belief in a moral law of nature? The solution that immediately occurred to Locke, and that he was still prepared to offer to Tyrrell in 1690 as a possible way forward, was that one could argue that it was possible that the law of nature existed, and that as long as there was a chance of its existing it was rational to act on the assumption that it really existed: in other words an application of Pascal's wager.

Probability had already been a central concept in the early drafts of the *Essay*.[43] It was probable knowledge, not deductive certainty, that led one to conclude that the Gospel story was well-attested and therefore true. Probability theory, as a theory of the reliability of testimony, thus underwrote the validity of revelation. Locke had already shown an interest, in 1676, in the possibility of using Pascal's wager to convince people who could see no proof of God's existence or of the immortality of the soul that they should act as if these were established truths.[44] He himself seems not to have had much doubt of the satisfactoriness of proofs of God's existence, but now in 1682 he was thrown back upon probability to establish the likelihood of immortality, and, we may suspect, to deal with God's attributes.[45]

Would such an argument work? Although Locke clearly continued to hope that it might, there is no evidence of his ever having found a formulation that seemed to him convincing. Pascal's wager was an argument for showing that one had little to lose and everything to gain by believing in revelation. Here was a specific doctrine that it was worth betting on. The problem about an argument from probability as Locke wanted to formulate it was that it depended not upon betting on a lottery whose terms had been set up by someone else, but devising one's own lottery on which one would then place bets. How could one know, for example, that an immortal life in another world was a significant possibility; might not reincarnation be more likely? How could one be sure that the rewards would, as Pascal insisted, be infinite and not finite? If one placed revelation entirely to one side it was hard to see how one could determine the terms of the bet.

There is a second problem at the heart of the idea of an argument from probability. Suppose one could hypothesize that a law of nature existed: could God be said to have promulgated such a law merely by making it possible to conceive of its existence? Could someone be held to be culpable merely because they miscalculated the odds, or placed their bet on a different outcome? It was hard to see that what would be involved in any such probability calculation would be anything other than a calculation of self-interest, whereas what Locke needed was something more than that. For while he believed that morality was the best policy, it was right not merely because it was the best policy but because it was recognized to be so by reference to a law. In an argument from probability the law became merely hypothetical and the moral guilt consequently uncertain. There were, in short, insurmountable problems which stood in the way of any probabilistic account of a law of nature.

Discovery and promulgation

As Locke was working on the final draft of the *Essay*, it seems that he had beside him a draft, intended to form part of a chapter, entitled 'Of Ethics in General'.[46] This text is of crucial importance for any attempt to make sense of the evolution of Locke's thought on the question of the law of nature. In it Locke asserts that demonstrating the law of nature depends on proving the immortality of the soul and a life after death, and this must now be done. Here the manuscript breaks off.

It would seem then that in 1688 Locke had not abandoned all hope of filling the great lacuna in his moral philosophy, and we are therefore under an obligation to take at face value his claims to Tyrrell and to Molyneux that he believed that one could indeed hope to make progress with the task of demonstrating the law of nature by natural reason. Who would have imagined, he asks in 1690, just what could be demonstrated in mathematics before the publication of Newton's *Principia*? In 'Of Ethics in General' he had written that the very existence of a discipline of moral philosophy (a discipline that so far had produced no certain knowledge of right and wrong) suggested the possibility of an authentic discovery in this field. That Locke had sincere hopes of such a discovery we need not doubt. What he seems not to have realized for some time is that such a discovery would scarcely serve his purposes.

Newton had discovered the physical laws of nature, laws that had previously been unknown and incomprehensible. Locke, similarly, might hope to establish a deductive natural theology, the foundation of a reliable moral philosophy. But the problem about any discovery in this field was that it would be a discovery of something previously unknown, and of something obviously extremely hard to discover. How could one claim that the law of nature had been promulgated to all reasonable men, and was binding at all times and in all places, if for six thousand years it had gone undiscovered?[47] Moreover, what would be the value of such a discovery? Would it not be possible for a reasonable man to have doubts about the reliability of the deductions involved?

By 1695, when he published *The Reasonableness*, Locke was clear about the difference between discovery and promulgation. There he said that it was likely that no philosopher had adequately understood the principles of natural law before the coming of Christ. But even if any philosopher had done so, the opinions of one man could have had no authority. Only the resurrection could be an effective proof of the truth of such arguments.[48]

Exploring alternatives

The evidence as we have looked at it so far fits in with a picture of a Locke slowly moving away from the idea of a rationally demonstrable law of nature, but who may well in good faith have still believed that some such law ought to be demonstrable. But it is important to recognize that the shift in Locke's views that occurred after 1689 had already been foreshadowed in his manuscript self-interrogations.

First, we may note that Locke considered an alternative type of deductive moral philosophy to the God-centred theory of the *Two Treatises* and the *Essay*. In a draft entitled 'Morality' he set out to provide what amounted to a refutation of his own claim (made in his journals in 1677) that 'A Hobbist with his principle of self-preservation whereof himself is to be judge will not easily admit a great many plain duties of morality.'[49] 'Morality' aims to show how, from mere principles of worldly self-interest, one might claim to deduce the principle that all men should obey the golden rule and could show that men would have good reason to invent a system of justice, even if they had no knowledge of a divinely ordained moral order.[50] Locke repeatedly insisted elsewhere that only those who were immoral could be drawn to atheism, and yet here we find him arguing as if an adequate concept of morality could be founded upon atheistical principles, without any reference to natural law at all.

What is the date of 'Morality'? In some respects it is reminiscent of the 'Ethica' of 1692, discussed above. There Locke set out to show that morality and this-worldly hedonism could be reconciled; his claim is that the best way to happiness in this life is to love your neighbour as yourself. But it seems clear that 'Morality' must have been written prior to the discussion of property in the *Two Treatises*, for in it Locke assumes that an explicit contract would be needed to establish property, a view refuted by the labour theory of property and the principle of 'enough and as good' presented in the *Two Treatises*. We know that Locke continued in later years to have a favourable view of his account of property there, and as 'Morality' runs counter to it we must assume that it was written before 1681.[51]

'Morality' amounts to an exploration of the possibilities of a Hobbist account of natural law; Hobbes, after all, was the great exponent of the possibilities of a deductive science of ethics. Had Locke continued along this road he would have sidestepped all the problems regarding the immortality of the soul that barred him from making further progress in moral theory after 1689. There were of course problems peculiar to a Hobbist approach, problems that Locke had explored in the *Essays on the Law of Nature*, and that blocked his path when he considered this approach in 1692. Self-interest could scarcely seem to provide a reliable basis for demanding the sacrifice of individual interests to the common good (the problem he sought to overcome in 'Ethica', where he discussed the pleasure of going without a meal to feed the starving), nor was it clear that principles based on immediate self-interest could properly be described as moral laws.

When Locke stated in *The Reasonableness* that the law of nature was also the law of convenience he knew that 'law' was only being used metaphorically in the second phrase; moral laws required sanctions deliberately imposed according to a rule. Locke held, from 1678 onward, that there were three possible sources of such sanctions: God, the state, and public opinion.[52] Public opinion was, he stressed, the source of most men's moral conceptions. The moral philosophy of the schools scarcely differed from it in character. Both served a valuable role in fostering the interests of society as a whole. In 1678 he formulated this position bluntly: 'That virtue is but the name of such actions as are most conducing to the good of the society and are therefore by the society recommended by all to the practise of the people seems to me very plain.'[53] In a note on 'credit and disgrace' he brought out the power of social sanctions to shape behaviour:[54] they were the primary factor to be appealed to in explaining human behaviour.

Locke was therefore clear that one could dispense with the idea of God in explaining the moral values people actually held. Indeed in most societies he claimed that religion had had little to say about morality; it was a peculiarity of Christianity that it inculcated morality. Pagan religion, as he stressed in *The Reasonableness* in 1695, in a note entitled 'Sacerdos' of 1698,[55] and already in a note on Cicero's *De Natura Deorum* of 1683, had little to say about moral behaviour, being concerned with explaining fortune and with winning the favour of the gods.[56]

It is not surprising that Locke should have had a clear grasp of the secular foundations of moral behaviour. The point had been stressed by Nicole, whom he was reading and translating in 1677, and by Bayle, whose *Pensées Diverses sur la Comète* (1682) Locke read in their first edition as early as October 1684.[57] Locke's repeated claim that atheists were incapable of being proper citizens ran counter not only to his understanding of men's knowledge of the moral law, as expressed in *A Paraphrase* in the last years of his life, but also to his thinking in the late 1670s.

For Locke to abandon the idea of a divinely ordained moral law, accessible to all men, an idea he so often insisted on from the *Essays on the Law of Nature* to the *Essay*, he needed an alternative account of where most men's moral values came from; this he had in the idea of collective self-interest. He also needed to be able to maintain that morality was not universally seen in terms of divinely ordained rewards and punishments, for otherwise one might be inclined to accept Herbert's claim that there was a universally accepted natural religion: his reading of Cicero and his study of travel literature confirmed him in his conviction that this was untrue. Finally, he needed, if he was to avoid an ultimate identification of morality with collective self-interest, an account of how the true moral code had been revealed in Christianity; thus the divinely ordained moral law could be restored as a fact of history, not reason.

It might be thought that this final element of his position in the last years of his life was one that was slow to suggest itself. His intensive study of theology seems for the most part to date to the 1690s and beyond; his access to the Socinian books which shaped his theology might be thought to begin with his exile to Holland in 1683. It is therefore a fact of considerable interest that Locke acquired a small collection of twelve Socinian and Unitarian works, bound in one volume, in 1680.[58] Among them was a copy of the Racovian catechism and works by Crell, Przypkowski, Stegmann and Biddle. Locke certainly acquired more Socinian books once he went into exile; he was buying and reading Crell's most important works in 1684.[59] And he was certainly reading on problems central to Socinian theology – the Trinity, original sin, resurrection – in 1688,[60] but from 1680 he had possession of a collection of very rare Socinian works, many of them works that had been sentenced to be burnt by the hangman, and was therefore much better informed than most English intellectuals on the fundamental principles of Socinian theology.

To possess books is one thing, to read them another, and to be persuaded by them a third. Have we any evidence that Locke was not what he appeared to be when he went into exile: a conforming Anglican whose theology was substantially orthodox, even if he believed in toleration? Certainly he had long had association with men like Firmin, a latitudinarian merchant with marked sympathies for Socinianism. And there are stray hints that he already saw orthodox religion from an outsider's point of view, even if he was not prepared to admit the fact. In the manuscript of the 1667 'Essay on Toleration', for example, references to 'your religion' (i.e. the Anglican religion) have been belatedly corrected to 'our religion'.[61] But I am aware of only one substantial piece of evidence that goes further than this: a discussion of divine justice in his journal for 1 August 1680.[62] Locke's argument here is that God's justice must take a form compatible with his goodness. He concludes that God can only punish for the good of his creation, just as, one might say, a father should only punish for the welfare of his child, or a magistrate for the welfare of his society. Locke does not pursue this essay in natural theology to the point of comparing the conclusion he has reached with orthodox Christian theology, but it is difficult to see how Locke would have been able to show that the punishment of all mankind for the sin of Adam met the standard he had established for divine justice. Moreover his standard for divine justice would seem to make it necessary that religion should primarily be concerned with the inculcation of morality, for it is hard to see how God could be justified in punishing people who were ignorant of the niceties of orthodox theology or deprived of the sacraments. Locke's discussion of divine justice seems therefore to foreshadow his mature theological position. It seems to be incompatible with the orthodox Christian doctrine of original sin, but entirely compatible with Socinianism.

Locke may have still been planning to use 'Of Ethics in General' in the *Essay* in 1688, but by 1680 he was well aware of the arguments he would employ to put together the quite different position of *The Reasonableness* and *A Paraphrase*. Furthermore, there is no evidence after 1682 that Locke seriously believed that he could find his way around the difficulties presented by his original position. Why then did it take Locke so long to change his mind? Was it merely that he was so committed to the idea of a universally applicable, theocentric moral order that he could not easily bring himself to adopt the Socinian alternative? Or had he in fact changed his mind long before 1688, and was he simply too cautious to expound, in public, heretical opinions (the *Essay* after all, unlike *The Reasonableness*, was to carry Locke's signature)? Was the *Essay*, as later readers claimed, the work of a covert Socinian? I doubt if there is any decisive answer to these questions, but it is to them we must now turn.

Possible interpretations

Dishonest Locke

Locke had a great capacity for secrecy.[63] He had first sought to conceal his political commitments from his colleagues in Oxford and had then been obliged not only to go into exile, but to go into hiding to avoid being kidnapped or assassinated. He was used to writing letters in cipher and took elaborate precautions to prevent his private papers from falling into the wrong hands.

He was also capable of lying. He lied in an effort to hold on to his Oxford position in 1684. He lied when he told Edwards he had read no Socinian books. He was capable of believing that the Church Fathers had practised a systematic economy with the truth in their exposition of Christian doctrine.

Is there then any reason to assume that he meant seriously what he said about the law of nature in the *Two Treatises* and the *Essay*? May not the law of nature in the first have been merely a logical prerequisite to a defence of a right of revolution, adopted for polemical purposes? May not the claim that one could have certain knowledge of moral principles in the second have been merely an attempt to deny the subversive implications for moral philosophy and theology of his own epistemology?

The primary argument against such a view is 'Of Ethics in General', which appears to herald a genuine attempt to resolve a problem that Locke, in this view, must have known was insoluble within his own system of ideas. This objection is not insuperable, for one could claim that 'Of Ethics in General' was not a statement of Locke's private thoughts but a draft of a chapter intended to mislead the public. One could point to its internal contradictions as evidence that Locke cannot have been thinking seriously when he wrote it.

In this view, the Locke of the *Essay* and the *Two Treatises* would be involved in a complicated strategy of deception. Already a Socinian by 1689, perhaps by 1680, his attempts to defend religious freedom and to establish a materialist epistemology would have led him to an outward acceptance of the idea of a universally applicable law of nature, though he believed no such idea could be effectively sustained. Indeed, there would be no need for the argument to stop there; behind a Socinian claim that morality and immortality are to be known only through revelation one could divine the existence of a secret Hobbism. It is clear that an argument of this sort leads precipitately to mere empty speculation.

Honest Locke

Let us consider the alternative. As early as 1671 Locke's drafts of the *Essay* were noticeably incomplete in their treatment of morality. From that date he was in quest of a solution. He made progress: the *Two Treatises* filled in the content of natural law; the theory of mixed modes helped explain the nature of moral concepts. But he also lost ground: arguments from God's attributes or arguments designed to prove the immortality of the soul became increasingly unconvincing to him. 'Of Ethics in General' shows a man wrestling with a problem he has been unable to resolve.

Only after 1690, under pressure both from his enemies, whose accusations of Hobbism infuriated him, and from his friends, who begged him to fulfil the promise implicit in the *Essay* of a deductive system of morality, did he finally begin to recognize that the problems were for the moment insuperable. *The Reasonableness* is the work of a man forced to recognize that in practice revelation would have to do the work that he had previously hoped reason could do. In *A Paraphrase* Locke faces the true implications of his defeat: before Christ there had been no law of nature promulgated to mankind.

John Dunn has carefully developed the possibilities of this line of argument,[64] and it has one very important thing to be said for it. We have Locke's letters, Locke's notebooks, Locke's library. We can catch him out in small deceptions and in large inconsistencies; but everywhere we look – in the *Two Treatises*, the *Essay*, *The Reasonableness*, *A Paraphrase* – we seem to find Locke honestly trying to convey convictions we know he held. Nowhere do we find any complex pattern of misrepresentation, any esoteric philosophy that he did not also seek to make public to the whole world.

Inconsistent Locke

Even this approach, however, seems hardly to work. First, it involves maintaining that Locke had managed to blind himself to the extent of his difficulties – and to the existence of a theological solution to them – until the 1690s. In defence of this view one can cite the honest indignation of the letters to Tyrrell and the confusions of 'Of Ethics in General'. And it does seem impossible to date conclusively Locke's conversion to a fundamentally Socinian set of theological principles before the 1690s. Nevertheless, I must confess to having lingering doubts. For it seems to me that this implies that Locke was extraordinarily slow-witted.

By 1674 Locke already had a Socinian view of the relationship between church and state.[65] In 1676 he adopted hedonism. In 1680 he purchased a collection of Socinian works. The same year he indirectly attacked the idea of original sin in his journals and in 1682 he explicitly rejected the most important proof of the immortality of the soul. We have the testimony of Damaris Cudworth, who knew Locke better than perhaps anyone else, that the main shift in his religious views took place not in the 1690s, nor while he was in Holland, but 'some years before he went to Holland'.[66] By 1683 he recognized Limborch as a theologian working along similar lines to his own. In the mid-1680s it would seem he was building up a library of Socinian books.

Why would it have taken him a further decade to recognize his predicament? By the mid-1680s, and perhaps earlier, all the building blocks required to construct *The Reasonableness* were to hand. Why not suppose, then, that 'Of Ethics in General' was an early draft which he kept by him because he knew he had to say something about ethics at the end of the *Essay*? Why not attribute his horrified reaction to Tyrrell's criticisms to a recognition that he had, in fact, been found out, even though he had tried to say nothing more damning in 1689 than he had said, quite innocently, in 1671?

This is the first problem, one of timing. The second problem is one of consistency. For Locke did not simply evolve from book to book. Each book was itself reshaped over time. Between the first and second editions the *Essay* became a more, not a less, radical work, tackling identity, for example, in a way entirely compatible with Socinianism but far from obviously compatible with orthodox Christianity.[67] But his discussion of morality was made in the second edition to seem as conservative as possible. Nor did *The Reasonableness* lead Locke, in still later editions of the *Essay*, to tone down his comments about the possibility of a deductive knowledge of morality. In his last years he was both writing *A Paraphrase*, which undermined the whole idea of a law of nature, and revising the *Two Treatises*. Both were intended for posthumous publication (in the case of the *Two Treatises* it would be the first time it had appeared under Locke's name), yet the two were directly at odds with each other. Nor for that matter would it be easy to reconcile *A Paraphrase* with the *Letter Concerning Toleration*: the latter argued that atheists were incapable of being good citizens, the former that reasonable Gentiles were in the same position as atheists until the apostles preached the Gospel to them.

Up until his death Locke could evade questions about the compatibility of the arguments of his major works, for to only one of them had he put his name. The problem of resolving the contradictions we may describe as Locke's bequest to posterity. He himself seems to have contented himself with believing different things when dealing with different problems. His epistemology was designed to undermine the claim of conscience to be infallibly reliable. Men's consciences were no better than the rules they judged by, and these varied from time to time and place to place. Thus Locke hoped to attack at the same time both tradition and enthusiasm, both custom and inspiration, but in doing so he undermined the possibility of a reliable moral philosophy. His political theory, on the other hand, was designed to justify the rights of the people against their rulers. It depended upon a principle of equality that could only be grounded in natural law. Finally, his theology was based upon the recognition that it was to Christ that we owed the promise of eternal life. It undermined the very idea of natural rights that could be recognized by all men with the aid of natural reason alone.

Locke's problem was that epistemology, political philosophy and theology all had differing implications for moral philosophy. His only solution was to try to minimize the threat that they posed to each other, for the only alternative was to allow one of them to eat up the others.

Let us suppose, for example, that Locke had decided that, since true morality was revealed only by God and the state was concerned only with earthly interests, self-interest was the proper law of political life. He then could have pursued the secular implications of the *Essay*. He was in a remarkably privileged position to develop a sociological account of politics and to try to integrate economic and political theory. He was, after all, familiar with the works of Hobbes, Nicole and Bayle, and he strongly believed that morality in general could be explained in terms of interests and that the intelligent pursuit of self-interest led to prosperity. He would, however, have had a double price to pay. Hobbes, Nicole and Bayle were all absolutists, and all three had denied the freedom of the will. It was hard to see how a theory of self-interest could provide the basis of a defence of political rights, or could be compatible with an adequate theory of moral responsibility.

Alternatively, of course, he could have concentrated on revealed religion. The New Testament, however, preaches obedience, not revolt; only a theory of natural law that claimed divine sanction but was detached from the Biblical text could lead to a comprehensive theory of rights. And to rely solely upon revelation was to abandon all hope of decisively overcoming the claims of tradition and inspiration.

Lastly, of course, he could take his stand upon moral philosophy, if, that is, he could find a set of principles that were solid, and if he could avoid the danger, common to all those who questioned the justice of God's imputing Adam's sin to all men, of proposing moral philosophy as a substitute for revealed truth.

Whichever way Locke turned he faced difficulties. He could not bring himself to admit that his principles could not be reconciled with each other, nor bring himself to abandon any one principle for the sake of the others. This is not, I think, a dishonest or an unreasonable position to be in. Consistency is an intellectual, not necessarily a moral or political, virtue. Locke, however, would not admit this to himself. He was prepared to admit that one could be wrong about how one had come by one's principles, but not that there might be no way of reconciling different sets of principles honestly come by. I take the following passage from *The Reasonableness* both as self-criticism, and as continuing self-deception.

> A great many things which we have been bred up in the belief of, from our cradles, (and are notions grown familiar, and, as it were, natural to us, under the Gospel) we take for unquestionable obvious truths, and easily demonstrable; without considering how long we might have been in doubt or ignorance of them, had revelation been silent. And many are beholden to revelation, who do not acknowledge it. It is no diminishing to revelation, that reason gives its suffrage too to the truths revelation has discovered. But it is our mistake to think, that because reason confirms them to us, we had the first certain knowledge of them from thence; and in that clear evidence we now possess them. The contrary is manifest.[68]

Even when prepared to admit that his moral principles originated in revelation, not, as he had long believed, in reason, Locke would not admit that they could not, in the end, be shown to be rational. Ultimately in Locke's case, I suspect, self-deception is more important than any plan to deceive others. But to recognize the evidence of that self-deception, to acknowledge that Locke left to us the task of reconciling his principles one with another, is to admit that what have been termed 'the foundations of modern political thought' were never solidly laid; hence some at least of the problems we encounter nowadays in doing political philosophy.

It was an assumption of the tradition in which Locke wrote when he discussed the law of nature that rights existed only where there were laws, and laws existed only once they had been promulgated and when they were accompanied by sanctions. Locke's defence of political rights was presented within this framework; natural rights were a side effect of the duties imposed upon men by the law of nature. Take away the sanctions accompanying that law and natural reason as a method of promulgating it, and there can be no universally valid natural rights. This was apparent to Hume and Bentham and, I am sure, to Locke himself. Like him, many of us doubt that reason adequately establishes what the law of nature is or how it is to be enforced. How then are we to justify the reluctance so many of us share with Locke himself when faced with an intellectual obligation to abandon the notion of natural right and commit ourselves to utilitarian principles? Seen from this point of view, Locke's private inconsistency has developed into the incoherence of an entire intellectual culture which accepts both the empiricism of the *Essay*, with its emphasis on the limitations of human reason, and at the same time the political principles of the *Two Treatises*, with their claim that all persons have inalienable and identifiable rights.

Acknowledgement

I would like to thank Ian Harris and John Dunn for discussing Locke's views on religion with me. Neither of them shares the views advanced here. Ian Harris's account of the development of Locke's thought is to be published by Cambridge University Press.

Notes

1 The most important discussion of this subject is J. Marshall, 'John Locke and Socinianism', in M. A. Stewart (ed.), *Oxford Studies in the History of Philosophy*, vol. 2, Oxford, Oxford University Press, forthcoming. I am most grateful to John Marshall for showing me this paper prior to publication. If I have reservations about his conclusion that Locke's Socinianism casts no light on the *Essay*, I am much in his debt in every other respect. See also M. Firpo's valuable 'John Locke e il socinianesimo', *Rivista storica italiana*, 1980, vol. 92, pp. 35–124; and the careful assessment of A. W. Wainright in his introduction to John Locke, *A Paraphrase and Notes on the Epistles of St Paul*, 2 vols, Oxford, Oxford University Press, 1987. Among earlier studies, H. McLachlan, *The Religious Opinions of Milton, Locke and Newton*, Manchester, Manchester University Press, 1941, and M. Montuori's studies collected in *John Locke: On Toleration and the Unity of God*, Amsterdam, J. C. Gieben, 1983 may be noted.

2 On the date of the composition of the *Two Treatises* see R. Ashcraft, *Locke's 'Two Treatises of Government'*, London, Allen and Unwin, 1987, pp. 286–97.

3 On the reception of the *Essay* see J. W. Yolton, *John Locke and the Way of Ideas*, Oxford, Oxford University Press, 1968; R. C. Tennant, 'The Anglican response to Locke's theory of personal identity', *Journal of the History of Ideas*, 1982, vol. 43, pp. 73–90; N. Jolley, *Leibniz and Locke*, Oxford, Oxford University Press, 1984; and S. A. Grave, *Locke and Burnet*, Perth,

University of Western Australia, 1981.

4 For a strong statement of the coherence claim see R. Grant, *John Locke and Liberalism*, Chicago, Chicago University Press, 1987.

5 See Q. Skinner, *The Foundations of Modern Political Thought*, 2 vols, Cambridge, Cambridge University Press, 1978.

6 On Tyrrell see J. W. Gough, 'James Tyrrell, Whig historian and friend of John Locke', *Historical Journal*, 1976, vol. 19, pp. 581–610.

7 J. Locke, *The Correspondence of John Locke*, 8 vols, ed. E. S. de Beer, Oxford, Clarendon Press, 1976–88, vol. 4, pp. 100–2, 107–9, 116–19.

8 ibid., vol. 4, pp. 110–13; vol. 5, pp. 79–80. J. Locke, *Essay Concerning Human Understanding*, ed. P. H. Nidditch, Oxford, Oxford University Press, 1975, bk II, ch. xxviii, sects 7–8 (compare the parallel passage at bk I, ch. iii, sect. 5), and bk II, ch. xxviii, sect. 11. J. Lowde, *A Discourse Concerning the Nature of Man*, London, 1694.

9 Presuming this to have been identical or similar to 'A' or 'B': for 'A' see sects 25–6 in *An Early Draft of Locke's 'Essay'*, ed. R. I. Aaron and J. Gibb, Oxford, Clarendon Press, 1936; for 'B' see sects 157, 160 in J. Locke, *An Essay Concerning the Understanding, Knowledge, Opinion, and Assent*, ed. B. Rand, Cambridge, Mass., Harvard University Press, 1931.

10 J. Locke, *Essays on the Law of Nature*, ed. W. von Leyden, Oxford, Clarendon Press, 1954.

11 Locke, *Correspondence*, vol. 4, pp. 507–9, 522–5, 599–602, 623–8, 647–52, 667–9, 700–1, 729, 767–78, 784–7, vol. 5, pp. 69–71, 253–5, 284–8. [C. Trotter], *A Defence of the Essay of Human Understanding*, London, 1702.

12 [Lord Shaftesbury], *Several Letters Written by a Noble Lord to a Young Man at the University*, London, 1716, pp. 38–41.

13 J. Locke, *Two Treatises of Government*, ed. P. Laslett, Cambridge, Cambridge University Press, 1960, and *Two Tracts on Government*, ed. P. Abrams, Cambridge, Cambridge University Press, 1967.

14 R. Cox, *Locke on War and Peace*, Oxford, Oxford University Press, 1960.

15 I am grateful to Richard Tuck for showing me this essay prior to publication.

16 Locke, *A Paraphrase*, Romans 2.14; also Romans 1.32, 5.13. For the earlier use of similar phrases see J. Colman, *John Locke's Moral Philosophy*, Edinburgh, Edinburgh University Press, 1983, p. 46.

17 Locke, *Essay* bk I, ch. iii, sect. 6; bk II, ch. xxviii, sect. 11; *The Reasonableness of Christianity*, in *The Works of John Locke*, 10 vols, London, 1823, vol. 7, p. 142: 'The law of nature is the law of convenience too.'

18 J. H. Tully, *A Discourse on Property: John Locke and his Adversaries*, Cambridge, Cambridge University Press, 1980; and I. Harris, 'Locke on justice', in M. A. Stewart (ed.), *Oxford Studies in the History of Philosophy*, vol. 2, Oxford, Oxford University Press, forthcoming.

19 H. Grotius, *De Iure Belli et Pacis*, 3 vols, ed. and trans. W. Whewell, Cambridge, 1853, vol. 1, p. xlvi. On the novelty of Grotius's approach see R. Tuck, 'The "modern" theory of natural law', in A. Pagden (ed.), *The Languages of Political Thought in Early Modern Europe*, Cambridge, Cambridge University Press, 1987, pp. 99–119.

20 R. E. Florida, 'British law and Socinianism in the seventeenth and eighteenth centuries', *Socinianism and its Role in the Culture of 16th to 18th Centuries*, Warsaw, PWN-Polish Scientific Publisher, 1983, pp. 201–10.

21 J. Edwards, *Some Thoughts Concerning the Several Causes and Occasions of Atheism*, London, 1695, and *Socinianism Unmask'd*, London, 1696.

22 Locke, *Correspondence*, vol. 4, pp. 599–602.

23 A valuable collection of documents, including extracts from the catechism, is G. H. Williams (ed.), *The Polish Brethren*, 2 vols, Missoula, Mon., Scholars Press, 1980.

24 There were of course other mortalists apart from Socinians; but Socinianism represented the most sustained attempt to face the theological implications of mortalism. See N. Burns, *Christian Mortalism from Tyndale to Milton*, Cambridge, Mass., Harvard University Press, 1972.

25 F. Pintacuda de Michelis, *Socinianesimo e tolleranza nell' età del razionalismo*, Florence, La Nuova Italia, 1975.

26 See W. M. Spellman, *John Locke and the Problem of Depravity*, Oxford, Oxford University Press, 1988, and D. D. Wallace, 'Socinianism, justification by faith, and the sources of John Locke's *The Reasonableness of Christianity*', *Journal of the History of Ideas*, 1972, vol. 33, pp. 3–22.

27 W. Chillingworth, *The Religion of Protestants*, Oxford, 1638.

28 H. Grotius, *De Veritate Religionis Christianae*, Paris, 1640.

29 P. van Limborch, *Theologia Christiana* (1686), Amsterdam, 1695, and *A Compleat System, or Body of Divinity*, 2nd edn, London, 1703. Although this translation is of a *Theologia Christiana* 'improved' by Wilkins, Tillotson and others, it reflects Limborch's thinking on the issue of most importance to us.

30 Locke, *Correspondence*, vol. 5, pp. 237–9, 368–72.

31 ibid., vol. 6, pp. 42-53.

32 Locke, *A Paraphrase*, vol. 1, pp. 39, 53, 58.

33 See John Locke's Commonplace Book for 1661, Harvard University Library, pp. 270-1, reprinted in Lord King, *Life and Letters of John Locke*, London, 1858, p. 289.

34 Locke, *Essay*, bk I, ch. iii, sect. 15; see draft 'B' (note 9 above), sect. 30.

35 Grotius, *De Veritate*, sect. 20; R. Cumberland, *A Treatise of the Laws of Nature*, trans. J. Maxwell, London, 1727, ch. 5; S. Parker, *A Demonstration of the Divine Authority of the Law of Nature and of the Christian Religion*, London, 1681, part 1, sect. 16. I do not agree with Richard Tuck's claim that the positions of Hobbes and Cumberland are closely comparable. Thus what Tuck describes as Cumberland's 'only answer' to the objection that wickedness may escape punishment is in fact one of three answers, the third of which (p. 257) involves an explicit appeal to divine providence. See R. Tuck, *Natural Rights Theories: Their Origin and Development*, Cambridge, Cambridge University Press, 1979, p. 166.

36 Locke MS f. 3, pp. 201–2 (15 July 1678), Bodleian Library; printed in W. von Leyden, 'John Locke and natural law', *Philosophy*, 1956, vol. 21, pp. 23–35.

37 Locke, *Essay*, bk IV, ch. iii, sect. 18.

38 Locke MS c. 42, in T. Sargentich, 'Locke and ethical theory: two MS

pieces', *Locke Newsletter*, 1974, no. 5, pp. 24–31.

39 Locke, *Essays on the Law of Nature*, pp. 263–72.

40 Locke, *An Early Draft*, pp. 121–3.

41 Locke MS f. 7, p. 107: 'Identity of persons lies not in having the same numerical body made up of the same particles, nor if the mind consists of corporeal spirits in their being the same. But in the memory and knowledge of one's past self and actions continued on under the consciousness of being the same person, whereby every man owns himself.'

42 Locke, *Essay*, bk IV, ch. iii, sect. 6.

43 For a discussion of probability in Locke see J. H. Tully, 'Governing conduct', in E. Leites (ed.), *Conscience and Casuistry in Early Modern Europe*, Cambridge, Cambridge University Press, 1988, pp. 12–72.

44 Locke, *An Early Draft*, pp. 81–2.

45 ibid., p. 123.

46 Printed in King, *Life and Letters*, pp. 308–13. On the date of this text see Locke, *Essays on the Law of Nature*, pp. 69–70.

47 Colman tries to solve this problem by arguing that Locke thought the law of nature had been promulgated in the law of opinion (Colman, *Locke's Moral Philosophy*, pp. 172–3), but the law of opinion is for Locke quite distinct from the law of nature; its coincidence with the law of nature is providential, for God's law corresponds with our interests, not historical (see note 17 above); it has nothing to do with 'tradition' or 'original morality' (and Locke denied that one should respect tradition as a source of authority). Colman, to reach his conclusion, has to misinterpret Locke's phrase about 'deriving these rules up to their original' to mean 'tracing back moral notions to their historical origins' rather than their 'logical origins'.

48 Locke, *Works*, vol. 7, pp. 138–47.

49 Locke MS f. 2, p. 120.

50 Locke MS c. 28, fols. 139–40, in Sargentich, 'Locke and ethical theory', pp. 26–8. I disagree with J. W. Gough, *John Locke's Political Philosophy*, Oxford, Clarendon Press, 1950, p. 7 and with Colman, *Locke's Moral Philosophy*, pp. 194-9 on the date and significance of this sketch; my view is closer to that of Tuck, *Natural Rights Theories*, p. 169. None of these commentators explains what on earth Locke was doing trying to devise a deductive moral system for men ignorant of divine sanctions.

51 It may also be noted that the account of 'desire' Locke gives in 'Morality' clearly predates the second edition of the *Essay*.

52 See Locke MS f. 3, p. 201 (15 July 1678). The threefold distinction thus occurs much earlier than is recognized by von Leyden in Locke, *Essays on the Law of Nature*, pp. 67–8.

53 Locke MS f. 3, p. 266 (26 August 1678). See also the passage from the 1661 Commonplace Book quoted in King, *Life and Letters*, pp. 292–3.

54 Locke MS f. 3, pp. 381–2; printed in King, *Life and Letters*, pp. 109–10.

55 Printed in King, *Life and Letters,* pp. 286–91. The date is from the MS of the 1661 Commonplace Book, contrary to H. R. Fox Bourne, *The Life of John Locke*, 2 vols, New York, 1876, vol. 1, p. 156, who describes it as undated.

56 Locke MS f. 7, pp. 17–18 (20 February 1683).

57 Locke MS f. 8, pp. 294–5.

58 Locke MS f. 4, pp. 10–12 (4 February 1680). I am grateful to Ian Harris for drawing this entry to my attention.
59 Locke MS f. 8, pp. 36, 41, 75, 268.
60 Locke MS c. 33, fols. 23–6.
61 Locke MS c. 28, fols. 21–32.
62 Locke MS f. 4, pp. 145–9; printed in King, *Life and Letters*, pp. 123–4, with incorrect date.
63 Richard Ashcraft, for example, says of the standard biography: 'The predominant conclusion one derives from a reading of Cranston's *Locke* is that he was an exceedingly secretive person'. Ashcraft, *Locke's 'Two Treatises of Government'*, p. 303.
64 J. Dunn, *Locke*, Oxford, Oxford University Press, 1984, pp. 60–70. See also T. Kato, *'The Reasonableness* in the historical light of the *Essay'*, *Locke Newsletter*, 1981, no. 12, pp. 45–59.
65 King, *Life and Letters*, pp. 300–6 (from Locke MS c. 27).
66 Fox Bourne, *Life*, vol. 2, p. 282.
67 Locke attributed this chapter to the prompting of Molyneux (Locke, *Correspondence*, vol. 4, p. 722), but as we have seen (note 41 above) the most important argument in it was one Locke had worked out long before; it therefore does not reflect a major evolution in his thought.
68 Locke, *Works*, vol. 7, p. 145.

Chapter three

The religious, the secular and the worldly: Scotland 1680–1800

Roger L. Emerson

In this essay, I want to trace in outline the increasing worldliness of
Scottish intellectuals during the eighteenth century, but I want also to
deny that they were secular in outlook. I shall try to support the latter
claim by showing that 'secular' does not quite adequately describe their
outlook and concerns. Most dictionaries tell us that 'secular' or its
equivalents mean 'temporal', or 'non-spiritual'. With the possible
exception of David Hume, Scottish intellectuals at no time during the
eighteenth century would have denied that a spiritual realm existed.
That realm was still seen as being of ultimate concern to men who are
not merely temporal creatures of this world. Scots had not, in short,
ceased to be Christians. Because most of them remained, at least in their
own minds, nominal Calvinists, they also saw this world as a scene of
activities which had or ought to have a spiritual purpose. To know, to
love and to praise God in thought, word and deed were obligations
incumbent upon Christians and truly, if not easily, fulfilled by those to
whom His grace had been given. These duties had also become the
obligations of all men living in civil states, but the sometimes rather
nominal subscription to Calvinist principles by 1800 shows that the
definition of 'religious' had greatly changed over the course of the
previous 100 years. It is to that we should direct our attention and that
which we need to understand. Central to that understanding is a
recognition that worldly obligations and activities, like knowledge of
the world itself, had increased but were now rooted in reason and sense
and in a rational religion.

To speak of 'religion' and 'religious' in the eighteenth century is to
speak ambiguously. The age understood religion in terms of supernatural revelations but also as natural and rational beliefs. The first
religion could be, and in Calvinist Scotland was, compatible with
worldly and temporal concerns, but not with a denial of spirituality.
Natural religion excluded a spirituality rooted in revelation and could be
aspiritual or *non-spiritual*. It was so in some forms of deism and in the
philosophy of Spinoza, where spirituality is taken to imply neither the

existence of a non-material soul nor of a non-material, transcendent God.[1] Epistemologically, the grounds of belief in the two kinds of religion were very different. Revelations had to be experienced by believers, made clear and evident to them in conversion experiences (which warranted what others or the biblical writers said) or accepted on the probable testimony of others. Rational religion was ultimately founded upon *a priori* or *a posteriori* arguments produced by reason, or reason and sense experiences of a different sort. For many or most seventeenth-century Scottish intellectuals, the warrant for the Christian religion was a lived experience, not the probable testimony of errant men or the proofs of rational religion which from sin-blasted intellects could hardly be infallible or beyond dispute. By 1800, the leading intellectuals were usually prepared to hold the truths of natural religion as merely probable. These justified the revelations given by a gracious God to the prophets, evangelists, and apostles. That reversal of certainties has been studied outside of Scotland but it is also clear that it had a Scottish history as well. There, too, moral certainty tended to replace that given by God's grace in an act of faith. When that happened, rational religion tended to become the only one interesting to philosophers as philosophers. It also became of greater importance to theologians and preachers whose Christianity approached but did not become a rational religion.

The impact of the new philosophy

Those who have looked at the crisis concerning the grounding of Christian faith and confidence in England and Europe have invariably traced it to a number of things: the controversies among Christians; the revival of ancient learning (including that of Sextus Expiricus); the competition of various parties all claiming to know something or other and, therefore, having a right to act upon that knowledge; and the disinterested pursuit of truth by a handful of men among whom are to be counted logicians, moralists, and men whom we anachronistically call 'scientists'. Scotland during the seventeenth century was not untouched by these various currents which all penetrated the universities and the clubs of the intellectual elite during the latter half of that period. Father John Russell and Christine M. Shepherd (née King) have shown that the new philosophy and science of Descartes, the academicians of Paris and London and the professors of Holland slowly made their way into the prelections of the College regents between 1650 and 1680.[2] By the late 1680s and 1690s, many regents held and taught Cartesian views of one kind or another. Perhaps from Gassendi and Boyle, but surely from Lucretius and Hobbes, came another sort of cosmology, as well as metaphysics, which was taught in its refutations by men like Edinburgh

University's Principal (1653–60) Robert Leighton. Leighton was particularly worried about atomism, the ability of the atoms to move and the determination of their movements by some force not providential in nature. In the 1650s, he seems to have refuted these errors, which were probably drawn to his attention during his long stay in France (*c*.1631–40) as well as by his reading of ancient and modern philosophers.[3] Less philosophical sources of scepticism can also be found in the antiquarian circles gathered about Sir James Balfour of Denmiln.[4] He and his friends sought to preserve, record, criticize and use the documentary evidence of the past to reconstruct the traditional history of Scotland, which they recognized as fabulous, error-filled and incomplete. For them, such an enterprise also demanded attention to natural history, a subject relatively new to Scots. Finally, these varied assaults made upon pious certainties by the religious, the philosophical and the scoffing doubters took their toll. Two late and obvious monuments to this hidden unbelief can be found in the 1697 trial records of Thomas Aikenhead and in the autobiography of Thomas Halyburton (1674–1714).[5] Halyburton ended as a bloody-minded Professor of Theology at St Andrews University but there must have been many days in the 1690s when he shared Aikenhead's alleged belief 'That Divinitie or the doctrine of Theologie was a Rapsodie of feigned and ill invented Nonsense patched up partly of the morall doctrine of Phylosophers and partly of poeticall ffictions and extravagant Chimeras.'[6] Doubts were, then, abroad in Scotland and they had a direct bearing upon how eighteenth-century Scots were to change their religious outlook. Perhaps one should look a bit longer at Leighton, who later became Bishop of Dunblane (1661–69) and Archbishop of Glasgow (1669–74), a rather odd progression for a one-time Covenanter.

Bishop Leighton was a gentle and sweet-tempered man cursed by having to live in a violent age among men whose certainties brooked no challenges and recognized little to respect in those who disagreed with them. He was, none the less, typical of his time and place in accepting revelations as certain and basing his religious and moral beliefs upon them and not upon erring reason. Natural and unaided reason could be of very little help to men:

> There are indeed very few demonstrations in philosophy, if you can except the mathematical sciences, that can be truly and strictly so called; and, if we inquire narrowly into the matter, perhaps we shall find none at all; nay, if even mathematical demonstrations are examined by the strict rules and ideas of Aristotle, the greatest part of them will be found imperfect and defective. The saying of that philosopher is, therefore wise and applicable to many cases: 'Demonstrations are not to be expected in all cases, but so far as the

subject will admit of them.' But if we were well acquainted with the nature and essence of the soul, or even its precise method of operation on the body, it is highly probable we could draw from hence evident and undeniable demonstrations of that immortality which we are now asserting: whereas, so long as the mind of man is so little acquainted with its own nature, we must not expect any such.[7]

Natural knowledge is not and cannot be certain. But, if it is to improve, we need to attend to the facts of experience, particularly those involving the nature of our minds. Leighton set out a somewhat contradictory and obscure theory of innate ideas. This, together with arguments from design, causes and being itself, he used to prove the existence of God or, rather, to confirm what was evident to men and evidently in men. What is of greater importance than the arguments themselves is the priority given to revelation and to the sanctifying of the light of reason which in men leads them to recognize the existence of God. With Leighton, as with the Cambridge Platonists, Stillingfleet and Tillotson, reason is not yet a wholly natural faculty but one given by God that we may know Him and other things.[8] It is still the candle of the Lord and known to be such. Like his English contemporaries, Leighton believed that natural reason could and should be improved by clear thinking and by attending to the facts of experience. This would fulfil some of the ends which pansophists from Bacon on had given to the advancement of knowledge. But, mere natural and unaided reason was errant, less sure than revelation and needing its correction. What Leighton and his generation had done was to pose questions about the status of reason and about natural knowledge which created tensions that were not easy to live with in an age that had seen too many revelations. His solution had been to turn uncritically to the Bible, to a book whose status in England had already been made much more problematic by Chillingworth, the sectaries and, after 1677, Père Richard Simon.[9] If reason could confirm revealed truths, could it not also arrive at these truths independent of the word of God? If it could use philosophical arguments to do this, was not philosophy, and the reason which produced it, more trustworthy than Calvinists like Leighton believed?[10] Positive answers to these questions were given by two influential Scottish physicians after the 1680s. In their works, Baconian pansophism and Newtonian metaphysics were fully expressed, as was the optimism implicit in both schools of thought. Leighton's certainties were given up by men who embraced erring reason as man's best hope for this world and who found in it the basis for their religious views. Their attitudes, like many of their practical concerns, were to characterize Scottish thought throughout much of the enlightenment period, just as similar ideas and activities marked thinkers elsewhere from around 1680 to the 1780s. The two prominent physicians of the 1680s who helped initiate these trends were Sir Robert Sibbald, M.D. (1641–1723) and Archibald Pitcairne, M.D. (1652–1713).

Elsewhere I have written at length about Sir Robert; here I wish only to summarize a few points made in that essay.[11] First, Dr Sibbald's autobiography tells us that Leighton's teachings made a great impact upon this idealistic young man. It also tells us that Sibbald was fascinated by the 'corpuscular' philosophy which he encountered in the works of Thomas White and Sir Kenelm Digby, two Catholic writers who were concerned with the problems of certainty. Among Sibbald's surviving manuscripts is a poem nearly contemporary with Dryden's *Religio Laici* (1682) which neatly poses the question of whether one should believe in an ordered world governed by the providence of a good and creative God or if one should accept a Lucretian cosmos of atoms whirling blindly without meaning in a void which no God made or haunts.[12] By the mid-1680s, Sibbald had perhaps not settled the issue. In 1687, he, like Dryden a year earlier, converted to Catholicism. Both men were probably less concerned to please patrons than they were to find the solace of infallible certainty that philosophy and Protestantism seemed to deny to them. Sir Robert's conversion was not permanent; indeed, it lasted only a few months, perhaps because he already had elaborated another way of assuaging his doubts. That way was the one outlined by Bacon and accepted by pansophists. Systematic study of the natural world would restore in part man's fallen intellect, allow him to know God better, to improve his own estate and to fulfil his duties to his fellow man. Progressive advances toward unrealizable truth and virtue were all that men could hope for in this world. The critical, but empirical methods of naturalists, physicians, and skilled workmen were to be preferred to those of the speculative philosophers just as those of the critical historians were to be employed by those who would rewrite the history of Scotland. Sibbald's active career (*c*.1660–1713) shows symptoms of the malaise of the men of that time and is an indicator of two ways in which dissonance might be reduced. That the doctor ultimately chose to be an Episcopalian Baconian may have been of some importance because of his prominence as a patron and supporter of modern learning in Scotland from 1670 to 1710.

Sir Robert's doubts seem to have led him to reject the certainties offered by Calvinists as well as those upheld by the teaching authority of the Church of Rome. The Bible was not self-warranting and one could hardly believe that the Roman Church possessed an uncorrupted tradition antecedent to the formation of the biblical canon and independent of it. Sibbald could not trust either his own or the conversion experiences of some of his Calvinist friends and came to disbelieve many of the historical fictions of the Catholics of his time.

Ultimately, he settled as a Scottish Episcopalian who believed that his Church's message, polity and rites had a validity shown by its history and the probable credibility of the Bible. Christianity was vindicated by the testimony of men which could pass the critical scrutiny of historians. The creeds, forms of worship and polity that Sir Robert accepted, reflected his sense of what the primitive church was like, as well as his beliefs about the ways in which it could adapt and had adapted to distinctive times and places. All this was a matter of fact, which, while it might not be certain, was sufficiently probable to be accepted. The existence of God, however, was more certain because both *a priori* and *a posteriori* arguments showed it. Of these he clearly found the argument from design most satisfying. All this is a rather giant step away from Leighton's views. Reason as a critical and natural faculty here has been desanctified to a great extent. It, not faith, grounds our acceptance of the Bible and our true belief in the existence of God. Reason judges the conflicting claims of Christians accepting the most probable. For Leighton, the externals of religion had mattered less than the graciously revealed message; that was still true of Sir Robert too, but the certainty had gone out of his life to be replaced by probable arguments and historical conclusions which the Bishop would have found dubious, perhaps impious and of little value. Sir Robert remained a Christian, but his beliefs now came with impedimenta.

How great an encumbrance such critical and philosophical views might be, can be seen in the reputation and beliefs of Sir Robert's sometime friend and colleague, Dr Archibald Pitcairne.[13] Dr Pitcairne was also an Episcopalian, a Jacobite and a Scottish patriot, but throughout his career he lacked any reputation for sincere religious conviction. He was called at times a deist, a scoffer and an unbeliever. The name-calling was probably unjustified, but his God was certainly made necessary by the requirements of Newton's physics more than by the traditional arguments for the being and attributes of God. Inert matter needed a living force to make it move and to sustain its regular motions in an apparently contingent world willed into existence by God, who might, in the twinkling of an eye, change it. Christianity might or might not be relevant to all this. Certainly other Newtonians – Samuel Clarke and William Whiston, to name only two – thought trinitarianism foolish and also agreed with other Socinian heresies. Pitcairne's beliefs are difficult to unravel, but he was hardly an ordinary or orthodox Episcopalian. What is not difficult to see is the use of reason to build a science which justified a belief in God. Both science and theology are probable but not certain and both have become tied to the analysis of empirical data. The material world can only be known by the senses and understanding, which in his mind seem also to have yielded a critical appraisal of religious beliefs and practice.[14]

Drs Sibbald and Pitcairne were cosmopolitan *virtuosi* well known to men in Dublin, London, Leyden, Amsterdam, Rotterdam, the Hague, Paris, Montpellier and Padua and in other places as remote as New York and Sumatra. The correspondents of the first included every considerable British naturalist of the period 1680-1710 and many of the most prominent natural or rational theologians who filled their works with arguments from design in nature. Pitcairne's friends were nearly equally prestigious but drawn from natural philosophy and the art of medicine. Within Scotland, both men had coteries and protégés who spread their outlook in the universities, in clubs and professional bodies and among the virtuosi.[15] As they did so they shaped Scottish scientific traditions that were to be long-lasting. Sibbald's work remained of interest to Scottish naturalists and improvers at least until the 1780s and 1790s. For distinguished naturalists like Drs David Skene and John Hope or the Reverend John Walker, natural historical pursuits never lost the religious relevance that Sibbald claimed for them and that had probably legitimized their pursuit in Scotland. The Newtonian views that Pitcairne helped to promote in Scotland offered, throughout the century, the basis for a powerful apology for a belief in a God compatible with Christianity. From George Cheyne and the Keill brothers, John and James, at the beginning of the period, to Thomas Reid at the end, both rational religion and Christian beliefs were defended by arguments drawn from natural philosophy and, in particular, from its Newtonian version. Both the naturalists and natural philosophers insisted upon the ability of men to know the world through observations and experiments carefully made and analysed. The knowledge that the scientific enterprise might yield was probable, but so was anything else we might claim to know. These conclusions about knowledge and the methods that produced it had an equal impact upon other areas of thought, notably history and law.

Among the friends of both Sir Robert and Dr Pitcairne were numerous antiquarians and historians. Most of them claimed to be critics; most had read or knew of the works of Bayle and of Père Mabillon and his associates at St Maur, and most eagerly sought manuscripts, artifacts and other 'vouchers' that would enable them to reconstruct Scottish history in a modern way. In short, most, though in varying degrees, had accepted a critical methodology as essential for the historian. This was also a legacy from Bacon, who saw no reason to separate sharply civil from natural history or to limit inductions to the facts of nature. The one great Scottish historian who emerged from this ambience was Father Thomas Innes whose *Critical Essay on the Ancient Inhabitants of . . . Scotland* appeared in 1729. It was the product of a generation of research. Innes's work provided an exemplary model of critical history as well as a new chronological framework for early and medieval Scotland. Like Sir Robert, he believed that historical reconstruction of the past would prop up the Church to which he belonged.

The growth of what can loosely be called scientific rationalism and empiricism was equally well reflected in moral philosophy, to which law remained intellectually tied. Lord Viscount Stair, the first real systematizer of Scots Law, drew heavily for his principles upon both ancient and modern versions of Roman law but he also expected to show that this harmonized with principles that had the force of divine revelation and were set out in the Old and New Testaments.[16] Within less than fifty years, Lord Kames was to argue that law was rooted in the faculties of the human mind, in sociability and in the development and employment of these in the various stages of human history.[17] These were largely to be periodized by their modes and means of production. Central to that development was Gershom Carmichael, whose teaching career ran from 1694 to 1729. In tracing his accomplishment, it is useful again to look briefly at Archbishop Leighton.

For Leighton, all morality was summarized in the two tables of the law revealed to Moses on Mount Sinai. Moral obligations to God, men and oneself were rooted in revelations that guaranteed their authority, warranted the obligations they imposed and made clear their sanctions. No one but a Christian could be truly moral and act from the only proper motive: the love of God made possible by His grace. Without that, the moral law only condemned sinful men whose consciences and reason told them they could not fulfil God's demands. Morality was an ideal to which men aspired as they did to happiness; neither was achievable without grace. Even as Leighton was penning such thoughts in the 1650s and 1660s, Thomas Hobbes was seeing both morals and law in rather different ways. Both were rooted in desires and the will of the strong, whose understanding of their needs made positive demands upon others. The interests of both the strong and the weak led to their recognition and adoption of rules, moral principles and laws based ultimately upon needs, fears or other natural and secular principles. This view of a graceless, unsociable, lawless and immoral world, as we all know, demanded and got refutation both in Britain and abroad. Stair's legal writing borrowed from foreign writers who had rejected Hobbes's ideas, notably from Pufendorf whose moral philosophy text was increasingly used in the arts colleges. Among those who taught *The Duties of the Man and the Citizen* was Gershom Carmichael who also published an edition enriched by his own notes.[18] Both the notes and surviving students' dictates show that Carmichael broke cleanly with Leighton's views and that he secularized moral judgments without following Hobbes.

For Carmichael, our experience shows us men who are social, caring of others for unselfish reasons and who are able to formulate rational standards of conduct. Moral life is obedience to these laws seen as principles of social order and as having a divine sanction found by man's reasons. Moral life is still doing what God wants us to do; it is still in harmony with biblical injunctions, but its principles can be known by all men who reflect upon their experiences. The natural law theories derived from Grotius, Pufendorf, Cumberland, Stair and Locke had thus found by around 1700 an academic expression which freed morals from the tutelage of the Christian religion. And as morality was made more rational, so too was law, which showed how moral principles were put in enforceable forms that varied with time and place.

Carmichael spent little time as a moralist puzzling over the nature of the mind and its faculties but throughout most of his career he had taught as a Regent, leading boys through the whole of the arts curriculum. In teaching logic, he would have dealt with the faculties of the mind and would have had to consider the ability, trustworthiness and character of the senses, consciousness, conscience and reason. There is not much evidence in his moral philosophy that pneumatology was of great interest to him, but we do know that he gradually gave up Cartesian beliefs in favour of Newtonian physics and methods. By 1729, when he died, the analysis of mind, which Locke had already put on an empirical footing, had become of considerable interest to Scots. Members of the Rankenian Club of Edinburgh (it included some of Carmichael's former students),[19] their friend Francis Hutcheson who succeeded Carmichael in his Glasgow chair and still more Scots, such as the future Lord Kames, were already trying to analyse the mind and the bases of morals in ways which Shaftesbury and Bishop Butler had set out. Thus, by the early 1720s, Scottish moral philosophy had assimilated empirical methods and had largely divorced itself from the Bible. Furthermore, moral judgments and laws had been made dubitable, progressive and subject to the kind of comparative analysis that Montesquieu would show the Scots how to do with verve and finesse.

Theology and the practice of religion

By the 1720s, Scottish intellectuals had not ceased to be religious, but their Christian beliefs, as opposed to their natural religious beliefs, had eroded somewhat and had been compartmentalized within a realm that had far less to do with worldly knowledge than had been the case earlier. After 1720 this trend continued on all fronts and can be easily seen in the progress of university teaching and in the extra-mural philosophizing of Scots. Perhaps, however, one should look first at the practice of religion itself.

By and large, the course of prestigious eighteenth-century Scottish religious writing and theology was one that increasingly separated feeling from argument. Enthusiasm, ecstasy or perceived manifestations of special grace were distanced from rational piety, calm assurances and hopes, and from the cool consideration of one's grounds for faith and its entailed obligations. In all this, Scots reflected and drew upon the experiences of others, notably the Dutch and English. Moreover, after 1690, some measure of toleration was expected in Scotland and it was mandated by Parliament in 1712. The power to make such changes lay with the English, who, after 1688, had forced upon Scots an Erastian settlement in the Kirk. Formally and almost annually protested by the General Assembly until 1780, this was a reality that probably no one after 1715 expected to change. By then, political control of the Kirk meant the cultivation within it by government politicians of a Moderate Party, which would manipulate affairs and discipline 'high-flying' laymen and clerics in the judicatories of the Kirk. Those clerics who led the Moderates (the name seems to derive from the 1720s)[20] included many whose religious stance differed little from that of Tillotson. Indeed, the party's preachers read, admired and even preached his sermons and certainly his messages.[21] Rational religion contained essential moral and religious truths which revelation impressively confirmed and joined to sanctions. Unfulfillable by sinful men, God's law required that they be redeemed with the blood of Christ who came not only to reveal the law, but to fulfil it and to atone for men's sins. Tillotson's moralistic Calvinist gospel and the reasons for accepting it were much the same for clerical leaders in Scotland and England after 1712. This was also the year when the hands of the increasingly Anglicized patrons of Scottish kirks were also strengthened by a Parliamentary act that restored the right of the gentry to choose their own ministers.[22] Most Scots might not be Episcopalians, but those in power generally agreed with Anglicans that only those forms of Christianity that conformed to those of the early churches in doctrine, rite and polity were to be allowed to exist. For both Presbyterians and Anglicans, that was largely a matter of history and political experience although, needless to say, history was very differently read.

Latitudinarians and tolerant Whig bishops dominated the English Church by 1715. In Scotland there were endless challenges to the Moderates' views from the ecstatics of all sorts. In the 1690s, the mystical theology of Episcopalians in Aberdeen was censured and Dr James Garden was removed from his Divinity Chair at King's College for teaching heresies of Antonia Bourignon. He later added more that were taken from another French Quietist, Mme Guyon. These heresies, along with those of the deists, were condemned by the General Assembly in 1736. Garden's errors were those that have always made mystics suspect: the apparent claims to revelation, the denial of our sinfulness, and the seeming irrelevance of Christ to our salvation. He and his many disciples sought to lose themselves in Christ and to be renewed by the spirit working in them.[23] Later Episcopalians in Scotland were largely notable for their non-juring views which resembled those of their English Jacobite brethren. By the 1780s, when their political sins were forgettable, they once again began to attract converts, particularly in the Anglicized upper class. By then their theologians were tamer and mystics hard to find.[24] With the Calvinists, the story was rather different.

From 1690 on, there were few years undisturbed by 'high-flyers' eager to reform the church in an evangelical manner. That placed a premium upon conversions and upon a special grace obtained by some but not available to all. The settlement in 1690 had been the cause of a near rebellion by Cameronian Covenanters. Evangelicals in 1697 had managed to hang for deism Thomas Aikenhead, an Edinburgh University student. They fretted before and after 1712 about the Kirk's loss of freedom and the tameness of its leaders. Indicative of those reactions is Thomas Boston's *Four-Fold State of Man* (1720), which was begun in 1712 as a protest against the restoration of patronage and the forcing of toleration upon a Kirk still largely unwilling to see Anglicans legally worship in Edinburgh Chapels. Boston's views on free grace and its manifestations led to the 'Morrow Controversy' of the 1720s and to the secession which followed the condemnation of Ebenezer Erskine and his friends in 1723. Similar but later movements stripped the Kirk of about 200,000 souls (15 per cent of the population) by 1800 while leaving many sympathizers still within it. Among them were those who tried for heresy a series of Scottish divines and professors beginning with the Glasgow Professor of Divinity, John Simson (1717, 1727). By the 1740s, the Evangelicals had lost control of the seminaries and were much feebler in the General Assembly. They could, however, still attract thousands to open-air religious meetings, such as the Cambusland Work of 1742.[25] Attacks by the same groups upon the clerical Moderates were unceasing and bitter well into the 1760s, by which time many of the old leaders were dead and increasing numbers of their followers had left the Kirk to join secession churches. Men like the prolific and learned John Brown of Haddington had become peripheral to the national intellectual life in which, however, the Moderates now played an important part.[26] As schisms split the established church, they also took from it those who were most vehement in arguing for a society that was not only religious, but thoroughly Christian in some particular way that usually gave a primacy to grace and revelation. It was a constant concern to the 'unco guid' of eighteenth-century Scotland that Moderatism was synonymous with a lessening of the importance of grace and the word of God which saved men. Moderates were berated as 'rational', 'legal' and 'moral' preachers who disbelieved in sin, most of the tenets of the creed they preached and in the biblical revelation. It was often claimed that they lacked learning and divinity, but not 'virtue', 'fellow feeling', 'good humoured vices', 'politeness' or the 'benefices', 'offices', important pulpits and university chairs from which to inculcate their heresies or to utter such pious ejaculations as 'O Lord, we thank thee for Mr Bayle's Dictionary. Amen.'[27] The reality was, of course, somewhat different.[28]

The theology of the Moderates was and remained a form of Calvinism in which an emphasis on sin, conversion, free grace and the knowledge of one's salvation was replaced by a rational and moral Christianity preaching about obligations in this world. Never denying the importance and necessity of grace to fallen men, or the faith that made it effective in their lives, the Moderates did strip Christianity of the anxieties and existential imperatives that evangelicals have often emphasized. Reason and history showed the Bible to be credible and its central message a moral one. Because men could not live up to its demands, a scheme of salvation had been devised for their benefit. One could hope to be included among the saved, but it was not entirely clear that faith (belief) was either a necessary or sufficient condition for this since God worked in mysterious and unfathomable ways. What was clear was the requirement that we love the Lord with all our heart and mind and our neighbours as ourselves. Hell had receded but man's duties in the world were much extended and made more specific by a rational moral theology still held to be inseparable from ethics, politics and law and from the concerns they touched. In the *Sermons* of Hugh Blair, in the doctrinal works of George Hill and among the moralizing Moderate *literati* not only of Edinburgh but elsewhere, Christianity had been reduced to a scheme of salvation that one might expect to benefit the polite church attender who was active in the world doing what was not only right but God's will. Thomas Boston's fourfold state of man (innocence, sin, grace and eternity), Thomas Halyburton's 'Christ and Him crucified' and the pursuit of the glory of God in actions inspired by the creeds or private manifestations of grace had all been replaced by a 'new light'. We should, however, be quite clear about several things. First, the Moderates seldom, if ever, denied confessional tenets that they had subscribed. There is no reason to think they rejected what they took to be the essentials of Calvinism or Christianity.[29] To a man they believed in and defended doctrines of 'free and special grace',[30] revelations, miracles and Christian mysteries. They wanted free inquiry and a purification of Christianity, but that, as they saw it, only allied them to the reformers. Reformation, they held, required men to rethink the Biblical messages so that they would be relevant to a modern and enlightened society. That demanded a thorough knowledge of Scripture which in the case of George Campbell still depended upon illumination but was tentative and suspect because men must not mistake their certainties for God's.[31] The text, not the illumination, was the trustworthy source. Moreover, it was a text that required critical scrutiny, a new translation and historical glosses. Christianity in Campbell's work was biblical more than it was confessional. Polity was, for him, merely a matter of expediency. The state had an obligation to support religion and a free, though established, church, because, Campbell wrote, Christ- ianity promoted the ends of every legitimate state: the happiness of citizens, good morals and sociability, lawful conduct and fidelity based upon equity, and government that secures the common good. It is not surprising that other Moderates used the established Church to further what we would think of as enlightened ends: agricultural improvement, the betterment of Highlanders, education for the under-privileged and numerous other activities ranging from missionary work to urban renewal schemes.[32] Presbyterianism had not been secularized but its relevance was now construed in worldly terms that did not so often address the spiritual condition of men but those institutions and roles that were now seen as shaping it. That view reflected changes in philosophical outlook that had raised the historical consciousness of Scots.

Empiricism in natural and moral philosophy

Scottish philosophers had consistently moved toward secularity in their epistemology and concerns with methods, but they had not broken the systematic mode of thinking. In logic and metaphysics, they had become increasingly empiricist in outlook and more sophisticated. Bacon and Locke had told them that all knowledge related to the mind of man and to experience. The first of these beliefs led to the ever-increasing number of senses and sensations discerned by Hutcheson, Lord Kames, Smith and some of the Aberdonians. It culminated in the elaborate rational psychology of Thomas Reid's common sense philosophy. For each and every one of these men, as well as for David Hume, a knowledge of the human mind, based on introspection, history and such things as a study of languages, was essential to the understanding of what could be known, of its extent and certainty.[33] Consciousness and its modes dictated the forms of thought, just as experience filled them with contents. It was equally clear that thought and language had changed over time and that the history of these changes was important in understanding man in what now became his new fourfold state:

(i)   the age of savagery and barbarism in which men lived in a 'natural' state as hunters and gatherers;

(ii) the age of rudeness and agriculture, which knew property but not civil institutions of much complexity;

(iii) the age of cities and commerce; and

(iv) the age of civility, politeness and luxury.[34]

Appropriate to each period were languages of a certain sort, forms of rhetoric and poetry, causal explanations and forms of discourse. If thought depended on human nature, then the expression of that nature was also bound to social institutions and to a time that in most conjectural histories did not begin on 23 April or October 4004 BC. Historicity had emerged with the employment of empirical methods to study human nature. The insistence that the base of all knowledge lay solely in human faculties to which that knowledge remained relative had undercut old certainties and made dubious both the self-evidence of the biblical message, the traditions of all churches and the moments of inspiration felt by the vatic in every age. Those might be believable, but their credibility had to be established and related to man not initially to something extrinsic to him.

Such ideas, if they did not originate in natural philosophy, found there great support. After 1710 or thereabouts, Newton was regularly taught in all the arts colleges. Newton gave not only an exciting new cosmology and general physics, but a method and a programme. His rules of reasoning in philosophy were general and called for extension to other areas of philosophy as certainly as his physics served as a model for those seeking to understand other attractive and repulsive forces at work in the world.[35] Newton's conclusion to the *Optics* specifically set forth his methods as the means of perfecting moral philosophy, means which, if followed earlier, would have 'taught us to worship our true Author and Benefactor, as their Ancestors [the Gentiles] did under the Government of *Noah* and his Sons before they corrupted themselves'. This comment was to inspire Scottish moralists from the 1720s to the end of the century. Attempting to apply Newtonian methods to morals were George Turnbull, Henry Home (Lord Kames), David Hume and Thomas Reid to name only four men who produced original systems. Only one of them uncoupled this enterprise from a religious apologetic. David Hume's empiricism and his skepticism were purer than those of his friends.

Empiricism applied to logic and metaphysics led to unexpected conclusions; that was equally true of natural philosophy in Scotland. With Hume and Reid, the philosophers ceased to search for causes and were reduced to a search for regular constant conjunctions in the physical world which Reid held to be merely between effects. These regularities or laws were contingent, probable, and likely to change with more rigorous inductions and analyses. They were merely descriptive and not ultimately explanatory, since they did not deal with active powers which alone were true causes for Reid.[36] His methodological commitments to the study of effects also placed a premium upon the collection and manipulation of data. They also offered him the basis for a critique of past scientific systems, which led to the acceptance of views much like those put forth in the essays of Adam Smith or the conjectural histories of Lord Kames or in the real ones of Kames's distant cousin, David Hume. While Reid's type of common-sense philosophy heightened the separation between physics and pneumatics, between the sciences of inert bodies and moral philosophy which dealt with agents, it also left a legacy which made it possible for Adam Ferguson, John Millar and others to look for regularities in social behaviour and to construct what were in effect social sciences. These were not composed of causal laws but of 'laws of nature, comprehending a multiplicity of diversified appearances, which the law may serve to explain'. In morals, Ferguson tells us the laws concern not 'a fact, but what is good; and [they are] addressed to the powers of estimation and choice'. He warns that moral science must always go beyond considering 'moral approbation and disapprobation [as] mere phenomena to be explained', but his own writings seem sometimes to fall short of that requirement.[37] By the 1770s much Scottish moral philosophy had become factual and rather unrelated even to rational religion in its accounts of past ages. The conjectural histories and social theory of most of the mid- and late-eighteenth-century Scots derived from the application of their scientific methods to the data of history, travel accounts and contemporary observation. To study man in this fashion, either collectively or individually but abstractly as was done by the logicians and rational psychologists, set up important tensions in Scottish moral philosophy which lasted into the nineteenth century.

The principal tensions in the Scottish moral philosophy courses lay in their ambiguous nature. Every moralist was expected to 'preach virtue' and thus to give the teenage boys, who took their course, values and standards by which to live. This purpose conflicted with the analytical and methodological aims of the teachers, all of whom were committed to an empirical analysis of mind and to the anatomizing of the moral faculties. Pneumatology and rational psychology were essential to their courses, but they did not lead to the kinds of statements upon which preachments easily rested. Moreover, the professors tried uneasily to draw a line between what could and could not be the study of a science of morals.[38] Normative questions and questions concerning agency simply had to be treated differently from those of physics or one would end up looking uncomfortably like Hume or Kames, both determinists and one little better than a Hobbist. Preaching Christian virtue was also an uncertain business when one had competing sources and texts. During the first half of the eighteenth century, Cicero's *De Officiis* was regularly taught as was Pufendorf in Carmichael's edition of his *The Duties of Man and the Citizen.* They competed in the early years with religious writers like Henry More and Henry Scougal, just as later texts did with other religious works or works designed to uphold Christianity. As the practical needs of North British students seeking jobs in an improving age changed, they were met by courses that dealt more with politics, law, political-economy and what we would call sociology. Such courses as Smith's lectures on police, justice, revenue and arms included conjectural-historical sections and were useful to Scots who expected to make careers abroad in the Empire or even in England, which many had to do. Scottish moralists after 1730 all aimed to meet these needs as well as to outline an analytical philosophy supportive of Christianity which preached virtue. James Beattie's *Moral Science* and Adam Ferguson's *Institutes* and *Principles of Moral and Political Science*, like most of Dugald Stewart's moral and political economy works, show how various were the demands made on lecturers in this subject. They also show the degree to which empirical methods had denuded these subjects of explicitly Christian elements while leaving intact natural or rational religious ones.[39] Christianity had been relegated to the theology schools at the same time that the rational bases for its defence were believed to be strengthened by Newtonianism, common-sense philosophy and the critical inquiries of scholars. Natural history and human history were thought to serve similar functions, but the historians had been driven further toward secularism than had the philosophers.

Religion in a rational world

Around 1700, Sir Robert Sibbald's historical framework was set by some traditional date of creation and by the providence of God whose dispensations of grace to mankind could be known. The ancient and modern world could be fitted into this order and studied within traditional schemes that went back to Greek and Roman historians, to the Fathers of the Church and the chronologists of the sixteenth and seventeenth centuries. Since Sibbald's historical concerns did not require him to alter this, he worked comfortably within it. That was not true of his contemporary Andrew Fletcher of Saltoun. For him, the medieval and modern worlds were different from slave-holding antiquity and from the eras discernible in the biblical narratives. Fletcher's history was that of Sir Thomas Craig,[40] Harrington and Machiavelli from whom his basic ideas derived. Its dynamics could be largely explained in secular terms and there was no need to dwell upon the grand providential framework.[41] A generation later, in the work of

Scotland 1680–1800

the younger Thomas Blackwell (his students nicknamed him 'ratio profana'), the framework itself had been shifted from the Old and New Testament to the fifth book of Lucretius' On the Nature of Things. Later, conjectural historians also gave accounts of human history beginning at some unspecified date, which ignored the Bible or used it only as one among many sources. By the 1750s, then, there existed an alternative framework in which to put the data of the past and in terms of which it could be understood.[42] It was precisely this framework that was used by William Robertson, Gilbert Stuart, and others whose histories contributed to the reputation of Scotland as an enlightened land. Seldom did these men attempt to harmonize this history with the one in Genesis, although most took some note of the problems of doing so.[43] Religion as a natural phenomenon now derived from man's search for causes or from his fears or his awe in the face of a designed world. It could be understood, but the history of Christianity was difficult to accommodate within such a scheme. Hume's attempts to do so in The Natural History of Religion (1757) met no applause. However, in the very years Hume was writing his works on religion, the Glasgow Professor of Ecclesiastical History, William Ruat, was telling his students that Montesquieu was correct to include religious institutions within the developmental scheme he had set forth in 1748.[44] What was true of religion was also clearly true of philosophy in many other works besides those of Montesquieu. By the middle of the century, then, Scots had set out secularized patterns of historical development and had brought within them both earlier systems of thought and religious beliefs and institutions. In so far as church history was to be privileged and unique, it would appear as such in the seminaries and not in the arts courses. Most of the history that undergraduates were then taught began with primitives and ran through the four stages to polite Britain.[45] It might have touched sacred history in various places, but its relation to it was merely tangential until the ends of both were considered. Complete secularization was yet a step away because the 'spontaneous order' generated in every age by a myriad of human actors was still the providence of God displayed in secondary causes.[46] This manifestation of the divine in history came not in miracles and myths but in the regularities of nature which a moralist using the proper methods could now understand as well or better than a theologian.

Nevertheless, the order of nature and the minds and actions of men were still seen as created and governed by God – a still Christian God – and the world could by no stretch of the imagination be called a secular one. It was still one to be understood systematically and one in which every art and science led to the divine ground for temporal being. God was still understood to be He who is and is without end, the same who spake unto Moses and to St Paul and whose revelations were cherished in the Church of Scotland. By that time, however, one returned to that premise only *after* one had finished with philosophy and its guides to worldly life. That might have been deplored by the 'high-flyers' but it was the Moderates' line and it pervaded the thinking of leading intellectuals in the last decades of the eighteenth century,[47] most of whom were also laymen who appear not to have considered clerical careers. Religion was still part of the philosophical system, but Christianity and its revelations and grace had been excluded, shunted aside to dogmatic theology. This did not mean that Scottish thought had been thoroughly secularized, but it did mean that the religion now important to or within philosophy had ceased to be one acknowledged to rest on revelation. Christianity had a new place in the Scottish world of learning. Despite the worldliness of the learned, they did not yet live in a secular world. Their world was still religious in a rational way, as the works of men like John Robison, James Hutton and the writers of *The Mirror* and *Lounger* essays amply show. That story ought not to be told by a historian of the enlightenment. It is sufficient for him to note that, for the majority of Scots in 1790, knowledge of the world and of our obligations in it no longer depended upon any revealed premises, but the acceptability of any revelations depended upon reason and sense.

Notes

1 The relevant literature is noticed in J. W. Yolton, *Thinking Matter: Materialism in Eighteenth-Century Britain*, Minneapolis, University of Minnesota Press, 1983. Claims that the major English deists were really atheists have recently been made by D. Berman in 'Deism, immortality and the art of theological lying', in J. A. Leo Lemay (ed.), *Deism, Masonry and the Enlightenment: Essays Honoring Alfred Owen Aldridge*, Newark, University of Delaware Press, 1987, pp. 61–78.

2 J. L. Russell, 'Cosmological teaching in the seventeenth century Scottish universities,' parts I and II, *Journal of the History of Astronomy*, 1974, vol. 5, pp. 122–32, 145–54; C. M. Shepherd, 'Philosophy and science in the arts curriculum of the Scottish universities in the seventeenth century', unpublished Ph.D thesis, Edinburgh University, 1975, and 'The arts curriculum at Aberdeen at the beginning of the eighteenth century', in J. Carter and J. Pittock (eds), *Aberdeen and the Enlightenment*, Aberdeen, Aberdeen University Press, 1987, pp. 146–54.

3 See R. L. Emerson, 'Science and moral philosophy in the Scottish Enlightenment', in M. A. Stewart (ed.), *Oxford Studies in the History of Philosophy*, vol. 1, Oxford, Oxford University Press, 1989.

4 For Balfour's predecessors, friends and successors see G. Donaldson, 'A lang pedigree: an essay to mark the centenary of the Scottish History Society, 1886–1986', *Scottish Historical Review*, 1986, vol. 65, pp. 1–16, esp. 8–9.

5 T. Halyburton, *Memoirs of Thomas Halyburton*, ed. J. W. Halyburton,

Edinburgh, 1715; for citations to the records of Aikenhead's trial and execution see G. E. Davie, 'The Scottish Enlightenment', The Historical Association, Pamphlet G 99, 1981, p. 32 note 7.

6 Cited from the Collections of Sir John Lauder of Fountainhall, Edinburgh University Library, Laing MS, II. 89/222.

7 R. Leighton, *The Works of Robert Leighton, D.D. ... [with] a Life of the Author*, ed. J. Aikman, Edinburgh, 1839, pp. 563–4.

8 R. T. Carroll, *The Common-Sense Philosophy of Bishop Edward Stillingfleet, 1635–1699*, The Hague, Martinus Nijhoff, 1975, pp. 56, 151–8; H. G. VanLeeuwen, *The Problem of Certainty in English Thought, 1630–1690*, The Hague, Martinus Nijhoff, 1970, pp. 13–48.

9 See G. Reedy, *The Bible and Reason: Anglicans and Scripture in Late Seventeenth Century England*, Philadelphia, University of Pennsylvania Press, 1985.

10 I have discussed some of these issues in 'Latitudinarianism and the English deists', in Leo Lemay (ed.), *Deism, Masonry and the Enlightenment*, pp. 19–48.

11 See R. L. Emerson, 'Sir Robert Sibbald, Kt., the Royal Society of Scotland and the origins of the Scottish Enlightenment', *Annals of Science*, 1988, vol. 45, pp. 41–72.

12 Sir Robert Sibbald, untitled poem beginning 'Oft did I wavor in a doubtful case;/Which of these two Opinions to embrace', National Library of Scotland, Sibbald MS, 5.2.8/244.

13 References to recent work on Pitcairne can be culled from W. S. Craig, *History of the Royal College of Physicians of Edinburgh*, Oxford, Blackwell, 1976; A. Cunningham, 'Sir Robert Sibbald and medical education, Edinburgh, 1706', *Clio Medica*, 1978, vol. 13, pp. 135–61; and A. Guerrini, 'The Tory Newtonians: Gregory, Pitcairne and their circle', *Journal of British Studies*, 1986, vol. 25, pp. 288–311.

14 Dr Pitcairne's reputation as a deist and scoffer rests in large part upon a passage in Robert Wodrow's *Analecta or Materials for a History of Remarkable Providences mostly relating to Scotch Ministers and Christians*, 4 vols, Edinburgh, 1842, vol. 3, p. 243. His interest in Newtonianism is documented in Guerrini, 'The Tory Newtonians', pp. 290–7.

15 On the Scottish context in which they worked see R. L. Emerson, 'Natural philosophy and the problem of the Scottish Enlightenment', *Studies on Voltaire and the Eighteenth Century*, 1986, vol. 242, pp. 243–91.

16 Stair's career has been commemorated in a special issue of the *Juridical Review*, 1981, vol. 26: G. Donaldson, 'Stair's Scotland: the intellectual inheritance', pp. 128–45; J. Cameron, 'James Dalrymple, 1st Viscount of Stair', pp. 102–9; R. H. Campbell, 'Stair's Scotland: the social and economic background', pp. 110–27; N. MacCormick, 'The rational discipline of the law', pp. 146–60; and D. M. Walker, 'The importance of Stair's work for the modern lawyer', pp. 161–76. MacCormick has also briefly traced the course of Scottish legal philosophy from Stair's rational and empirical grounding of human law in divine law to George Bell's legal positivism, in his 'Law and enlightenment', in R. H. Campbell and A. S.

Skinner (eds), *The Origins and Nature of the Scottish Enlightenment*, Edinburgh, John Donald, 1982, pp. 150–66.

17 I. S. Ross, *Lord Kames and the Scotland of His Day*, Oxford, Oxford University Press, 1972, pp. 203–46.

18 See J. Moore and M. Silverthorne, 'Gershom Carmichael and the natural jurisprudence tradition in eighteenth century Scotland', *Man and Nature/L'Homme et la nature*, 1982, vol. 1, pp. 41–54, and 'Natural sociability and natural rights in the moral philosophy of Gershom Carmichael', in V. Hope (ed.), *Philosophers of the Scottish Enlightenment ... in Honour of George Davie*, Edinburgh, Edinburgh University Press, 1984, pp. 1–12.

19 On the Rankenian Club see M. A. Stewart, 'Berkeley and the Rankenian Club', *Hermathena*, 1985, vol. 139, pp. 22–45, and 'George Turnbull and educational reform', in Carter and Pittock (eds), *Aberdeen and the Enlightenment*, pp. 95–103.

20 Charles Erskine seems to have given currency to the term 'moderate' in correspondence of 1729 when discussing the case of a heretical professor of divinity at Glasgow University; National Library of Scotland Erskine–Murray MS 5073/135-6. Richard Sher prefers to restrict the use of the term 'Moderate Party' until after 1754, but he ignores the many similarities of purpose and outlook which the Moderates of that time shared with Erskine's friends of 1729; R. Sher, *Church and University in the Scottish Enlighten= ment: The Moderate Literati of Edinburgh*, Edinburgh, Princeton University Press, 1985, pp. 16–17.

21 The best evidence of this is to be found in the numerous and expanded editions of H. Blair, *Sermons* (1777), 5 vols, Edinburgh, 1802.

22 The Toleration and Patronage Acts are discussed from somewhat different viewpoints by W. Ferguson, *Scotland 1689 to the Present*, Edinburgh, Oliver and Boyd, 1968, pp. 110–13, and T. C. Smout, *A History of the Scottish People, 1560–1830*, London, Collins, 1969, pp. 80, 229–34.

23 See G. D. Henderson (ed.), *Mystics of the North East*, Aberdeen, Aberdeen University Press, 1934, pp. 11–33, *passim*.

24 See M. Lochhead, *Episcopal Scotland in the Nineteenth Century*, London, John Murray, 1966, pp. 30–46.

25 The most succinct account of their efforts is contained in J. MacLeod, *Scottish Theology in Relation to Church History since the Reformation*, 3rd edn, Edinburgh, Banner of Truth Trust, 1974, pp. 133–269, *passim*. For the Cambusland Work see p. 180.

26 The Moderate/Evangelical frays c.1750–1800 are covered by Sher, *Church and University in the Scottish Enlightenment*, *passim*; for Brown see R. Mackenzie, *John Brown of Haddington* (1918), London, Banner of Truth Trust, 1964.

27 J. Witherspoon, *Ecclesiastical Characteristics: or the Arcana of Church Policy ... the Character of a Moderate Man ...* (1753), Edinburgh, 1843, pp. 26, 22, 46, 43, 37.

28 The orthodoxy of leading Moderates could even be defined by their opponents. For example, see the references to William Robertson in a widely read funeral sermon by John Erskine included in his *Discourses*

Preached on Several Occasions (1798), 2nd edn, Edinburgh, 1801, pp. 262–77.

29 See F. Voges, 'Moderate and evangelical thinking in the later eighteenth century: differences and shared attitudes', *Records of the Scottish Church History Society*, 1985, vol. 22, pp. 141–57.

30 The phrase is from *The Westminster Confession of Faith*, ch. 10, Art. II.

31 I wish here to thank the Revd Mr Donald MacCallum for allowing me to read his unpublished study of Campbell's theology and ecclesiology.

32 See J. Walker, *The Rev. Dr John Walker's Report on the Hebrides of 1764 and 1771*, ed. M. M. McKay, Edinburgh, John Donald, 1980, an outstanding example of the Moderate's interest in most of the listed causes; Sher, *Church and University in the Scottish Enlightenment, passim.*

33 For Reid and the work of his protégé, Dr James Gregory, on language see M. Barfoot, 'James Gregory (1753–1821) and Scottish scientific metaphysics, 1750–1800', unpublished Ph.D. thesis, Edinburgh University, 1983, pp. 87–196.

34 For a discussion of the conjectural histories in which these four states are detailed and examined see R. L. Emerson, 'Conjectural history and Scottish philosophers', *Historical Papers 1984/Communications Historiques*, Canadian Historical Association, pp. 63–90.

35 See C. M. Shepherd, 'Newtonianism in Scottish universities in the seventeenth century', in Campbell and Skinner (eds), *The Origins and Nature of the Scottish Enlightenment*, pp. 65–85.

36 See R. Olson, *Scottish Philosophy and British Physics, 1750–1880*, Princeton, NJ, Princeton University Press, 1975, pp. 42–8; P. B. Wood, 'Thomas Reid, natural philosopher: a study of science and philosophy in the Scottish Enlightenment', unpublished Ph.D. thesis, University of Leeds, 1984.

37 A. Ferguson, *Principles of Morals and Political Science* (1792), 2 vols, Hildesheim and New York, Georg Olms Verlag, 1975, vol. 1, pp. 114–19, 159–61, 114, 118, 160-1.

38 See R. Sher, 'How moral was academic moral philosophy in eighteenth century Scotland?', and P. B. Wood, 'Science and the pursuit of virtue in the Aberdeen Enlightenment', in M. A. Stewart (ed.), *Oxford Studies in the History of Philosophy*, vol. 1, Oxford, Oxford University Press, 1989.

39 This is also apparent from the lists of authors used and recommended in the Edinburgh moral philosophy dictates and lectures. For example, *c.*1670: Aristotle, William Ames, Richard Baxter, Henry More; *c.*1700: More, Cumberland, Pufendorf, Grotius, Henry Scougal; *c.*1740: Cicero, Marcus Aurelius, Pufendorf, Bacon; and *c.*1780: Hutcheson, Ferguson, Smith, Hume.

40 Sir Thomas Craig (1538–1608) was the author of *Jus Feudale* (*c.*1603), *De Unione Regnorum Britanniae Tractatus* (*c.*1604), *De Hominio, Or Scotland's Sovereignty Asserted* (*c.*1605), and of much poetry. His political works are notable for their claim that all European systems of feudalism resembled one another, were produced by similar causes and developed in similar ways.

41 J. G. A. Pocock, *The Machiavellian Moment*, Princeton, NJ, Princeton University Press, 1975, pp. 426–36.

42 See Emerson, 'Conjectural history and Scottish philosophers', *passim.*

43 See, for example, H. Blair, *Lectures on Rhetoric and Belles Lettres* (1783), New York, 1817, p. 54.

44 W. Ruat, 'Lectures on church history' (*c*.1754), National Library of Scotland, Ruat MS 4992, ff. 39–150.

45 Exempletive of this history are J. Dunbar, *Essays on the History of Mankind in Rude and Cultivated Ages*, London, 1780; W. Barron, *History of the Colonization of the Free States of Antiquity*, London, 1777; A. F. Tytler, *Plan and Outline of a Course of Lectures on Universal History*, Edinburgh, 1783; J. Millar, *The Origin of the Distinction of Ranks*, London, 1771, and *An Historical View of the English Government: From the Settlement of the Saxons in Britain to the Accession of the House of Stewart* (1787), 4 vols, London, 1803; and R. Hamilton, *The Progress of Society*, London, 1830.

46 At least one insightful commentator sees the Scottish 'doctrine of spontaneous order' as too secular, R. Hamowy, 'The Scottish Enlightenment and the theory of spontaneous order', *Journal of the History of Philosophy*, Monograph Series, 1987; in support of which see the final sentence of A. Ferguson, *An Essay on the History of Civil Society* (1767), ed. D. Forbes, Edinburgh, Edinburgh University Press, 1966, p. 280.

47 Much of the discourse in which their thought is clothed is analysed by J. Dwyer, *Virtuous Discourse: Sensibility and Community in Late Eighteenth-Century Scotland*, Edinburgh, John Donald, 1987. Interesting as Dwyer's book often is, he too underestimates the Christian content of the thought of his subjects and their audience.

Chapter 4

Science and secularization in Hume, Smith and Bentham

Douglas G. Long

This essay is concerned with the work of David Hume (1711-76), Adam
Smith (1723-90) and Jeremy Bentham (1748-1832) as 'philosophers of
science' in the broad and indeed fluctuating sense in which they would
have used that expression. It is not – cannot be – concerned with evalu-
ating or characterizing them as 'scientists', for they never referred to
themselves by that name. In fact, as we shall see, they predate the use of
that term. As this essay attempts primarily to clarify their judgements,
rather than retrospectively to impose judgements on them, the label
'scientist' must be set aside, at least initially. Although all three men
dedicated much of their prodigious energies to making contributions to
the 'sciences' of morals, politics, political economy, human nature,
legislation and/or jurisprudence, they maintained that such organized
bodies of knowledge (or conjecture, or hypothesis, or even imaginings)
as these were 'arts' as well as 'sciences'. Individuals who studied them
seriously or contributed to their development were regarded as
philosophers in one sense or another, never as 'scientists' in anything
like the modern sense.

The first use of the term 'scientist' identified by the *Oxford English
Dictionary* occurs as late as 1840, when William Whewell, in the
'Introduction' to his *The Philosophy of the Inductive Sciences,* observes
that 'We need very much a name to describe a cultivator of science in
general. I should incline to call him a scientist.'[1] By Whewell's time, at
least in some quarters, confidence in and enthusiasm for 'those
[sciences] which are concerned about the material world' had grown so
great that Whewell could envision the 'progress of knowledge' as
proceeding with a seemingly irresistible momentum:

> the nature of truth is in all subjects the same, and . . . its discovery
> involves, in all cases, the like conditions. On one subject of human
> speculation after another, man's knowledge assumes that exact and
> substantial character which leads us to term it SCIENCE.[2]

The tone here is reminiscent of Bentham's at the beginning of his *Fragment on Government* (1776): 'The age we live in is a busy age; in which knowledge is rapidly advancing towards perfection. In the natural world, in particular, every thing teems with discovery and improvement.'[3] Yet Whewell's lengthily expounded 'new method of pursuing the philosophy of human knowledge', based on a blithe faith in the cumulative quality of the intuitive insights of exceptional thinkers from generation to generation, exhibits neither the epistemological scepticism that put limits on the claims made in the name of science (or about science) by Hume and Smith, nor the anti-intuitive character of Bentham's consequentialist calculus. All three of our protagonists, we may surmise, would have found Whewell's work naïve at its foundations and, as such, philosophically deficient. His vision of 'SCIENCE' as a single vast repository of 'exact' and 'substantial' knowledge, and of truth as both homogeneous and conclusively attainable 'in all subjects', would surely alarm both the author of the *History of Astronomy* and the poser of the problem of induction. Bentham's approach to science would seem at first glance to have much more in common with Whewell's than would the reflections of Hume and Smith. Bentham might appear to constitute what Whewell called a 'scientist', even though he would not – could not – have used the name. But this apparent similitude stems largely from the non-specific character of Whewell's use of 'scientist': it denotes a kind of enthusiasm rather than a type of method. Bentham would have been loath to rest his hopes for the progress of science on the exceptional intuitive capacities of a few gifted thinkers. What made progress in the sciences possible for Bentham was not the continuing refinement of men's intellectual sensibilities, but the discovery of simple and evident regularities in the relationships among objects in the external, material world. Lacking an external standard for the evaluation of judgements about the world, Whewell's system lacked, by Bentham's criteria, the essential feature of a science. Intuitive judgements, Bentham held, are irreparably subjective, expressive of sentiments of 'sympathy' and 'antipathy' which can only be obstacles to scientific objectivity. Surely Bentham would have rejected Whewell's intuitionism as what he called (*c.*1815) a 'phantastic' or 'calculation scorning' mode of 'sentimentalism':

> Utilitarianism, working by calculation, is consistent and solicitous beneficence. Sentimentalism, in so far as independent of utilitarianism, is in effect a mask for selfishness or malignity, or both for despotism, intolerance, tyranny.[4]

The 'sentimentalist' is that uniquely Benthamic creation, the abhorred 'ipse-dixitist'.[5] 'Ipse-dixitism', created (though not, of course, so named) in England by the third Earl of Shaftesbury, represents a triumph of 'sense' over science, for it repudiates calculation and demonstration:

> Demonstration necessitates study and admits scrutiny, sense excludes it. Demonstration may err, sense can not. Demonstration is for drudges, sense for gentlemen. If demonstration fail of producing your assent: 'You are no Mathematician. If you have no sense, you are no man.'[6]

In contrast to Whewell's picture of a science arising directly from (and thus congruent with) our intuitions, Bentham conjured up an image of science as 'shackling the will' while it 'enlightened the understanding': 'In politics, religion and morals every man clings to the notions most accordant to his prepossession and all turn a deaf ear to truth which might shackle their will while it enlightened their understanding.'[7] In principle, Whewell's intuitionism need pose no insuperable obstacles to the continuance of traditional (i.e. theological) modes and structures of moral and political authority. But Bentham's enthusiasm for the pursuit of truth via the elaboration of a 'science of Man' involved an evident and explicit attack on all 'establishments' purporting to be sources or vehicles of moral authority. The present discussion aims ultimately to show by what stages a social science like Bentham's, so thoroughly secularized as to constitute a direct threat to the moral authority of religious doctrines, emerged in eighteenth-century Britain.

Perhaps partly because of the suppression of Bentham's more blatantly atheistic works by his philosophical radical companions in his lifetime and by his literary executor after his death, the reaction against the atheistic implications of untrammelled enthusiasm for science took time to gather momentum, but by the 1870s writers in popular magazines were expressing an anxiety that presumably was widely shared. The *Oxford English Dictionary* finds the first use of the pejorative term 'scientism' in a fascinating article, titled 'Modern Prophets', in *Fraser's Magazine* of September 1877.[8] The author, who signs himself 'Unus de Multis', finds himself in the middle of a war declared against 'theologic dogmatism' by modern science. Despite youthful 'intellectual and moral animosity' toward the 'Theologian' and continuing hostility toward 'Dogmatic Theology', 'Unus' is alarmed by the consequences of all-out warfare:

> Science has of late been carrying all before it; and I must own that I am not entirely satisfied with the result. Science is carrying too much before it to please me ... Those teachers and preachers who have most the ear of the present time, aim at ... the destruction, not merely

of Dogmatism but of Religious Faith. . . . The present age will be noted or notorious for this, that for the first time in the history of modern civilization ATHEISM is publicly and authoritatively inculated.[9]

The 'modern prophets' of this atheistic 'scientism', we are told, preach that 'there is nothing perceptible anywhere in the universe but Matter', and that '"Morality" is consideration, in a rational and logical shape, for the welfare of the community or of mankind; and apart from this there are no moral obligations'.[10] The anger of 'Unus de Multis' was primarily aimed at such alleged perpetrators of 'scientism' as Huxley and the Darwinians, with some reference to Comte as the 'Science-Prophet' of Sociology.[11] Had 'Unus' wished to trace the genealogy of 'scientism' back to more distant generations than these, however, he might easily have done so, and that is what I now propose to do. The seeds of what 'Unus' denounced as 'Atheism' were discovered by William Warburton, the Bishop of Gloucester, in David Hume's *Natural History of Religion* in 1757,[12] and although Adam Smith prudently avoided association with Hume's religious views, there is no evidence that those views did anything to estrange the two dear friends.

The genealogy of 'scientism'

The most substantial reference – at least on Smith's part – in the Hume/Smith correspondence to Hume's holding immoral or dangerous views is a playful one. Referring to the Duke of Buccleugh, with whom he is travelling in France, Smith says:

He has read almost all your [i.e. Hume's] works several times over, and was it not for the more wholesome doctrine which I take care to instill into him, I am afraid he might be in danger of adopting some of your wicked Principles.[13]

The term 'agnostic', coined though it was in 1869 by that very Dr Huxley against whom 'Unus de Multis' railed, would seem to be appropriate to characterize the thought of Hume.[14] It is difficult to say how closely the religious views of Smith, holder of a University post that would surely be threatened should he utter opinions – let alone publish works – tinged with atheism, resembled those of Hume. Smith was certainly aware of what it had cost Hume to maintain the views expounded in *The Natural History of Religion*, and this alone would have given him powerful motives for circumspection on the subject. Perhaps Smith would qualify as a deist or theist. His view, very reminiscent of Hume's as given in the *Natural History*, was that religious convictions, whether Christian or otherwise, rest on sentiment, and specifically on the opinion 'first impressed by nature, and afterwards confirmed by reasoning and philosophy, . . . that [the] important rules of morality are the commands and laws of the Deity, who will finally reward the obedient, and punish the transgressors of their duty'.[15] He treats the subject of religious belief as Montesquieu might have approached a problem in comparative sociology:

> Men are naturally led to ascribe to those mysterious beings, whatever they are, which happen, in any country, to be the objects of religious fear, all their own sentiments and passions. They have no other, they can conceive no other to ascribe to them. Those unknown intelligences which they imagine but see not, must necessarily be formed with some sort of resemblance to those intelligences of which they have experience.[16]

Thus do men make their Gods in their own image – or at least in a form *originating* in the human imagination. In Hume's *Natural History*, in Smith's essay on *The History of Astronomy* and in *The Theory of Moral Sentiments*, the picture is the same: religious sentiments are natural to man. This is something very different from saying that the object(s) of religious sentiments exist, or that we can know of their existence, or that religious doctrines postulating their existence or attributing to them certain powers and qualities are true. Religion here is accepted as a 'natural' and even necessary phenomenon because of its functional relationship to basic human sentiments. It may be a fairy story, a fantasy or fiction, but it is a natural and useful one. Bentham, on the other hand, thought it both possible and necessary to divest men's imaginations of fictional notions about 'unknown intelligences which they imagine and see not'. Too much evil, he felt, had already come of men's attachment to religious fictions, and too much evil had been done by men prepared to manipulate and exploit the 'religious sanction'.

In the works of both Hume and Smith, religious scepticism accompanies epistemological scepticism, and is conjoined with a view of the nature, development and purposes of 'science' that reflects the inability of humankind to be certain of the nature of the 'external' material world. In Bentham, the case is strikingly different. Recent work has made it clear that in Bentham an assertively simplistic materialist metaphysic, a distaste for the niceties of epistemological scepticism, and a breathless enthusiasm for the very sorts of sciences Whewell admired – those 'concerned about the material world' – were united with a militant atheism: a determination to achieve not only 'the abolition of religion', but 'the elimination of religious beliefs as influential psychological factors in the human mind'.[17] In Hume and Smith, philosophy, religion and science are all seen as attempts to allay the inevitable anxiety of men in a condition of incorrigible uncertainty about things natural and divine. Such uncertainty was exactly what Bentham refused to accept. His metaphysics, his moral theory (of which his atheism forms a part), and his 'constructivist'[18] conception of social science depend on the prior demolition by Hume of human certainty about 'first causes', but insist on the possibility of a full and sound moral and legislative science in a world of inter-related and intersecting secondary causes. In Bentham, philosophical analysis is placed in the service of this science of secondary causes. It is asked to supply precise language in which to convey the interaction of forces in the material world, and to develop a 'logic of the will' and a logic of human action, like a navigator's bearing for the path of least resistance through a field of pleasurable and painful stimuli.[19] In Hume and Smith, science is placed in the service of philosophy. Scientific theories are produced and sustained because they help humankind deal with the problems of moral and metaphysical uncertainty.

I have suggested that there is a sense in which science achieves an ascendancy over philosophy in Bentham's thought that is in contrast with the order of priority on Hume and Smith. But as I have already pointed out the distinction on which this judgment rests was not consistently observed in the eighteenth century. Indeed, Bentham was in the habit of referring to metaphysics itself *as* a science. We shall learn more by asking not 'Were they scientists?', which will only lead to further terminological entanglements, but 'Did they contribute to the rise of "scientism"?' And the answer is that in very different ways and at different stages of the process they did. We can see how they did by postulating three different contexts within which the philosophy of science might be pursued:

(i) a theological context in which science is the study of men and nature as God's handiwork;

(ii) an agnostic context in which men denied certainty concerning the attributes and works of the Creator of the universe in the attempt to come to terms with their place in it as best they can; and

(iii) an atheistic context in which it is assumed that science can progress toward some kind of completeness and conclusiveness in situating humanity in the natural world without recourse to any metaphysical hypotheses concerning a God.

These sharply differing contexts may be thought of as characterizing successive phases in the emergence of a fully secularized modern science. In stage one, the philosophy of science is a branch of theology, and scientific inquiry arrives at truth, or achieves certainty, by confirming religious truth. In stage two, science has been 'secularized' in a negative sense: confined to the realm of the secular, cut off from ultimate truth, having lost the capacity for unmitigated certainty as a believer might lose the capacity for faith. In stage three, however, science is assertively secularized; the sense of loss is replaced by one of release, power and liberation. Not agnostic uncertainty but atheistic militancy sets the tone. The notion of certainty, metaphysical and moral, is redefined and revived. I shall argue that Hume and Smith made brilliant and subtle contributions to the philosophy of science in an intellectual context essentially like that sketched in stage two, whereas Bentham stands out as a remarkably unqualified proponent of a phase three philosophy of science. For all three men the question 'Does God exist?' was of extreme importance. In all three cases the answer to that question shaped the theorists' views as to two other questions: 'What things exist?' and 'How and how much can we know about such things?' Only after these two stages of interrogation had been completed could the question be asked: 'What is the nature of a science of man and society, and by what method can one go about constructing one?'

Scepticism versus certainty

Analyses of David Hume's contribution to the development of science, or the philosophy of science, usually gravitate (if the Newtonianism may be allowed) toward a consideration of his theory of causality. Thus, as Professor Popkin tells us, 'With Hume, we have often been told, theological and metaphysical notions of causality were exploded, clearing the way for a purely scientific theory of causality.'[20] But as Professor Popkin also points out, the transformation that occurs in the concept of science as one moves from, say, Newton to Hume is a change from science as the study of '*divine* causality' to science as the 'natural history' of the appearance and development of certain human sentiments and activities: 'God as first cause dwindled in importance as Hume transformed Malebranche's denial of the efficacy of secondary causes into a commentary on the inefficacy of first causes – God's action.'[21] Sir Isaac Newton before Hume, and David Hartley and Joseph Priestley after him, would hold the study of natural causality to be subsumed under the study of divine causality. All three made their scientific achievements subordinate to their millenarian religious views. For these thinkers natural history proceeded 'within divine history and would last only as long as necessary to fulfill God's prophetic history'.[22] Popkin points out that while 'this sort of science seen within a religious framework' was very much in 'the mainstream of intellectual activity' in the eighteenth century, the influence of the French Enlightenment produced a movement away from it: 'the mainstream of *scientists* tended toward the deism, agnosticism, and atheism of the French Enlightenment, culminating in LaPlace's Newtonian cosmology without God that he presented to Napoleon'.[23]

Hume's monumental attempt in the *Treatise of Human Nature* to show how all other sciences might refer back to a 'science of Man' and of 'human nature', and how such a master science might be founded on the use of an 'experimental method',[24] is in this context interesting not only because it is Baconian, but because it is not particularly Newtonian. In 1787, however, Adam Smith's great student John Millar was to assert, with reference to the field of jurisprudence, that 'The great Montesquieu pointed out the road. He was the Lord Bacon in this Branch of Philosophy. Dr Smith is the Newton.'[25] Bentham's attitude toward Montesquieu was more mixed, but his vision of his own role was more immodestly Newtonian:

> every . . . work of mine that has been or will be published on the subject of legislation or any other branch of moral science is an attempt to extend the experimental method of reasoning from the physical branch/department/world to the Moral. What Bacon was to the physical world, Helvétius was to the moral: The moral world has therefore had its Bacon, but its Newton is yet to come.[26]

All three authors were consciously attempting to extend somehow the great work in the fields of physical and moral science by Newton and Bacon. None, it can safely be said, shared the millenarian mentality of Newton, whom John Maynard Keynes, no mean Newton scholar, once characterized not as the first of the empiricists but as 'the last of the magicians'.[27] Moreover, all three exhibit more than a shift from a Newtonian emphasis on divine causality to a secularized emphasis on natural causality. They also reconsider the metaphysical presuppositions of causal theory. Indeed it might be said that they direct attention away from causality (although certainly not to the point of neglecting its study), seeking to focus our gaze as well on the shape, nature and origins, the 'what' as well as the 'why', of action. The accounts given by Hume, Smith and Bentham of human actions and natural phenomena all assume the validity of a Humean analysis of causality as a working hypothesis. Each then goes on to explain human sentiments and actions as responses to natural stimuli. The analysis of 'first causes', traditionally theological, gives way to the analysis of secondary, natural, efficient causes, and this, as J. S. Mill was to argue in his study of the principle of utility,[28] is a necessary and central feature of a utilitarian mode of thought. But utilitarianism, fully developed, also presupposes a metaphysics and an epistemology of a particular sort. It was with regard to the basic questions of what things exist and of how and how fully we can know what exists that the approaches of Bentham and the two Scots diverged irreparably. We can see the nature of this divergence more clearly if we bear in mind the passage quoted above in which Bentham alluded to his Newtonian aspirations.

We know that Bentham had read Hume. He referred positively to the *History* and some of the *Essays*, and called the *Treatise* 'that celebrated book: of which the criminality in the eyes of some, and the merits in the eyes of others, have since been almost effaced by the splendour of more recent productions of the same pen'.[29] Why, we may ask, when Bentham was in the process of identifying his entire *oeuvre* with the attempt to 'extend the experimental method of reasoning from the physical world to the moral', seemingly a most Humean task, did he defer instead to a peripheral figure in the dramatis personae of the French Enlightenment, Claude Adrien Helvétius, author of *De L'Esprit*? The answer will give us a clue to the differences between Bentham's and Hume's understandings of the philosophical foundations of scientific inquiry.

Hume was a 'penetrating and acute metaphysician', yet Bentham 'would not wish', he said, to 'send the Reader' to any volume of the *Treatise* but the third; 'As to the two first, the Author himself, I am inclined to think, is not ill disposed ... to join with those who are of opinion, that they might, without any great loss to the science of Human Nature, be dispensed with.'[30] 'The like might be said', he suggested, even 'of a considerable part' of volume three, 'But, after all retrenchments, there will still remain enough to have laid mankind under indelible obligations.'[31] If we follow David Fate Norton in categorizing Hume as a sceptical metaphysician and a common-sense moralist,[32] the passage we have just examined from Bentham constitutes a rejection of Hume's thought as characterized by all but the last word of the description: Hume was somehow an important 'moralist' despite the fact – or rather Bentham's contention – that his metaphysical and epistemological work as well as the 'common sense' or 'moral sense' component of his moral theory were all intellectually dispensable.

In saying that the first two volumes of the *Treatise* could 'be dispensed with', Bentham was acknowledging a major methodological difference between his approach to science and Hume's. Hume's metaphysical and epistemological reflections, however 'acute and penetrating', seemed to him not so much unpersuasive or unacceptable as useless and unnecessary. Such speculations, in Bentham's view, merely reflected the seductive nature of introspection and subjectivity for sensitive and gifted philosophical minds. One sometimes senses that Bentham almost *feared* introspection. Clearly he was quite determined, in his philosophical work, to look 'outward' from the human subject to the 'external' world of actions and events. His arena was the 'universal system of human actions',[33] and his search was for an external, demonstrable standard to govern it. In his early (and as yet unpublished) manuscripts Bentham made his position quite clear:

> I assume and take for granted, that among the objects or supposed objects that offer or are supposed to offer themselves to our sense, are some that actually exist . . . I assume in a word the existence of what is called the material world . . . I assume for example that I who am writing this exist . . . that the Table which the paper seems to rest upon exists, and so forth. All this I say I assume; and that without scruple: notwithstanding it has been the subject of so much controversy. I assume it boldly for this reason: because in point of practise, no bad consequences can as every one is ready to acknowledge possibly arise from supposing it to be true; and the worst consequences can not but arise from supposing it to be false.[34]

Hume could have written these words himself, but he would have written them in a spirit and with an intent very different from Bentham's. In this as in other respects Bentham does not actually repudiate Hume's ideas; rather he seems to set aside the sceptical 'mentalité' which informs them, replacing it with his own architectonic enthusiasm. Does Hume undermine the metaphysical status of 'substance'? Bentham asserts that 'The only objects that really exist are *substances*',[35] and that the building blocks of language (and thus the materials of metaphysical inquiry) are 'substantives'. Does Hume reduce the idea of personal identity to the notion of the individual as a mere 'bundle of sensations'? Bentham builds an entire philosophy of action and of law on the basis of that notion, making 'physical sensibility' the very 'ground of law'. Does Hume assert that reason is but the 'slave of the passions'? Bentham will 'rear the fabric of felicity by the hands of reason and of law'.[36] In each case (and more could be cited), Hume's work is presupposed, his insight indispensable. In each case, the thrust of his argument is somehow reversed. Hume was not to be 'censured', Bentham wrote, for having entered the realm of metaphysics, but for having 'lost his way' while there. The 'acute metaphysician' had caused the scales to fall from Bentham's eyes, but the latter's newly received vision was entirely his own.

It simply does not seem to have mattered to Bentham that assertions carrying the weight of axiomatic certainty in his system (such as his 'axioms of mental pathology') might under careful philosophical scrutiny turn out to be mere probabilities. What he wanted were fruitful working hypotheses. Refined metaphysical/epistemological reflection on their status seemed to him beside the point. In this regard – and it is a crucial one – his philosophy of science and Hume's (from which, in this respect, Smith's did not differ significantly) were virtually antithetical.

Bentham thus simply spurned the great labours of volumes I and II of Hume's *Treatise*. Yet, as we have seen, he also questioned the validity of 'a considerable part' of volume III. This was a way of saying that he rejected the 'common sense' or 'moral sense' legacy of Hume's teacher Frances Hutcheson. In some 'observations' appended to his ethical work, *A Table of the Springs of Action*, Bentham denounced the introspective, subjective doctrine that each man has a 'moral sense' which tells him what is right and what is wrong as both incompatible with utilitarianism and self-contradictory:

> 612. Hume acknowledges the dominion of utility, but so he does of the moral sense: which is nothing more than a fiction of IPSE-DIXITISM.
> 613. So before him Hutchinson [sic] of Glasgow.
> 614. Here then is a compromise of incompatible contradictions – necessary result, inconsistency.[37]

The result of the application of such a personal, impressionistic standard to practical moral judgements and actions will be inconsistency, indeed arbitrariness. Most cases will be governed by the criterion of utility (which Bentham thinks many moralists employ without knowing it), but some will be exempt. Sometimes actions will be assumed to be self-interested, sometimes not. Sometimes the evaluation of actions will rest upon calculations of consequences affecting happiness, sometimes not. Bentham waxed vitriolic about the result: 'Morals is what a gentleman pleases. Every man dreams he understands morality and wishes not to be awakened.' And again:

> In politics, religion and morals every man clings to the notions most accordant to his prepossession and all turn a deaf ear to truth which might shackle their will while it enlightened their understanding. Each man wishes to do his will. Truth, if subservient to this, is acceptable; if obstructive, odious.[38]

Finally, Bentham launched a blanket indictment of the entire Scottish Enlightenment school of moral thought (he referred to them as 'a host of Scotch sophists'),[39] including both Hume and Smith in the broadside:

> When everything is done by feeling and talking about feeling, the task of a teacher is not difficult. ... Hume, Reid, Smith, etc., vied in cultivating it. No wonder ... it fitted everyone and proved all

DESIDERATA without skill or practice.... In morals, instruction could be delivered without thought, so as to please every man.[40]

Nevertheless, Bentham was quite willing to acknowledge his indebtedness to the third volume of Hume's *Treatise* in two major respects. First, as we shall see later in this discussion, from its moral analysis he learnt 'that UTILITY was the test and measure of all virtue'; learnt it even if it was not exactly the lesson Hume had intended to teach.[41] Second, when he read 'that part of the [*Treatise*] which dealt with the subject of the original contract', he remarked, 'I felt as if scales had fallen from my eyes. I then, for the first time, learnt to call the cause of the people the cause of virtue.'[42] Once again, Bentham had extracted a radicalizing message from Hume's work, whether Hume had intended to convey such a meaning – which seems most unlikely – or not. In sum, the most accurate encapsulation of Bentham's response to volume three of the *Treatise* is probably the following: 'That the foundations of all VIRTUE are laid in UTILITY, is there demonstrated, after a few exceptions made, with the strongest force of evidence: but I see not, any more than Helvétius saw, what need there was for the exceptions.'[43]

Hume had not intended to found all virtue on utility, and his 'few exceptions' were not the results of absence of mind, but evidence of Hume's reasoned commitment to a 'moral sense' account of obligations. There are in this view fundamental moral duties 'to which men are impelled by a natural instinct or immediate propensity, which operates on them, independent of all ideas of obligation, and of all views, either to public or private utility'.[44] The 'science of human nature' envisioned by Bentham had less in common with that developed by Hume than a superficial reading of the relevant evidence might suggest.

A thoroughly secularized social science

It was Helvétius whose critique of Hume Bentham endorsed, and Helvétius whose vision of the 'genius', the 'censor' as contributor to the interdependent sciences of morals, manners, legislation and education inspired Bentham to develop his own 'genius' for legislation. Bentham said that his reading of *De L'Esprit* changed his life. Where he was critical of Hume, he was utterly unqualified in his praise of Helvétius. Hume, as it happens, sent a copy of *De L'Esprit* to Smith shortly after its publication in 1759. He assessed it as follows:

It is worth your Reading, not for its Philosophy, which I do not highly value, but for its agreeable composition. I had a Letter from him a few days ago, wherein he tells me that my Name was much oftener in the Manuscript, but that the Censor of Books at Paris [Males-herbes] oblig'd him to strike it out.[45]

Hume was quite right; *De L'Esprit* was a work far more rhetorical than rigorous, a work 'agreeable' enough for its colourful flights of fancy and its flowing prose but exhibiting no solid philosophical foundations at all. It was an outburst of enthusiasm, and it seems to have infected Bentham. Even a summary view of all of the points of convergence between Bentham's approach to the sciences of morals and legislation and that of Helvétius would require a separate essay, but a single illustration may suffice to give the flavour of *De L'Esprit*'s influence. Having established that 'public utility' was the 'principal end of [his] work', and that men with a 'genius' for the 'invention' of moral ideas must be relied upon to advance society toward the goal of maximum public utility, Helvétius challenged the moralist to join the legislator in reconciling private with public interest:

> I say, that all men tend only towards their happiness; that it is a tendency from which they cannot be diverted; that the attempt would be fruitless, and even the success dangerous; consequently, it is only by incorporating personal and general interest, that they can be rendered virtuous. This being granted, morality is evidently no more than a frivolous science, unless blended with policy and legislation: whence I conclude that, if philosophers would be of use to the world, they should survey objects from the same point of view as the legislator. Though not invested with the same power, they are to be activated by the same principle. The moralist is to indicate the laws, of which the legislator ensures the execution, by stamping them with the seal of his authority.[46]

The role sketched here for the 'philosopher' was that of 'jurisconsulte': social and political architect, advisor to statesmen, maker of policies. This role called not for lengthy and subtle philosophical reflection but for the building of an ambitious social edifice. It suited Bentham perfectly. It left Hume cold. It convinced Bentham that he possessed a 'genius' for legislation, and it also seems to have convinced him that the essence of genius in relation to the sciences lay in the capacity for the 'invention' of ideas.[47] Helvétius asserted that 'genius is derived from GIGNERE, GIGNO; I bring forth, I produce; it always supposes invention, and this quality is the only one which belongs to all the different kinds of genius'.[48] Innovation, reform, invention – these kinds of activities indicated genius, if performed with sufficient efficacy to earn the interest and approval of an inherently self-interested public. For that purpose not philosophical subtlety but 'obstinacy' was required: 'the man of genius has no advantage over other men but the habit of application, and a method of study'.[49] Bentham's 'habit of application' will be all too apparent to anyone who has ever surveyed the voluminous (250,000 sheets) collection of Bentham manuscripts housed at University College London. It is, at times, the bane and the nemesis of the Bentham scholar. But the manuscripts do provide abundant evidence of Bentham's inventing activities and, as I have argued at length elsewhere,[50] Bentham seized on Helvétius's conception of invention as a central methodological principle in the development of his work in moral and legislative science.

In the course of his analysis of 'imagination and sentiment', Helvétius had made a distinction between genius and imagination: 'Imagination is ... invention with respect to images, as genius with respect to ideas.'[51] The precise relationship between an idea and an image here is characteristically unclear, but the formulation none the less enables us to articulate a contrast between Bentham's moral and legislative science on one hand and the philosophy of science of Hume and Smith on the other. Bentham distrusted the imagination. His theory of fictions and his entire analysis of language were designed to dissolve the products of the imagination into real, concrete referents or components, or into deserved nothingness. He cultivated his genius for inventing ideas in the form of a passion for the redefinition and invention of words, then of propositions, of laws, of codes, and thence of reality itself. His science was founded on construction, and his constructs were taken to be not imaginative but real, for they were fashioned from the stuff of pleasure and pain. That 'physical sensibility' was the 'ground of law' Bentham regarded as a proposition both 'obvious' and 'incontestible'.[52] The uniqueness, on the other hand, of the understanding of science found in Hume and Smith lies precisely in their subtle recognition, expressive of their epistemological and metaphysical scepticism, that science is and must be founded upon 'images' and the 'imagination'.

'Philosophy', wrote Smith, 'is the science of the connecting principles of nature.'[53] To add to the terminological confusion, he went on to describe it as 'one of those arts which address themselves to the imagination'.[54] Philosophy, as art and as science, had an essential task to perform in the process which we would now call cognition. It must assist men in allaying that sense of chaos which accompanied experience and observation of the natural world:

Nature, after the largest experience that common observation can acquire, seems to abound with events which appear solitary and incoherent with all that go before them, which therefore disturb the easy movement of the imagination; which makes its ideas succeed each other, if one may say so, by irregular starts and sallies; . . . Philosophy, by representing the invisible chains which bind together all these disjointed objects, endeavours to introduce order into this chaos . . . to allay this tumult of the imagination, and to restore it, when it surveys the great revolutions of the universe, to that tone of tranquillity and composure, which is both most agreeable in itself, and most suitable to its nature.[55]

Here we see that 'emphasis on the constructive role of the imagination', which in Professor Raphael's view characterizes Smith's 'theory of scientific method', and which clearly, as Raphael observes, 'must . . . have come from an appreciation of Hume'.[56] Indeed, the passage just quoted at length could have come from Hume's very text. As Raphael and A. S. Skinner in another place point out,

Smith thinks that philosophy or science is an enlargement of commonsense belief as represented by Hume. . . . Hume himself says that systems of philosophy are also a product of the imagination, but his description of the processes of the imagination . . . comes into his account of our ordinary belief in an external world, and that is what Adam Smith uses in his account of scientific theory.[57]

Philosophy would replace 'tumult' with 'tranquillity' of the imagination by replacing the fear of 'chaos' with the sense, however illusory, of 'system':

Systems in many respects resemble machines. A machine is a little system, created to perform, as well as to connect together, in reality, those different movements and effects which the artist has occasion for. A system is an imaginary machine invented to connect together in the fancy those different movements and effects which are already in reality performed.[58]

No doubt the utility of systems and machines is very great. Still, Smith denies that the pursuit of such utility motivates philosophers:

Their imagination, which accompanies with ease and delight the regular progress of nature, is stopped and embarrassed by . . . seeming incoherences; they excite their wonder. . . . Wonder, therefore, and not any expectation of advantage from its discoveries, is the first principle which prompts mankind to the study of Philosophy, of that science which *pretends* to lay open the concealed connections that unite the various appearances of nature.[59]

The famous 'obvious and simple system of natural liberty', which in Smith's *Wealth of Nations* 'establishes itself of its own accord',[60] is thus a metaphor – a construct only in the imaginative sense. It is not something to be built in the external world, but something conjured up in the mind. Systems are never more than working hypotheses. Thomas Kuhn would surely approve of Smith's approach to philosophy of science.[61] As one interested scholar has remarked,

> The great significance of Smith's doctrine is that since it measures the value of philosophical systems solely in relation to their satisfaction of the human craving for order, it sets up a human rather than an absolute or natural standard for science, and it leaves all science essentially hypothetical. Furthermore, Smith implied that unceasing change rather than permanence must be the characteristic of philosophy.[62]

'Systems' of philosophy, *a fortiori* in science, must be understood as effective but frequently illusory hypotheses which endure and carry force because of their imaginative appeal to human sentiments and needs. Thus the appeal of utility, as Hume had argued, is essentially aesthetic.[63] It is the sense of utility which gives birth to a 'love of system, [a] regard to the beauty of order, of art and contrivance, [which] frequently serves to recommend those institutions which tend to promote the public welfare'.[64] And the fact that the poor in society admire and defer to, rather than loath and despoil, the rich is to be explained by the fact that Smith believes that the many apply a peculiar aesthetic principle in their evaluation of 'the palaces, the gardens, the equipage, the retinue of the great'.[65] When we observe 'the beauty of that accommodation which reigns in the palaces and oeconomy of the great' we are not appalled but 'charmed'. Why? Because,

> We naturally confound it in our imagination with the order, the regular and harmonious movement of the system, the machine or oeconomy by means of which it is produced. . . . And it is well that nature imposes upon us in this manner. It is this deception which rouses and keeps in continual motion the industry of mankind. It is this which first prompted them to cultivate the ground, to build houses, to found cities and commonwealths, and to invent and improve all the sciences and arts, which ennoble and embellish human life . . .[66]

Here the contrast noted earlier between the moral theories of Bentham on one hand and the philosophers of the Scottish

Enlightenment on the other finally bears practical fruit. Smith's 'principle' of 'utility', based on sentiments and resting in the context of his theory of philosophical hypotheses as appeals to the imagination, is a comforting delusion, an aesthetically pleasing fairy-tale about a fantastic social machine. Bentham scoffed at this subjective approach to 'politics, religion and morals', as we have seen. Such imaginings could only obstruct the path to a science of morals and legislation by inviting every man to 'cling to the notions most accordant to his prepossession' and 'turn a deaf ear' to any 'truth which might shackle [his] will while it enlightened [his] understanding'.[67] The moral discipline imposed by the rule of our 'two sovereign masters, PAIN and PLEASURE' was by comparison rigid and inescapable, but Bentham had no doubt that it was rooted in reality rather than fiction:

> They govern us in all we do, in all we say, in all we think: every effort we can make to throw off our subjection, will serve but to demonstrate and confirm it. In words a man may pretend to abjure their empire: but in reality he will remain subject to it all the while. The PRINCIPLE OF UTILITY recognizes this subjection . . . Systems which attempt to question it, deal in sounds instead of sense, in caprice instead of reason, in darkness instead of light.

And he added, in a dismissal which could epitomize his differences with Hume and Smith, 'enough of metaphor and declamation: it is not by such means that moral science is to be improved'.[68]

Bentham's constructivism

The modern reader is not alone in finding Jeremy Bentham's writings on the subject of metaphysics dry, tedious and voluminous: Bentham felt the same way about them. Yet he felt bound to persist with his metaphysical researches, and with good reason. He was quite consciously and deliberately attempting to construct a new philosophy of scientific inquiry, replacing scepticism with a kind of metaphysical positivism as its foundation. F. A. von Hayek has described the approach to social science that emerged from this transformation as 'constructivist' and has connected it with the rationalism of the French Enlightenment. Strangely, he has never to my knowledge identified Bentham as its leading English-speaking exponent. Hayek has, on the other hand, given famous accounts of Hume and Smith as forefathers of the mode of minimal state liberalism which is now in vogue. These highly influential analyses of Smith and Hume are entirely secularized in nature, lacking a theological dimension which, as the present discussion has shown, is essential to a proper understanding of the idea of a science of man and society in Hume or Smith. One wonders why Hayek pays no attention to the one eighteenth-century philosopher of social science whose perspective *is* entirely secularized: Bentham. For whereas distortion must be the result of secularized interpretations of theorists in whose thought divine causality or divine laws still play a role (even if that role is to leave a void when their epistemological status is undermined), no such distortion need result from such a reading of Bentham. 'Warts and all', he represents modernity methodologically to such a remarkable degree that it calls for a far fuller critical study of his works than has in the past been thought either possible or desirable. Full secularization of the concept of science, especially of social science or the social sciences, was a crucial step in the process by which moral and political theory came to assume their twentieth-century forms. Nothing less than the taking of that momentous step was involved in the metaphysical researches that generated the philosophical and linguistic underpinnings of Bentham's social science.

Notes

1　I should perhaps note that I cannot locate this statement in the 1847 edition of William Whewell's *Philosophy of the Inductive Sciences founded upon their History*, London, 1847, 'with corrections and additions'. The *Oxford English Dictionary* cites the 1840 edition, 'Introduction', p. 113.
2　Whewell, *Philosophy of the Inductive Sciences*, Introduction, pp. 2, 3.
3　See J. Bentham, *A Comment on the Commentaries and A Fragment on Government*, ed. J. H. Burns and H. L. A. Hart, London, Athlone Press, 1977, p. 393.
4　J. Bentham, *Deontology together with A Table of the Springs of Action and the Article on Utilitarianism*, ed. A. Goldworth, Oxford, Clarendon Press, 1983, pp. 33, 35.
5　ibid., pp. 46–7.
6　ibid., p. 45.
7　ibid., p. 47.
8　'Modern prophets' by 'Unus de Multis', *Fraser's Magazine*, vol. 16, September 1877, pp. 273–92.
9　ibid., pp. 273–4.
10　ibid., pp. 274, 275–6.
11　ibid., p. 283.
12　See D. Hume, *The Natural History of Religion, and Dialogues concerning Natural Religion, by David Hume*, ed. A. W. Colver and J. V. Price, Oxford, Clarendon Press, 1976, p. 9: 'The design of the . . . essay is the very same with all Lord Bolingbroke's, to establish NATURALISM, a species of atheism.'
13　Smith to Hume (August 1765), *The Correspondence of Adam Smith*, ed. E. C. Mossner and I. S. Ross, Oxford, Clarendon Press, 1977, p. 105.

14 See the *Oxford English Dictionary* entries for 'agnostic' and 'agnosticism'.

15 A. Smith, *The Theory of Moral Sentiments*, ed. A. L. Macfie and D. D. Raphael, Oxford, Oxford University Press, 1976, part III, ch. V, p. 163.

16 ibid., pp. 163–4.

17 See J. E. Crimmins, 'Bentham on religion: atheism and the secular society', *Journal of the History of Ideas*, 1986, vol. 67, no. 1, p. 105.

18 The term is borrowed quite deliberately from F. A. von Hayek, who surprisingly does not focus on Bentham as the perfect example of two of his favourite corruptions: 'scientism' and 'constructivism'. See F. A. von Hayek, *New Studies in Philosophy, Politics, Economics and the History of Ideas*, Chicago, University of Chicago Press, 1978, ch. 1, 'The errors of constructivism', pp. 3–22; and for 'scientism' see ch. 2, 'The pretence of knowledge', pp. 23–34, esp. p. 23.

19 For Bentham on the 'logic of the will' see J. Bentham, *An Introduction to the Principles of Morals and Legislation*, ed. J. H. Burns and H. L. A. Hart, London, Athlone Press, 1970, pp. 8–9.

20 R. H. Popkin, 'Divine causality: Newton, the Newtonians, and Hume', in P. J. Korshin and R. R. Allen (eds), *Greene Centennial Studies: Essays Presented to Donald Greene in the Centennial Year of the University of Southern California*, Charlottesville, University Press of Virginia, 1984, p. 41.

21 ibid., p. 40 (my emphasis).

22 ibid., p. 41.

23 ibid.

24 D. Hume, *A Treatise of Human Nature: Being An Attempt to Introduce the Experimental Method of Reasoning into Moral Subjects* (1888), 3 vols, ed. L. A. Selby-Bigge, Oxford, Clarendon Press, 1973, Introduction, pp. xv–xix.

25 J. Millar, *An Historical View of the English Government: From the Settlement of the Saxons in Britain to the Accession of the House of Stewart* (1787), 4 vols, London, 1803, vol. 2, pp. 429–30 note, cited by D. Stewart, 'Account of the life and writings of Adam Smith, LL.D.', ed. I. S. Ross, in *Adam Smith: Essays on Philosophical Subjects*, ed. W. P. D. Wightman and J. C. Bryce, Oxford, Clarendon Press, 1980, p. 275.

26 Bentham MSS, University College London, Box 157, fol. 32 (UC 157/32), quoted and discussed in D. G. Long, *Bentham on Liberty: Jeremy Bentham's Idea of Liberty in Relation to his Utilitarianism*, Toronto, University of Toronto Press, 1977, p. 164.

27 J. M. Keynes, 'Newton the man', in *Essays in Biography*, London, Macmillan, 1961, p. 311.

28 On the inappropriateness of proofs resting on notions of 'first causes' in attempts to demonstrate the validity of the principle of utility see J. S. Mill, *Utilitarianism*, in *Utilitarianism, On Liberty, and Considerations on Representative Government*, ed. H. B. Acton, London, Dent, 1972, ch. 1, 'General remarks', p. 4.

29 Bentham, *A Fragment on Government*, p. 439.

30 ibid., pp. 339, 440. But see also Bentham MSS, 'Prep.[aratory] Princ.[iples] Ins.[erenda]', UC 69/152, p. 298: 'Hume censurable not for having enter'd

into Metaphysics but for having lost his way.'

31 Bentham, *A Fragment on Government*, p. 440.
32 D. F. Norton, *David Hume: Common-sense Moralist, Sceptical Metaphysician*, Princeton, NJ, Princeton University Press, 1982.
33 See J. Bentham, *Of Laws in General*, ed. H. L. A. Hart, London, Athlone Press, 1970, p. 120.
34 See Bentham MSS, UC 69/52, headed 'Key. What things exist'.
35 Bentham MSS, UC 69/241, headed 'Preparatory Principles Inserenda'.
36 Bentham, *Introduction to the Principles of Morals and Legislation*, p. 11.
37 Bentham, *Deontology/Springs of Action*, p. 57.
38 ibid., pp. 55, 47.
39 ibid., p. 28.
40 ibid., p. 55.
41 Bentham, *Fragment on Government*, p. 441.
42 ibid., p. 440.
43 ibid.
44 D. Hume, *Essays Moral, Political, and Literary*, ed. E. F. Miller, Indianapolis, Liberty Classics, 1985, part II, essay XII, 'Of the Original Contract', p. 479.
45 See Hume to Smith (12 April 1759), *The Correspondence of Adam Smith*, p. 34.
46 C. A. Helvétius, *De L'Esprit, or Essays on the Mind and its Several Faculties*, Eng. trans. (1810), New York, Burt Franklin, 1970, essay II, ch. XV, p. 124.
47 See *The Works of Jeremy Bentham*, ed. J. Bowring, 11 vols, Edinburgh, 1838–43, vol. 10, pp. 26–7; and Helvétius, *De L'Esprit*, essay IV, ch. II, p. 373. The story of how, on reading Helvétius at the age of 21, Bentham declared that he had a genius for legislation, is also told in M. P. Mack, Jeremy Bentham: An Odyssey of Ideas, 1748–92, London, Heinemann, 1962, pp. 55–6.
48 Helvétius, *De L'Esprit*, essay IV, ch. I, 'Of genius', p. 365.
49 ibid., p. 370; and essay III, ch. XXX, p. 360.
50 Long, *Bentham on Liberty*, part II, 'Invention', pp. 65–119, esp. p. 70.
51 Helvétius, *De L'Esprit*, essay IV, ch. II, 'Of imagination and sentiment', p. 373.
52 Bentham MSS, UC 69/10; discussed in Long, *Bentham on Liberty*, p. 17.
53 A. Smith, 'History of astronomy', *Essays on Philosophical Subjects*, p. 45.
54 ibid., p. 46.
55 ibid., pp. 45–6.
56 D. D. Raphael, 'The impartial spectator', in *Essays on Adam Smith*, cited in A. S. Skinner, *A System of Social Science: Papers Relating to Adam Smith*, Oxford, Clarendon Press, 1979, p. 17.
57 Smith, *Essays on Philosophical Subjects*, General Introduction by D. D. Raphael and A. S. Skinner, p. 18.
58 Smith, 'History of astronomy', *Essays on Philosophical Subjects*, sect. IV, p. 66.
59 ibid., sect. III, pp. 50, 51 (my emphasis).
60 A. Smith, *An Inquiry into the Nature and Causes of the Wealth of Nations*,

2 vols, ed. R. H. Campbell, A. S. Skinner, and W. B. Todd, Oxford, Oxford University Press, 1976, vol. 2, bk. IV, ch. IX. p. 687.

61 See T. Kuhn, *The Structure of Scientific Revolutions*, Chicago, University of Chicago Press, 1970.

62 R. Olson, *Scottish Philosophy and British Physics, 1750–1880*, Princeton, NJ, Princeton University Press, 1975, p. 123, cited by Raphael and Skinner in Smith, *Essays on Philosophical Subjects*, General Introduction, p. 12.

63 See Smith, *Theory of Moral Sentiments*, part IV, ch. 1, 'Of the effect of utility upon the sentiments of approbation', ch. 1, pp. 179–87: 'Of the beauty which the appearance of UTILITY bestows upon all the productions of art, and of the extensive influence of this species of Beauty'; and Hume, *Treatise*, bk. II, part II, sect. V, 'Of our esteem for the rich and powerful', pp. 363–5.

64 Smith, *Theory of Moral Sentiments*, part IV, ch. 1, p. 185.

65 ibid., p. 182.

66 ibid., p. 183.

67 Bentham, *Deontology/Springs of Action*, p. 47.

68 Bentham, *Introduction to the Principles of Morals and Legislation*, p. 11.

Chapter five

Edmund Burke and John Wesley: the legacy of Locke

Frederick Dreyer

John Wesley and Edmund Burke are not often talked about in the same context: one man's career belongs to the church, the other's to the state. There is no evidence that the two ever met. However, their meeting is neither impossible nor unlikely. Each of them knew Dr Johnson and might be counted as a member of Johnson's circle. Johnson admired both. Of Burke, he said, 'Take up whatever topick you please, he is ready to meet you.' Of Wesley, 'John Wesley's conversation is good, but he is never at leisure. He is always obliged to go at a certain hour.' This, Johnson went on, 'is very disagreeable to a man who loves to fold his legs and have out his talk as I do'.[1] A second point of contact for Burke and Wesley was supplied by the politics of Bristol. The Methodist revival had taken its start in Bristol and the city remained a stronghold of Methodist influence. Burke was member of parliament for Bristol from 1774 to 1780. Wesley never hesitated to tell the Bristol Methodists how they should vote. On the question of the American revolution, Burke and Wesley chose different sides. Burke supported the revolution and Wesley opposed it. In the election of 1780, he almost certainly instructed the Methodists to vote against Burke. Burke blamed his defeat on Methodist opposition. 'Wesley', he complained, 'carried over that set men to the Court, and to all the slavish doctrines of Charles 2ds reign in their utmost extent'.[2]

However, our concern here is with what unites Burke and Wesley and not with what divides them. In the common conception of the eighteenth century, both men figure as conservatives. Both in a sense are regarded as enemies of the enlightenment. Against the rights of man, the text-book Burke asserts the authority of tradition; against the claims of reason, the text-book Wesley asserts the imperatives of faith. Burke's conservative credentials in this regard need no demonstration. His *Reflections* stands today as the classic argument against the French revolution. If some of Burke's admirers are right, it represents the classic argument against the New Deal as well. Wesley is often seen as a kind of mass-market Burke. For left-wing historians, it was his function to tame the English working-man and reconcile him to the hardships of the industrial revolution. Puritanism made men revolutionary democrats; Methodism made them submissive tories. According to E. P. Thompson, Wesley 'nearly destroyed' the 'democratic and anti-authoritarian' legacy which the Puritans had left to the English working-class. 'Between the people and their revolutionary heritage', Methodism inculcated 'a callow emotionalism'.³ Right-wing historians do not disagree. In a recent work, J. C. D. Clark cites Burke and Wesley to exemplify the conservative and authoritarian complexion of eighteenth-century thought. In Burke and Wesley he finds a profound rejection of the individualist values and assumptions that are found in the thought of John Locke. For Clark the central orthodoxy of the eighteenth century was prescribed by the Caroline divines. This orthodoxy was at bottom patriarchal and anti-individualist in its assumptions. If Locke's individualism found any audience in the age, it was only as a minority preference. Burke and Wesley both testify against the 'quick triumph of Lockeian empiricism and the swift demise of the divine right of kings'.⁴ As we shall see, however, it is in the thought of Burke and Wesley that the individualistic, indeed, the Lockeian character of eighteenth-century thought finds its most pronounced and decisive expression. The text-book reactionaries of common conception are in fact men whose basic thought rests upon principles that are ultimately Lockeian and liberal. Locke's influence is as crucial to the interpretation of Burke and Wesley as it is to the interpretation of Voltaire.

Lockeian epistemology

Locke's theory of knowledge constitutes his main contribution to the thought of the eighteenth century. In the *Essay concerning Human Understanding*, he argued that the proper realm of philosophical enquiry was not what truly exists but what the human mind can possibly know. In other words, philosophers had to concern themselves with psychology and not ontology. Things may be true independently of our powers of perception, but such things are not objects of human knowledge. 'It will be no excuse to an idle and untoward servant, who would not attend his business by candle light, to plead that he had not broad sunshine. The candle that is set up in us shines bright enough for all our purposes.' The human mind on Locke's account comes by its knowledge only by exercising the powers of sensation and reflection. Sensation informs us of things external to ourselves; reflection, about the operation of our own minds. Knowledge that cannot be attributed to either source is not knowledge fit for human understanding. 'All those sublime thoughts, which tower above the clouds and reach as high as heaven itself, take their rise and footing here.' The mind knows nothing that it cannot perceive. 'In all that great extent wherein the mind wanders, in those remote speculations it may seem to be elevated with, it stirs not one jot beyond those ideas which sense or reflection have offered for its contemplation.'[5] Much of the eighteenth-century enlightenment can be read as a sympathetic response to Locke's claim that knowledge is psychology. It is this that Voltaire asserts in *Candide* (1759) and *Micromégas* (1752). Ultimately, it is the central contention of Hume in the *Treatise of Human Nature*:

> 'Tis evident, that all the sciences have a relation, greater or less, to human nature; and that however wide any of them may seem to run from it, they still return back by one passage or another. Even mathematics, natural philosophy, and natural religion, are in some measure dependent on the science of man; since they lie under the cognizance of men, and are judged of by their powers and faculties.[6]

On this point, Burke and Wesley, no less than Voltaire and Hume, are indebted to Locke.

Burke's adherence to Locke's epistemology manifests itself first in his *Philosophical Enquiry into the Origin of our Ideas of the Sublime and Beautiful*. Here the commitment to empiricism is, in J. T. Boulton's estimation, 'uncompromising'.[7] Burke attempts to show that our standards of beauty are things which are prescribed not by the nature of existence but by the constitution of the human mind. Our knowledge of the sublime and the beautiful is ultimately psychological in character. Like Locke, he believed that our ideas were derived from experience. The senses are 'the great originals of all our ideas'. The imagination of man could never invent anything truly new. It could only 'vary the disposition' of those ideas that we learn from experience.[8] Nothing that man could experience possessed a metaphysical identity whose essence could be encompassed in the terms of a definition. 'I have no great opinion of a definition,' writes Burke:

> For when we define, we seem in danger of circumscribing nature within the bounds of our own notions. . . . A definition may be very exact, and yet go but a very little way towards informing us of the nature of the thing defined.[9]

With Locke, he denied that the mind could ever transcend the information it received from the senses. 'When we go but one step beyond the immediate sensible qualities of things, we go out of our depth. All we do after is but a faint struggle, that shows we are in an element which does not belong to us.'[10] What identifies man is his capacity to feel and not his capacity to reason. Burke subordinates reason to an auxiliary role in the operation of the human mind. 'Whenever the wisdom of our Creator intended that we should be affected with anything, he did not confide the execution of his design to the languid and precarious operation of our reason; but he endued it with powers and properties that prevent the understanding, and even the will; which seizing upon the senses and imagination, captivate the soul before the understanding is ready.'[11] In agreement with Locke, Burke conceives of man as a creature who is motivated not by reason but by feeling.

Wesley's commitment to empiricism was not something proclaimed in a formal treatise. It is, nevertheless, as explicit and as unmistakable as Burke's. Wesley had read Locke as an undergraduate and as a young fellow at Lincoln, he had used an abridgement of the *Essay* for teaching purposes. Later he often recommended Locke as suitable reading for Methodists. In the 1780s, extracts from the *Essay* were published in the *Arminian Magazine*.[12] Wesley's endorsement of Locke was not unqualified. He disapproved of Locke's criticism of formal logic. But this was a minor objection:

> From a careful consideration of the whole work, I conclude that, together with several mistakes (but none of them of any great importance,) it contains many excellent truths, proposed in a clear and strong manner, by a great master both of reasoning and language.[13]

In explaining how the mind acquired the knowledge it possessed, Wesley's agreement with Locke was complete. 'For many ages it has been allowed by sensible men, *Nihil est in intellectu quod non fuit prius in sensu.*'[14] He gave Locke full credit for refuting the argument for innate ideas:

> I think that point, 'that we have no innate principles', is abundantly proved, and cleared from all objections that have any shadow of strength. And it was highly needful to prove the point at large . . . as it was at the time an utter paradox both in the philosophical and religious world.[15]

Unlike John Norris and Thomas Reid, Wesley saw no objection to Locke's somewhat unclear and arbitrary assumption that the idea was the medium by which the mind received the information it possessed. For Wesley as for Locke, the idea remained the basic and indispensable postulate for the explanation of human thought.

> To talk of 'thinking without ideas' is stark nonsense. Whatever is presented to your mind is an idea; so that to be without ideas is not to think at all. Seeing, feeling, joy, grief, pleasure, pain are ideas. Therefore to be without ideas is to be without either sense or reason.[16]

No less than Burke, Wesley supposed that our knowledge of things was limited to their sensible properties. Without sensation there could be no knowledge.

> I endeavour . . . not to account for things, but only to describe them. I undertake barely to set down what appears in nature; not the cause of those appearances. . . . That things are so, we know with certainty; but why they are so, we know not. In many cases we cannot know; and the more we inquire, the more we are perplexed and entangled.[17]

This commitment to empiricism cannot be dismissed as some occasional profession of an academic formality. For both Burke and Wesley, empiricism is crucial to the exposition of any theory that we can legitimately attribute to them. Without Locke, it is impossible for us to understand what either man is trying to say. In Burke's case the commitment to empiricism is the central issue in his dispute with Richard Price over the American and French revolutions.

Price espoused a theory of knowledge that denied the primacy of the senses. This theory was argued at some length in his *Review of Morals*. Rational intuition, independent of all sense perception, could be a source of new ideas. 'Sense sees only the *outside* of things, reason acquaints itself with their natures.' He believed that the laws of physics could be discovered *a priori*. 'Such is the fecundity of reason, and so great is the injury done to it, by confining it within the narrow limits of sense, fancy, or experience.'[18] Had Price never dabbled in politics, Burke, no doubt, would have ignored his objectionable metaphysics. But Price did dabble, and he did it in support of Burke's enemy, Lord Shelburne. In the *Observations on Civil Liberty*, Price attacked Burke's friends for supporting the Declaratory Act. It was in this work that Price first defined civil liberty as the absence of restraint on the will of the citizen. 'To be free is to be guided by one's own will; and to be guided by the will of another is the characteristic of servitude.' In 1790, Price again attacked Burke's friends with the publication of his *Discourse on the Love of our Country*.[19] Here Price greeted the dawning in France of a new age of liberty. On both occasions Burke made a reply to Price. On both occasions he grounded his reply on empiricist suppositions. Political truths were no different from ordinary truths of human knowledge. They were valid or invalid not with reference to the necessities of existence but to the perceptible realities of human nature. 'There are people', Burke wrote in the *Sheriffs of Bristol*, 'who have split and anatomized the doctrine of free government as if it were an abstract question concerning metaphysical liberty and necessity, and not a matter of moral prudence and natural feeling. 'Liberty was not something to be discovered in the 'depth of abstruse science'; nor did it resemble 'propositions in geometry and metaphysics which admit of no medium, but must be true or false in all their latitude'.[20] The same argument was restated in the *Reflections*:

> I cannot stand forward, and give praise or blame to anything which relates to human actions and human concerns on a simple view of the object, as it stands stripped of every relation, in all the nakedness and solitude of metaphysical abstraction.[21]

The rights of man as Price had defined them were nothing more than speculative inventions. They existed merely by virtue of their definition. 'In proportion as they are metaphysically true, they are morally and politically false. The rights of man are in a sort of *middle*, incapable of definition, but not impossible to be discerned.'[22] If such rights were to be asserted as real things, then their reality had to be derived from the nature of man and not from the nature of being. 'The science of constructing a commonwealth, or renovating it . . . is, like every other experimental science, not to be taught *a priori*.' The rights that men could assert under government could only be claimed as derivations from human psychology. 'Government is a contrivance of human wisdom to provide for human wants. Men have a right that these wants should be provided for by this wisdom.'[23] Burke's *Reflections* represents one of the major celebrations of Lockeian epistemology in the literature of the eighteenth century. The relationship that exists between Burke and Price in the *Reflections* corresponds exactly with the relationship between Voltaire and Leibniz in *Candide*.

It is Locke's epistemology also that supplies Wesley with the suppositions that account for his theory of salvation. As a protestant, Wesley knew that man was saved by faith, 'not having my own righteousness, but that which is through faith of Christ, the righteousness which is of God by faith'. The doubt that troubled him was whether he could himself claim the possession of this faith. It was an issue for him of psychological status and not ontological truth. One might conceivably know the truth and still not claim the knowledge as belief. 'That I am not a Christian at this day I as assuredly know as that Jesus is the Christ.' Doubting his salvation, he appealed to the only evidence of truth that a Lockeian could admit, that is, the evidence of sensation. 'I feel this moment I do not love God; which therefore I *know* because I feel it. There is no word more proper, more clear, or more strong.'[24] Once converted, he appealed to the same evidence to prove his salvation. 'I felt my heart strangely warmed, I felt I did trust in Christ, Christ alone for salvation.'[25] Knowledge of salvation for Wesley was knowledge of something true about ourselves as individuals. This knowledge was to be obtained the same way all other knowledge was obtained, that is through the testimony of the senses.

> How does it appear to you, that you are alive, and that you are now in ease, and not in pain? Are you not immediately conscious of it? By the same immediate consciousness, you will know if your soul is alive to God. . . . By the same means you cannot but perceive if you love, rejoice, and delight in God.[26]

To account for our consciousness of belief, Wesley postulated our possession of a spiritual sense. Natural man in his regeneration acquired this sense through the intervention of the Holy Ghost. The spiritual sense was not unlike the ordinary senses. What the believer actually felt in its operation was indescribable to the non-believer who lacked it. To explain belief to the infidel was like explaining sight to the blind or sound to the deaf. 'He who hath that witness in himself, cannot explain it to one who hath it not; nor indeed is it to be expected that he should.'[27] Locke, of course, had never written about any spiritual sense. Yet its supposition on Wesley's part serves to confirm his commitment to Locke's epistemology. What the mind knows can only be accounted for on the supposition of an appropriate sense. In this respect, Wesley's spiritual sense corresponds to Francis Hutcheson's moral sense. Both are contrivances devised by men who are determined to understand the world in the way that Locke had taught them to see it.

Lockeian contractarianism

The second contribution that Locke made to the thought of the eighteenth century was in the realm of political theory. Here Locke made two critical suppositions. The first was that man is ultimately governed by the law of nature. This law remains in force even after man has left the state of nature and become a member of civil society. No law that is merely political and positive can be understood to annul any natural law. 'The municipal laws of countries' are 'only so far right as they are founded on the law of nature, by which they are to be regulated and interpreted.' The second supposition was that political authority can only be derived from contract. Without consent no man is deemed subordinate to the authority of another. 'Men being . . . by nature all free, equal, and independent, no one can be put out of this estate and subjected to the political power of another without his own consent.'[28] The debt that Burke and Wesley owe to Locke in this respect is less explicit than their debt to Locke's epistemology. There is no political equivalent of the *Sublime and Beautiful* where Burke formally avows an academic discipleship to Locke on matters of natural right and contract. Nor did Wesley ever republish extracts from the *Letter on Toleration* or the *Treatise of Government* for the edification of Methodist readers. What is at issue here is more a matter of silent agreement than open endorsement. Nevertheless, the extent of that agreement is substantial. Both subscribe to a doctrine of natural rights and a doctrine of contract. In the fundamentals of their respective theories both are Lockeians.

Wesley's commitment to contract theory lapsed in the debate over the American revolution. In his zeal to condemn rebellion, Wesley repudiated contract without reservation. The supposition of contract as the basis of public authority was 'utterly indefensible' even 'though Mr Locke himself should attempt to defend it'.[29] If government was to be regarded as a trust, it was not a trust instituted by the people. '"There is no power but of God." It is a delegation, namely, from God; for "rulers are God's ministers", or delegates.'[30] Here, Wesley had borrowed his political theory from St Paul, Rom. 13:1-7. But in denying contract, Wesley did not deny the theoretical premise that prescribed contract as a necessary assumption to account for the existence of political authority. The premise is that men in nature possess a right to liberty. He admitted that the Americans as 'naked sons of nature' might claim life, liberty and property. These rights he did not deny. What he objected to was the failure of the Americans to distinguish clearly between claims of natural liberty and claims of civil privilege. With respect to the same things, Americans could not claim both the rights of man and the rights of citizenship.[31] How Wesley could consistently admit natural-right premises and reject social-contract conclusions, is not at all clear. Yet it is obvious that he asserted natural liberty in its broadest terms and had no desire to minimize its relevance to civil life. Wesley was no Hobbist. His entire case against negro slavery rested on the supposition of natural liberty which all men possessed by virtue of their humanity. 'Liberty is the right of every human creature, as soon as he breathes the vital air; and no human law can deprive him of that right which he derives from the law of nature.'[32] If Wesley is a Tory in his denial of contract, in his assertion of natural liberty he is a Whig.

To find the positive assertion of contract theory in Wesley's thought, we must look not at his conception of the state but of the church. Methodists never claimed for themselves any ecclesiastical status. Wesley discouraged the use of any terms that might imply such a claim.

Methodists were not to call their association a church, nor were they to call their preachers ministers. In Scotland he warned Methodists against doing anything in imitation of the Presbyterians. To an unfortunate preacher in Glasgow who had presumed to convene a Methodist *session*, Wesley sent an immediate prohibition: 'I require *you* . . . immediately to disband that session (so called). . . . Discharge them from meeting any more. And if they will leave the society, let them leave it. . . . You ought to have kept to the Methodist plan from the first.'[33] When Francis Asbury in America began to call himself a bishop, Wesley's reaction was identical:

> How can you, how dare you suffer yourself to be called a Bishop? I shudder, I start at the very thought! Men may call me a knave or a fool . . . and I am content; but they never shall by my consent call me a Bishop! For my sake, for God's sake, for Christ's sake put a full end to this![34]

In Wesley's mind the Methodists figured not as a church but as a society. It was as a society that he preferred to speak of them. This was done with evident deliberation. Describing their origins, he wrote, 'Thus arose . . . what was afterwards called a *Society*; a very innocent name, and very common in London, for any number of people associating themselves together.'[35] As a society the Methodists received their collective authority from the consent of its members. In his leadership of the society, Wesley acted by virtue of his temporal appointment and not by virtue of some spiritual office. He acted as 'one whom that Society had voluntarily chosen to be at the head of them'.[36] When delinquent Methodists were to be censured or expelled, Wesley invoked no supernatural right:

> I took upon me no other authority . . . than any steward of a Society exerts by the consent of the other members. I did neither more nor less than declare that they who had broken our rules were no longer of our Society.[37]

Whenever his authority within the movement was disputed, it was to the terms of the original contract that he made his appeal. Methodism had started when individual penitents had placed themselves under his direction. 'Here commenced my power; namely a power to appoint when, and where, and how they should meet; and to remove those whose lives showed that they had not a desire "to flee from the wrath to come".' Wesley claimed no status in the Methodist society that could not be accounted for on the assumption of contract. 'All I affirm is . . . the people who choose to be under my care, choose to be so on the same terms they were at first.'[38] In the end, Wesley acknowledged no church, whether ancient or modern, that could claim authority independently of the believer's consent. If submission to supernatural authority were the issue, Wesley asserted, 'I could be a member of no church under heaven.' He insisted on the right of private judgement. 'I dare call no man Rabbi. I cannot yield either implicit faith or obedience to any man or number of men.'[39] Against the authority of the church, Wesley opposed an uncompromising claim to natural liberty:

> Every man living, as a man has a right to this, as he is a rational creature. The Creator gave him this right when he endowed him with understanding. And every man must judge for himself, because every man must give an account of himself to God. Consequently this is an indefeasible right; it is inseparable from humanity. And God did never give authority to any man, or number of men, to deprive any child of man thereof, under any colour or pretence whatever.[40]

The relationship between the believer and the priest depended on contract alone. 'I cannot guide any soul unless he consent to be guided by me. Neither can any soul force me to guide him, if I consent not.'[41] In their respective assumption of contract, there is no difference between Wesley's theory of the church and Tom Paine's theory of the state.

Burke did not state a contract theory of the church that matched Wesley's in explicitness. Yet it is clear that Burke did not think of the church as a spiritual institution authorized by God. Burke's church is always an artificial contrivance that is made by man. Scholars who sometimes interpret Burke as a late Laudian or an early tractarian are profoundly mistaken. Whenever he undertakes to defend the Church of England, he describes it as a temporal association and asserts for it the same rights that can be claimed for any other temporal association. In the debate on the Feathers-Tavern petition, he spoke for the right of the church to insist upon clerical subscription to the Thirty-Nine Articles. Nowhere in the debate did he attribute spiritual authority to the church. The right to insist upon subscription was a right it enjoyed simply as an artificial association. If the church was to be regarded as a corporation, then, like any other corporation, it might devise its own regulations. 'The Church, like every body corporate, may alter her laws without changing her identity.'[42] If the church was merely a voluntary society, then like any club it might prescribe the terms of membership for those who sought admission.

It is essential to this voluntary society to exclude from her voluntary society any member she thinks fit, or to oppose the entrance of any upon such conditions as she thinks proper. For, otherwise, it would be a voluntary society acting contrary to her will, which is a contradiction in terms.[43]

When Burke came to defend the Catholic Church in France against the depredations of the National Assembly, he did not change his conception of what it is that constitutes a church. In France as in England, the church was defended as an artificial body. The crimes he denounced were not offences committed against a supernatural jurisdiction but offences against property rights, ultimately property rights possessed by individuals. 'Who but a tyrant . . . could think of seizing on the property of men, unaccused, unheard, untried, by whole descriptions, by hundreds and thousands together.' The status of the victims as clergymen did nothing in Burke's eyes to aggravate the offence. They suffered injustice in their natural capacity. 'Of what import is it, under what names you injure men.' In the context of the French revolution, clergymen and laymen were indistinguishable for Burke. 'It is in the principle of injustice that the danger lies, and not in the description of persons on whom it is first exercised.'[44]

Edmund Burke was an eighteenth-century thinker. As a thinker, it was his misfortune to find his first disciples among late nineteenth-century historicists like John Morley and Leslie Stephen. Both admired Burke primarily as an early champion of their own historicism. Leslie Stephen's Burke condemned the French revolution because it offended against the requirements of the historical process. 'To him', wrote Stephen, 'a nation was a living organism of infinitely complex structure, of intimate dependence upon the parts, and to be treated by politicians with a careful observation of the laws of its healthy development.'[45] For the historicist Burke, the objection to the French revolution was a question of method. Indifferent to history, the revolutionaries attempted to do the wrong thing, in the wrong way, at the wrong time. In fact, however, the issue he addressed was that of jurisdiction and not method. At bottom his attack on the revolution rested on legitimist assumptions. What was wrong with the revolution was that the revolutionaries lacked a valid title to authority. They were usurpers and whatever they did and however they did it, their government was illegitimate. Burke's complaint over jurisdiction was clearly stated in the *Reflections* in his attack on the National Assembly:

I can never consider this assembly as anything else than a voluntary association of men who have availed themselves of circumstances to seize upon the power of the state. They have not the sanction and authority of the character under which they first met. They have assumed another of a very different nature, and have completely altered and inverted all the relations in which they originally stood. They do not hold the authority they exercise under any constitutional law of the state.[46]

Short of abandoning the revolution and restoring the government of the three estates, there was nothing the revolutionaries could conscientiously do to justify themselves. 'If they mean honestly', Burke asked, 'why do they not strengthen the arms of honest men to support their ancient, legal, wise and free government, given to them in the spring of 1788?'[47] Burke never made the slightest distinction between the successive regimes that were thrown up in the course of the revolution. The National Assembly, the Convention, the Directory: all were the same. All were condemned in identical terms. Whether a regime was more or less radical, more or less violent or bloodthirsty, made little difference. All were equally illegitimate. Each was objectionable as a usurpation. When the Terror ended and the Directory came to power, we do not find Burke rejoicing as a practical man over the termination of a practical evil. On the contrary! The Directory differed 'nothing from all the preceding usurpations'. Like the other regimes, it exercised power without title. 'The whole of their government, in its origination, in its continuance, in all its actions, and in all its resources, is force and nothing but force.'[48]

Burke's case against the legitimacy of all revolutionary regimes presupposed a contract theory of the state. The state like the church was an artificial institution. 'The idea of a people is the idea of a corporation. It is wholly artificial, and made, like all other legal institutions, by common agreement.'[49] Members of an existing corporation could not repudiate their constitution and still retain their old corporate identity. If the people of France wished to act in their corporate capacity as the people of France, they were bound in logic to act under the forms prescribed in their corporate constitution. To act under a different constitution was not to act as the people of France. What gave the existing, the legitimate, constitution its validity was the consent of the people it governed. If that consent were withdrawn and the constitution effectively repudiated, what resulted was not a new incorporation acting under a new constitution but rather an accidental collection of disconnected individuals. For Burke, there was no way that the presumed consent that had authorized the old constitution could be transferred to authorize a new constitution.

When men, therefore, break up the original compact or agreement which gives its corporate form and capacity to a state, they are no longer a people, – they have no longer a corporate existence, – they have no longer a legal coactive force to bind within, nor a claim to be recognized abroad. They are a number of vague, loose individuals, and nothing more.[50]

The National Assembly and its successors were usurpations because their government lacked a valid basis in consent. In spite of the revolution, the old corporation endured. Its legal representatives were to be found in the emigration:

If we look for the *corporate people* of France, existing as corporate in the eye and intention of public law . . . they are in Flanders, and Germany, in Switzerland, Spain, Italy, and England. There are all the princes of the blood, there are all the orders of the state, there are all the parliaments of the kingdom.[51]

In the controversy over what Burke really meant, it is often assumed that contract theory implies a commitment to democracy. It does not. We need only think of Hobbes to find a contractualist who is not a democrat. Whether a supposition of contract entails a supposition of democracy, depends entirely on what we imagine the initial terms of the contract to be. Burke supposed that the social compact in France and England committed the citizen to constitutions that were not democratic. In defending the validity of these undemocratic constitutions, Burke is not rejecting the assumption of contract. Indeed, he is asserting it and opposing the sanctity of contract against the danger of political innovation. Contracts, after all, are not only relationships that parties may assent to, but on the supposition of assent are relationships that may be enforced. 'The constitution of a country being once settled upon some compact, tacit or expressed, there is no power existing of force to alter it, without breach of the covenant, or the consent of all the parties.' The parties are bound by the terms of their agreement. 'Such is the nature of contract.'[52]

Wesley and Burke as Lockeian theorists

In the study of Burke and Wesley, conventional wisdom often denies the capacity of either man for systematic thought. Both are represented as doers rather than as thinkers. The affirmation of Wesley's intellectual incoherence has become almost an article of faith in American Methodist circles. In the celebrated Wesleyan quadrilateral, Wesley is supposed to acknowledge four different sources of truth: reason, Scripture, experience, and tradition. 'The four', it is asserted in a popular teaching manual, 'are interdependent and no one can be subsumed by another.' As a matter of fact, Wesley never spoke of a quadrilateral; nor did he ever argue that reason, tradition, Scripture and experience were joint authorities for the believer to consult. The quadrilateral has nothing to do with the historical Wesley. Yet the attribution of the quadrilateral to Wesley nicely illustrates his rather low reputation as a systematic thinker. A man who proclaims the quadrilateral may say anything and everything. He has emancipated himself from the restraints of logic. Albert Outler (possibly, the real author of the quadrilateral) regards Wesley as a figure who is 'by talent and intent, a *folk* theologian'. Outler's Wesley is 'an eclectic who . . . mastered the secret of plastic synthesis, simple profundity, the common touch'.[53] What Outler celebrates as a merit in Wesley's thought, others, understandably, have condemned as a fault. In *The Making of the English Working Class*, E. P. Thompson describes Methodist theology as 'opportunist, anti-intellectual, and otiose'.[54] For Thompson, Methodism represents not a system of thought but an expression of social tension and sexual repression in the mass-psychology of eighteenth-century England. In his reputation as a theorist, Burke has fared little better than Wesley. In a recent essay Harvey Mansfield has identified Burke as a thinker who denies the validity of all theory. 'It is theory as such that he rejects. . . . Sound theory, to him, would seem to be self-denying theory.' In Isaac Kramnick's *Rage of Edmund Burke*, Burke is studied not in terms of any theory that he may have enunciated but in terms of the social and sexual ambivalences which underlie his conscious thought. Kramnick's Burke is half homosexual and half heterosexual, half middle-class and half upper-class. This is the reality that governs Burke's thought and not any theory he happened to subscribe to. 'Deep and persistent tensions arising from the issues of ideological and sexual identity conflict . . . helped shape the content of his social and political ideals.'[55] Possibly the fiercest attack on Burke's status as a thinker has come from political historians, particularly those political historians who are disciples of the late Sir Lewis Namier. For the Namierites, it is the interest and not the argument that is the main consideration in the study of any political text. John Brooke dismisses the *Reflections* as Burke's 'apologia for his devotion to Rockingham'. In the crusade against the French revolution, Burke on Brooke's account, 'spent the last years of his life fighting to make the world safer for future Rockinghams to rule'.[56] Namierite orthodoxy on Burke has received its most absolute statement in Frank O'Gorman's *Edmund Burke: His Political Philosophy*. Here we are reminded that Burke was 'not inclined to abstract, rational philosophy'. Those who read Burke and seek a system are said to 'seek in vain'. No one should undertake to look for 'key notions' or 'fundamental concepts' in the text of his writings. On O'Gorman's instruction the reader should abandon all efforts to find consistency of thought. All one can do is emphasize 'the *absence* of system in Burke's political ideas and underline his characteristic lapses into inconsistency'.[57] One of the pieties of Namierism is that nobody thinks very much in politics and Edmund Burke thinks less than most.

Neither Burke nor Wesley, to be sure, ever claimed any status as a theorist. Burke did not write a political treatise; nor Wesley a systematic theology. What they tended to write in the main were occasional pieces which addressed some particular controversy or other. This was always true of Burke and largely true of Wesley. Both also affected an indifference to formal statements of theory. 'I do not pretend', wrote Burke, 'to be an antiquary, a lawyer, or qualified for the chair of professor of metaphysics.' He never defended the interests of his constituents on 'speculative grounds'. He refused to justify the *Reflections* as an expression of his philosophy of government. 'I was throwing out reflexions upon a political event, and not reading a lecture upon theorisms and principles of Government. How I should treat such a subject is not for me to say, for I never had that intention.'[58] Theory was repudiated by Wesley in equally decisive terms. 'I design plain truth for plain people: . . . of set purpose, I abstain from all nice and philosophical speculations; from all perplexed and intricate reasonings; and as far as possible from even the show of learning.'[59] He refused to define Methodism in terms of its doctrine. He thought of religion not as a matter of assenting to some kind of truth but of feeling the right sort of way. 'We do not lay the main stress of our religion on any opinions, right or wrong. . . . The weight of all religion, we apprehend, rests on holiness of heart and life.'[60] If Burke and Wesley were not formal philosophers, they were, nevertheless, controversialists and debaters. Everything they wrote can be read as an argument that is intended to have us believe something or assent to something. Burke wants us to vote with Lord Rockingham and Wesley to have us submit to the inspiration of the Holy Ghost. Without subscribing to formal theory one may do many things, but to state an argument without reference to theory is a logical impossibility. All arguments claim validity with reference to some standard. The standard may be implicit or explicit, but in the end it supplies the context in which the argument is stated. If we do not know the theory, we cannot understand the argument. To study Burke and Wesley without reference to their theory, is to ignore their identity as advocates and controversialists. To say that a controversialist assumes a theory that is crucial to our analysis of him as a controversialist does not mean that his assumption of theory is necessarily consistent. Some people argue consistently and some do not.

But no argument can be understood if it is analysed merely with reference to its non-theoretical historical circumstances. This is to make a mush-minded equation between arguments and interests. The identification of the interest that prompts a man to state an argument does not identify the argument that he states. Saying that a motive describes an argument is as absurd as saying that an argument describes a motive.

The importance of theory in the thought of Wesley and Burke is often denied because we confuse questions that are essentially different. If we ask whether Burke and Wesley intended to formulate theory, then the answer is probably no. They did not write treatises and disclaimed all intention of doing so. If the question is whether they were inspired by the theories that they assumed in debate, then the answer is: we cannot tell. Burke may not have believed all the things he professed; Wesley may not have understood everything he believed. There are no infallible tests for sincerity. But if the question is what theory did they assert or assume in debate, then the importance of Locke is undeniable. Theory exists not by virtue of the fact that it is believed or that it serves to inspire. It exists because it is assumed in argument. In this sense, Burke and Wesley are indebted to Locke. Both subscribe to Locke's theory of knowledge: truth is what the individual knows through the report of his senses. Both subscribe to Locke's theory of authority: associations are instituted by the consent of their members. These commitments constitute the basis of Locke's individualism. The same commitments identify Burke and Wesley as individualists. Moreover, it is the inheritance from Locke that supplies the distinctive elements in the thought of Burke and Wesley. Burke's conservatism rests on contractualist foundations. Once promises are made they must be kept. On the other hand, the freedom of individuals to create associations allows Wesley to form Methodist societies and carry on his evangelical campaign in England. Assuming Locke's theory of knowledge, Burke can dismiss reason as an authority in political matters. On the same assumption, Wesley can urge the Christian to seek the evidence of his conversion in the experience of his heart. Without Locke, Burke and Wesley would have been profoundly different in the theories they assert. This is not to say that Locke's doctrine functions as some kind of motive in their minds that caused them to say what they said and do what they did. Without Locke, Burke might still have become a conservative and Wesley an evangelical, but not the same kind of conservative or the same kind of evangelical. It is Locke's influence that explains how they argued and what they understood by the arguments they stated. In short, Locke explains what they meant.

Notes

1 J. Boswell, *Boswell's Life of Johnson*, 2 vols, London, Everyman's Library, 1960, vol. 2, pp. 167–8, 329.
2 E. Burke, *The Correspondence of Edmund Burke*, 10 vols, ed. T. W. Copeland, Cambridge, Cambridge University Press, 1958–78, vol. 4, p. 271.
3 E. P. Thompson, *The Making of the English Working Class*, New York, Random House, 1966, p. 54.
4 J. C. D. Clark, *English Society, 1688–1832: Ideology, Social Structure and Political Practice During the Ancien Régime*, Cambridge, Cambridge University Press, 1985, pp. 44, 57–8, 81, 152, 227, 237, 258, 279.
5 J. Locke, *An Essay Concerning Human Understanding*, 2 vols, London, Everyman's Library, 1961, vol. 1, pp. 7, 89.
6 D. Hume, *Treatise of Human Nature*, London, Pelican Classics, 1969, p. 42.
7 E. Burke, *A Philosophical Enquiry into the Origin of our Ideas of the Sublime and Beautiful*, ed. J. T. Boulton, London, Routledge and Kegan Paul, 1958, Introduction, p. xxxvi.
8 E. Burke, *The Writings and Speeches of Edmund Burke*, 12 vols, Boston, Little, Brown and Co., 1901, vol. 1, pp. 87, 95.
9 ibid., pp. 80–1.
10 ibid., p. 209.
11 ibid., p. 184.
12 V. H. H. Green, *The Young Mr Wesley: A Study of John Wesley and Oxford*, London, Edward Arnold, 1961, pp. 191, 315; J. Wesley, *The Letters of the Rev. John Wesley, A.M.*, 8 vols, ed. J. Telford, London, The Epworth Press, 1931, vol. 4, p. 249, vol. 7, pp. 82, 228; and J. Wesley (ed.), *Arminian Magazine for the Year 1782*, London, vol. 5, pp. 27–648; *1783*, vol. 6, pp. 30–652; and 1784, vol. 7, pp. 32–302.
13 J. Wesley, *The Works of John Wesley*, 14 vols, ed. T. Jackson, Grand Rapids, Mich., Baker Book House, 1979, vol. 13, pp. 460–4.
14 ibid., vol. 7, p. 231.
15 ibid., vol. 13, p. 455.
16 Wesley, *Letters*, vol. 6, p. 229.
17 Wesley, *Works*, vol. 14, p. 301.
18 R. Price, *A Review of the Principal Questions in Morals*, ed. D. D. Raphael, Oxford, Clarendon Press, 1974, pp. 20, 35.
19 R. Price, *Two Tracts on Civil Liberty* (1778), New York, Da Capo Press, 1972, p. 11, and *A Discourse on the Love of our Country*, London, 1790, p. 30.
20 Burke, *Writings and Speeches*, vol. 2, pp. 228–9.
21 ibid., vol. 3, p. 240.
22 ibid., p. 313.
23 ibid., pp. 310–11.
24 J. Wesley, *The Journal of the Rev. John Wesley*, 8 vols, ed. N. Curnock, London, Robert Culley, 1909–16, vol. 1, p. 424; vol. 2, pp. 125–6.
25 Wesley, *Journal*, vol. 1, p. 476.
26 Wesley, *Works*, vol. 5, p. 114.
27 ibid., pp. 120–2.

28 J. Locke, *The Second Treatise of Government*, New York, The Library of the Liberal Arts, 1952, pp. 9, 54.
29 Wesley, *Works*, vol. 11, p. 104.
30 ibid., p. 105.
31 ibid., p. 83.
32 ibid., p. 79.
33 Wesley, *Works*, vol. 8, p. 321, and *Letters*, vol. 8, p. 136.
34 Wesley, *Letters*, vol. 8, p. 91.
35 ibid., vol. 2, p. 294.
36 ibid., p. 239.
37 ibid.
38 Wesley, *Works*, vol. 8, pp. 311, 313.
39 Wesley, *Journal*, vol. 3, p. 243.
40 Wesley, *Works*, vol. 11, pp. 37–8.
41 J. Wesley, *Minutes of the Methodist Conferences, From the First Held in London by the Late Rev. John Wesley A.M., in the Year 1744*, London, 1862, pp. 27–8.
42 Burke, *Writings and Speeches*, vol. 7, p. 7.
43 ibid., p. 17.
44 ibid., vol. 3, pp. 371, 372, 432.
45 L. Stephen, *History of English Thought in the Eighteenth Century* (1902), 2 vols, London, Rupert Hart-Davis, 1962, vol. 2, p. 211.
46 Burke, *Writings and Speeches*, vol. 3, p. 450.
47 ibid., vol. 4, pp. 53–4.
48 ibid., vol. 6, p. 70.
49 ibid., vol. 4, p. 169; see also W. D. Love, 'Edmund Burke's idea of the body corporate: a study in imagery', *Review of Politics*, 1965, vol. 27, pp. 184–97, and 'Meaning in the history of conflicting interpretations of Burke', *Burke Newsletter*, 1965–6, vol. 7, pp. 526–38.
50 Burke, *Writings and Speeches*, vol. 4, p. 170.
51 ibid., p. 421.
52 ibid., p. 162.
53 L. H. Weems, *The Gospel According to Wesley: A Summary of John Wesley's Message*, Nashville, Discipleship Resources, 1982, p. 5; and J. Wesley, *A Library of Protestant Thought*, ed. A. Outler, New York, Oxford University Press, 1964, p. 119.
54 Thompson, *The Making of the English Working Class*, p. 39.
55 E. Burke, *Selected Letters of Edmund Burke*, ed. H. C. Mansfield, Chicago, The University of Chicago Press, 1984, p. 4; and I. Kramnick, *The Rage of Edmund Burke: Portrait of an Ambivalent Conservative*, New York, Basic Books, 1977, pp. 10–11.
56 Sir L. Namier and J. Brooke (eds), *The House of Commons 1754–1790*, The History of Parliament, London, Her Majesty's Stationery Office, 1964, vol. 2, p. 153.
57 F. O'Gorman, *Edmund Burke: His Political Philosophy*, Political Thinkers, London, Allen and Unwin, 1973, pp. 12–14.

58 Burke, *Writings and Speeches*, vol. 2, p. 222, and *Correspondence*, vol. 6, p. 304.
59 Wesley, *Works*, vol. 5, pp. 2, 3, 7.
60 ibid., vol. 8, p. 243.

Chapter six

Religion, utility and politics: Bentham versus Paley

James E. Crimmins

It is commonly assumed that 'radicalism' and the doctrine of utility are natural allies in the British political tradition, a view largely due to the fact that Jeremy Bentham (1748-1832), the ideologue-in-chief of post-French Revolution British radicalism, is also revered as the founding father of British utilitarianism.[1] But the progress of utility as the cornerstone of a new secular philosophy in the eighteenth and early part of the nineteenth centuries was neither inexorable nor comprehensive in its reach. Indeed, it is still little appreciated that, for the most part, it was the religious version of the doctrine of utility which dominated English moral thought in the age before Bentham. Exponents of this theological variant, influenced by Locke's ethics with its deference to revelation, included George Berkeley, John Gay, John Brown, Abraham Tucker, and Edmund Law, among others. Even into the early decades of the nineteenth century it was the Cambridge Divine William Paley (1743-1805) who was most often toasted as the standard-bearer of the general doctrine, not Bentham. I have discussed elsewhere the Anglican advocates of an ethics based on utility in eighteenth-century England.[2] It is my purpose here to take the analysis a step further: to contrast the religious and the secular versions of the doctrine of utility set forth by their most well-known proponents, Paley and Bentham, by demonstrating the implicit relationship that exists between the theological and metaphysical presuppositions upon which their respective systems were constructed and the political positions they embraced. For both men remained to the end creatures of their intellectual formation. Even so, what emerges is a paradox. If there appears to be a distinct correlation between Paley's theological orthodoxy and political conservatism, and between Bentham's atheistic, materialist philosophy and political radicalism, out of the juxtaposition of their respective brands of the doctrine of utility surfaces a more profound contrast which muddies the picture emphatically. It becomes apparent that while Paley's Christian ethics depended absolutely on individual autonomy, Bentham developed a secular legislative science which sought to circumscribe that autonomy and to give 'enlightened' *direction* to the activities of individuals. The issue, in other words, takes on a subtle twist: the 'paternalist' Bentham versus the 'liberal' Paley – a very different contrast from the one to which the body of this essay is devoted. Before proceeding, however, I might be forgiven a few general observations on the nature of the relationship between the thought of Paley and Bentham and how this came to be perceived later on. They were, after all, near contemporaries, who in some respects vied with each other for the ear of the public, and this rivalry adds piquancy to the comparison I wish to present.

Competing exponents of utility

A few years before Bentham published his now famous *Introduction to the Principles of Morals and Legislation* (1789) Paley had published his *Principles of Moral and Political Philosophy* (1785), for John Maynard Keynes 'an immortal book'.[3] Bentham's work had in fact been completed and printed in 1780 and when Paley's *Principles* appeared Bentham's friends, fearing that he would not receive the accolades they believed to be his due, urged that he quickly circulate his own rendering of the doctrine of utility.[4] In response, Bentham initially affected indifference to Paley's success and held back the *Introduction* for another three years.[5] Nevertheless, thus introduced to Paley's work so early in his career, he subsequently had several occasions to refer to the thought of his religious counterpart, at times to enlist him as an ally in the cause of utility but most often to attack aspects of his philosophy that on Bentham's account of the doctrine should be swept away. Paley was thus an ally, because in a hostile world Bentham perpetually felt himself in need of supporters (of whatever stripe) when arguing for the virtues of utility as the criterion of action and social policy; and an enemy, because he was 'a false brother', an apologist for the *status quo*, a founder member (along with William Blackstone) of the 'everything-as-it-should-be-school'.[6]

Bentham's criticisms greatly outweigh the praise he has for Paley and fairly reflect the basic differences between their systems. For example, Paley is consistently lauded as a fellow advocate of utility in *Supply Without Burthen* (1795), in the marginals for *A Table of the Springs of Action* (1817), and again in a letter to Etienne Dumont (6 September 1822)[7] On the other hand, he is criticized by Bentham for his non-utilitarian defence of the death penalty in a collection of manuscripts of 1809,[8] for his favourable remarks on juries in a further collection of manuscripts c.1791 and again in 1809, for his vindication of England's episcopal hierarchy in manuscripts on the 'Church' in 1812, and for his equivocal position on subscriptions to articles of faith in *Church-of-Englandism and its Catechism Examined* (1818).[9] In *An Analysis of the Influence of Natural Religion on the Temporal Happiness of Mankind* (1822), Bentham confronts Paley's argument from design, and in his polemical piece entitled *Not Paul, but Jesus* (1823) Paley's eulogistic version of the life and miracles of St Paul is subjected to an intemperate examination.[10]

Despite these differences, however, in the literature on utilitarianism, Paley is commonly cited as a precursor of Bentham, albeit one whose thinking barely approached the rigour and precision of the latter's calculative and scientific doctrine.[11] Bentham himself occasionally thought of 'parson Paley' in these terms: as a moralist who had fathomed the fundamental motivating factors of human nature but had failed to associate pleasures and pains correctly with the quest for general happiness, and who had confused the analysis of human action by positing a religious dimension which, by the strict standards of utility, could not be justified.[12] Nevertheless, the tendency to see the doctrine of utility as all of a piece, with a general progress within the tradition from crude or primitive Christian versions to Bentham's final, secularized mature doctrine, is misleading.

One more point needs to be aired before moving on. Bentham's utilitarianism is often acknowledged to be in some sense 'secular', but what is meant by this it is rarely thought necessary to explain. It goes without saying that in the course of the eighteenth century ethical and social thought had undergone a large measure of secularization. But the term, as Jacob Viner and others have noted, is liable to deceive. In Viner's view it represents 'a lessening of the influence . . . of ecclesiastical authority and traditional church creeds, and a shifting of weight from dogma and revelation and other-worldliness to reason and sentiment and considerations of temporal welfare'.[13] From this perspective the issue of secularization is one of degree: how far were ethical and social thinkers prepared to go in their secularism? Bentham's penchant for the scientific (as Douglas Long has explained), his rejection of superstition, idealism and abstraction in favour of the strictly perceptible, verifiable and useful, places him at one extreme pole on this secular spectrum. Yet we might pause to consider that Paley's philosophy was also in some sense secular. Within the ranks of the clerics, Paley typified the eighteenth-century effort of the church to make its religion more accessible to its congregation. There is indeed in Paley's thought a shifting of weight from revelation and other-worldliness to reason and considerations of temporal welfare. However, the shift here is one of emphasis merely: it is the basically theological constructs of Paley's ethics which remain dominant, and which provide me with the substance of the contrast I want to draw between his version of the doctrine of utility and that advanced by Jeremy Bentham.

The religious version of the doctrine of utility

It is only recently that Bentham's early philosophical radicalism of the 1770s, influenced by his reading of Locke and the continental *philosophes*, has been given the attention it deserves.[14] The essentials of this social science can be briefly stated: it rests on the assumption of a universe in which all 'real' entities are either discrete physical objects or else ultimately reducible to other 'real' entities, and which, via the medium of descriptive language, can be made intelligible free from the verbal foibles, mysticism and fictions which commonly pose obstacles in the path of human understanding. These presuppositions, together with Bentham's studious commitment to the 'dichotomous' mode of classification and analysis, provide and shape the information (the empirical data) – whether it be in the field of law, economics, politics, or theology – upon which utility, the greatest happiness principle, is then applied as the one, true test of social value.[15] This is an important development; understanding the philosophical tenets of Bentham's science of society is crucial to an appreciation of the many and varied features of his efforts on behalf of social (economic, legal, juristic, penal and educative) improvement.

In contrast, Paley expounded an ethics which – though it gives prominence to utility as the criterion of moral judgement – depended as much on orthodox Christian teaching as Bentham was to depend on empiricism, reason, and an abhorrence for traditional metaphysics.[16] But if utility is so central to Paley's analysis (as he argued), and therefore fundamental to explaining his attitude toward public institutions, then we must be careful what is meant by 'utility' in this context. What do we mean when we describe Paley as an exponent of utility?

First, Paley adhered to the hedonist psychology that sees man as a creature motivated by considerations of pleasure and pain, and he was a consequentialist who defined right conduct in terms of the benefits that accrue from it to the individual and to society. Necessarily, therefore, he was concerned with the problem of moral choice and with the best means to ensure the moral end of happiness. Second, he recognized the potential for conflict between or among interests in social and political life. It was the religious solution he offered to such potential conflict which distinguished his version of the doctrine of utility. He defined virtue as 'the doing good to mankind, in obedience to the will of God, and for the sake of everlasting happiness'.[17] In this way, religion provided the solution to the puzzle of how a person can will something that apparently conflicts with his own personal interest, but that is for the good or benefit of others. The assumptions or beliefs involved are that

(i)   it is the will of God that all men be happy;

(ii)   all men at all times ought to contribute to the best of their ability to the fulfilment of God's purpose (the good to be sought);

(iii) all men have the means of knowing what enhances the happiness of others;

(iv) all men possess an immortal soul; and

(v)   there will be a future day of reckoning at which time goodness will be rewarded and evil punished.

On this view of the matter, the harmony between the private interests of the individual and those with whom he associates is based on the necessity that each man take into account in all his thoughts and deeds his own eternal happiness.[18] And the teachings of Christ dictate that each individual is responsible not only for his own spiritual well-being, but (toward this end) also for the temporal well-being of those about him. To 'be good' means that we actively pursue the happiness of others whenever it is within our power, for only by so doing can we secure our own happiness in the most encompassing sense of this term: eternal happiness.

The notion of a life after death, the cornerstone of Paley's moral thought in the *Principles*, is a recurring theme in his work; in the *Evidences of Christianity* (1794) he claimed that the assurance of a future life was the primary object of revelation. In the *Natural Theology* (1802) he wrote of life on earth as a state of probation, preparatory to another world, and several of his sermons focused on related questions.[19] Although he admitted that the belief in an after-life was strictly a matter of faith, it provided his ethics with a powerful moral sanction readily apprehended by his fellow men. Its deployment convinced him that he had bridged the gap between self-interest and social interest, thereby solving one of the pivotal problems of eighteenth-century ethics.

Paley's conservatism

For long the common view of Paley – beginning with his first biographer George Wilson Meadley – was that of a proto-liberal, a reformer, sometimes cautious but always with his heart in the right place. Elie Halévy echoes this view in *The Growth of Philosophic Radicalism*. Ernest Barker followed suit, describing Paley as 'half a Bentham and half a Blackstone', a man whose liberal elements, particularly his enlightened views of religious toleration and religious institutions 'prove that, for his age, he belonged if not to the Left, at any rate to the Left of Centre'.[20] The anachronism of applying twentieth-century ideological categories to eighteenth-century thought need not be belaboured. More to the point, Paley's reputation as a 'liberal' no longer carries the lustre (perhaps one should say stigma) it once did.[21] Based on his arguments for reforming the practice of imposing subscriptions to the Thirty-nine Articles, abolishing slavery, and giving relief to the Irish Catholics, this view of the liberal or 'Whiggish' Paley was always the product of a highly selective reading of the evidence.[22] Against these reforming efforts – invariably hedged about with qualifications and words of caution to those who would move too quickly – one must weigh Paley's general defence of England's religious and political establishments and the accepted traditions upon which they were founded.

There is not the space here to give a comprehensive rendering of Paley's theology. A. M. C. Waterman has recently traced a development in Paley's thought from an early disposition to maintain communication with the reformers within the church in the 1760s and 1770s (especially the Cambridge circle that formed around John Jebb), to the period following the collapse of the Feathers Tavern petition of 1772, when leading Anglicans (Paley included) were obliged to make up their minds about subscription and, to a significant degree, Trinitarian orthodoxy. From this point on, Waterman argues, Paley is properly situated in the ranks of the orthodox.[23] It is with this period of 'orthodoxy' that I am concerned, since it was in the years after the subscription controversy had died down that Paley wrote the major works upon which a credible assessment of his system must be based.

One might have expected a man like Paley, who believed that expediency was the measure of the value of social institutions, to have found a good deal in contemporary Britain that could be improved. In fact his attitude toward established institutions as it developed in later life was in essence that of a thoroughgoing conservative. To be sure, he did not regard the constitution as sacrosanct, but he found little about either its ecclesiastical or secular wings bad enough to require reform. In sermons, in pamphlets, and in his major work on ethics and politics, the *Principles*, he vigorously supported a host of established practices and institutions on the grounds of utility.

In 'A Distinction of Orders in the Church, Defended upon Principles of Public Utility' (1783), for example, Paley defended the English ecclesiastical establishment and particularly the role of the clergy.[24] Here he stated the difference between Christianity in its vital principles, on the one hand, and in its external forms, on the other. He candidly admitted that the Christian religion could exist under any form of church government, but defended the English ecclesiastical establishment as congenial to the character and habits of the various orders of the community and best calculated to enhance the efficacy of the clergy in their ministrations.

When he published the *Principles* in 1785 Paley likely disappointed contemporary reformers not only by his lukewarm views on proposals to reform the practice of subscription, but also by his apology for the existing electoral system and for various other incongruities of the constitution. In his discussion of the role played by reform in shaping the British constitution the essentially conservative character of his politics is revealed:

> Political innovations commonly produce many effects beside those that are intended. The direct consequence is often the least important. Incidental, remote, and unthought-of evil or advantages, frequently exceed the good that is designed, or the mischief that is foreseen. It is from the silent and unobserved operation, from the obscure progress of causes set at work for different purposes, that the greatest revolutions take their rise.[25]

English history, Paley held, was replete with examples to support this theory of unintended consequences: for example, when Queen Elizabeth helped enact laws that encouraged commerce and trade she had unconsciously contributed to the growth of a strong, oligarchical House of Commons.[26] More importantly, it was this doctrine, together with the Burkeian sentiment that Parliament should represent only the landed and moneyed interests (those who counted in English society), which formed the theoretical thrust of Paley's opposition to electoral reform, which he feared would lead to the unintended consequence of mob rule. Every innovation, he argued, diminishes the stability of government, and some absurdities are to be retained and many small inconveniences endured in every country, so that established usage will not be violated, nor the course of public affairs diverted from their old and smooth channel. On these grounds Paley defended the rights of property and contract as then stipulated by law; the right of bishops to sit in the House of Lords; the need for oaths of allegiance and for subscription to articles of faith; and the need to reinforce the duty of submission to civil government (invoking Scripture here to support his arguments from utility).[27]

Finally, in the pamphlet *Reasons for Contentment* – summoned forth by the revolutionary events in France and published in 1792 as a riposte to Thomas Paine – Paley warned England's labouring masses against radical reform, since it 'is not only to venture out to sea in a storm, but to venture for nothing'.[28] The poor have much to be thankful for, and should count their blessings. The only change to be desired is gradual change, that progressive improvement of our circumstances, which is the natural fruit of successful industry; . . . This may be looked forward to, and is practicable, by great numbers in a state of public order and quiet; it is absolutely impossible in any other.[29]

Coleridge's judgement on this tract was succinctly put: 'Themes to debauch Boys' minds on the miseries of rich men & comforts of poverty.'[30]

Utility was vital to Paley's support for the political establishment, and it was no less influential on his views of the role of religion. Prescribing spiritual perfection and happiness as the indispensable criteria of the good life in this world and in the world to come, the principle of utility nestled comfortably in the proselytizing arms of the Anglican church during this period. For Paley utility, as he understood it, added substance to the claim that for the sake of the well-being of the community the privileged position of the clergy as the guardian of the nation's morals should be protected by the state. Just as heretical theology tended to foster political radicalism, so theological orthodoxy was the seed-bed of political conservatism.

The authority of the established church, proclaimed Paley, is 'founded in its utility', in its usefulness in inculcating the principles of Christianity and in the support it gives to secular government. The abstract theory of a hypothetical alliance (popularized earlier in the century by Bishop Warburton) had no role in this justification.[31] Church and state were simply aspects of the same society. The moral role of the state was defined by the fact of its Christianity, and the sanctions behind its claim to obedience were rooted in Scripture and in the doctrines of the established church. In other words, the limits to the claims of the state are prescribed by the law of God as interpreted by the national church. And what was meant by 'national' demanded not only official recognition by secular government of the status of the church, but also its active support in maintaining both the position and privileges that the church and its ministers enjoyed.[32]

The connection between Paley's theology and his attitude to society and politics is unequivocal: his defence of the church and its role in civil society necessarily involved him in the defence of the established political order of which it formed an integral and indispensable part. To this end Paley advocated, in their mutual interest, a strengthening of the ties between church and state.[33] The underlying assumption is that the constitution is the best that man can conceive. Reforms are to be introduced for purposes of conservation not transformation. And throughout the exposition of these Burkeian sentiments the essential interdependence of church and state is primary.

Whatever desire for moderation and balance, and whatever liberal principles one discerns in Paley's work, therefore, they were never those of a political or parliamentary reformer. Of course, there was always room for improvements, but in general terms the existing institutions and electoral arrangements provided all the security society required.[34]

A secular utilitarian society

Bentham recognized the attraction of the religious version of the doctrine of utility to his Christian contemporaries. He opposed it both on metaphysical and on moral grounds. Materialism and nominalism dictated that the ideas of the soul, of a future state, and of an all-seeing omnipotent God were fictions irreducible to 'real' entities; Bentham's descriptive theory of language, with its attendant classificatory and paraphrastic techniques, revealed that these ideas, lacking physical referents, could not be made intelligible to the human understanding.[35] But even assuming the metaphysical credibility of such notions, Bentham was surely correct to doubt the validity of the claim that conflicting social and political interests could be overcome in the manner Paley suggested. Adherence to Christian dogma may well serve the interests of the individual soul, but to what extent could this be said to elicit socially beneficial actions? Added to this, the invocation to benevolence in the name of eternal happiness could hardly be expected to be persuasive to those who doubted or simply denied the existence of an immortal soul.

More importantly, it was to the belief in futurity and in Divine benevolence that Bentham traced the complacency that lay behind Paley's conservative attitude toward public institutions. Even if we grant, says Bentham, that the world was created by a designing intelligence, we are still not justified on this account of the matter in ascribing any intentions to its creator other than what are actually realized in the visible constitution of things. In so far as nature and history testify to a certain degree of justice and beneficence in the distribution of pleasure and pain, the author of nature can be credited with justice and benevolence; but if on examination we perceive inequalities of fortune in the world irreconcilable with our notions of morality, we have no grounds for inferring that God's intentions have been thwarted in the execution.[36]

If religion could not supply the sanction to ensure public happiness, what could? The answer is adumbrated at length in Bentham's writings of the 1770s and 1780s: legislation. At one point he described the superiority of his own ethical system over that of the 'religionists' in these terms:

The laws of perfection derived from religion, have more for their object the goodness of the man who observes them, than that of the society in which they are observed. Civil laws on the contrary have more for their object the moral goodness of men in general than that of individuals.[37]

There is a curious tension here between Bentham's nominalism with its regard for discrete entities and the emphasis he places on the abstract and collective notion of 'men in general'. But the shift in focus indicated clearly distinguishes the central aim of his work from that of the religious exponents of utility. Moreover, in thus allying utility with law Bentham announced – albeit prematurely – the imminent demise of the religious version of the doctrine of utility as a persuasive theory of morals. Accordingly, in the course of the attempt to prove the worth to society of a rational system of jurisprudence, founded on materialism and a nominalist logic, he took great pains to discredit religion as a necessary motivational factor in effecting the occurrence of actions conducive to general happiness. The probing of the deficiencies of religion as an agency of social welfare in the *Introduction to the Principles of Morals and Legislation* was integral to the endeavour (influenced by Helvétius and Beccaria) to establish the primacy of legislative science as a means to advance the happiness of the greatest number.

Bentham's opposition to the religious trappings of the moral thought expounded by Paley and others was complemented by his explicit opposition to the political philosophy it nourished. To appeal, as Paley did, to a questionable revelation weakened the utilitarian system, but the use he made of his philosophy to justify current rules of conduct, rather than to press for improvement, made his deviation doubly reprehensible. Paley had tried to show that the worth of the church, and of the political constitution of which it formed an integral part, could be established on the grounds of his religious version of utility. Bentham sought to establish the deleterious effects of the church and other public institutions by testing them against his own secular form of the doctrine.

The relationships between the various aspects of Bentham's system have still to be satisfactorily worked out.[38] It is generally accepted today that his political radicalism, defined in terms of the advocacy of democratic institutions, came much later than either his philosophic or his religious radicalism. It was only in 1809 or thereabouts, we are told, that Bentham, frustrated by the repeated failure of his efforts to instigate reform in other areas (and encouraged by James Mill), came to accept that the institutionalization of democracy was the only way to resolve the impasse between the movement for social improvement and the barricades thrown up by reactionary 'sinister' interest.[39] By comparison, the essential groundwork for philosophic and religious radicalism had been laid in the 1770s, though Bentham wisely deemed it expedient not to publicize his views in these areas until long after.[40] Around 1815 he set about elaborating systematically the materialist, nominalist and linguistic principles that had informed his social science from the outset of his philosophic career, and these appeared posthumously in the Bowring edition of the *Works*.[41] On the religious front, however, Bentham's critique took on a far more urgent character. During the decade or so following his democratic conversion, i.e. between the years 1809 and 1823, he conducted not only an attack on England's political constitution but also a much ignored but exhaustive examination of religion with the declared aim of extirpating religious beliefs, even the idea of religion itself, from the minds of men.[42] Applying the utilitarian test at every turn – first in *Swear Not at All* (1817) and *Church-of-Englandism*, then in *An Analysis of the Influence of Natural Religion* and *Not Paul, but Jesus* – his analysis was squarely focused on the supposed perniciousness of man's reverence for other-worldly beings, for the authority of 'holy books' and the sanctity of churches and their clerical officiates.

The critique of the Anglican establishment was always the strong arm of Bentham's offensive against religion during this period. His attack on the redundancies and immorality of requiring subscriptions to articles of faith and on the imposition of compulsory oaths in *Swear Not at All*, on penal laws against religious dissent, and on the Common Law crime of 'blasphemy', and his defence of the non-sectarian Lancasterian schools,[43] were all undertaken against a church determined to resist the movement to a more tolerant (and, admittedly, secular) society. Even his discussion in *Church-of-Englandism* of the political motives of the bishops in opposing seemingly rational proposals for reform was, while fanciful in part, not entirely ungrounded in experience. Had not the lack of public spirit on the part of the ecclesiastical establishment served to quash Bentham's hopes for his cherished Panopticon: a circular prison in which to 'grind knaves honest'?[44] Were not the bishops the ones who watered down the Unitarian Toleration Bill in 1813,[45] who helped to delay the repeal of the Test and Corporation Acts, and who threw their weight behind the government of the day whenever the tide of seditious, libellous, or blasphemous literature seemed to threaten the traditional order of society?[46]

Church-of-Englandism in its final form became a general exposé of the corruption and corrupting effect of the ecclesiastical establishment in England. In the *Plan of Parliamentary Reform* (1817), which Bentham started to write in 1809, he had given a sketch of the 'temporal' nature of the constitution and expounded the democratic causes of annual parliaments, secret and universal male suffrage. In *Church-of-*

Englandism he promised to tackle the 'spiritual' nature of the constitution.[47] In the event he went to extraordinary lengths to point out all the absurdities inherent in both the structure and doctrines of the church. It occurred to Bentham that 'the main root of all abuse in the field of religion and Government [is] an Established Church'.[48] In other words, the very fact that it was an 'establishment' made it a fertile soil for political patronage, and as such ensured clerical compliance with the wishes of secular government. The actions of the bishops in the House of Lords and as local magistrates in upholding the wishes and statutes of their political masters, and the general moral and intellectual corruption perpetrated by the church through a combination of incredible doctrines and obsequious practices, were convincing proof of the clergy's thraldom. The reward for all this came in the form of Crown patronage and legal protection for the privileges of the church.

Bentham had particularly harsh words for the Anglican National Schools Society, established in 1811 to set up schools throughout the land to combat the spread of the dissenting academies of Joseph Lancaster. According to Bentham, education was seized upon by the church as an effective weapon in its fight for survival. Organized on a national basis, education was enlisted to protect the vested interests and influence of the Anglican clergy, whose sole objective was to preserve 'their own worldly and anti-Christian power, their own factitious dignities, their own overpaid places, their own useless places, and their own sinecures'.[49] That a national school system should be based on the national religion was an idea rooted in the siege-mentality of the clergy. To Bentham's mind, it was nothing more than 'a state engine . . . employed in the manufactory of the matter of corruption, for a cement in the *Warburton Alliance* between *Church* and *State*'.[50] Radical remedies were required. The hierarchy was too entrenched to expect piecemeal reform to have any real impact – 'euthanasia', and nothing less, would do.[51] The church would have to be disestablished, her secular functions taken over by the state, and (with fair compensation to the clergy) her property redistributed. Utility could no longer be used as an aid in the philosophical justification of things as they are; it was now the foundation of the demand for the reconstruction of things as they ought to be.

Experience, it appears, had taught Bentham that moderation and the apparent reasonableness of the legal, economic and social reforms he proposed were not persuasive to those who held positions of authority in church and state. In politics, the radical remedy was to remove the distinction between rulers and ruled by vesting sovereignty in the people. However, the ultimate success of this remedy in facilitating the creation of a rational utilitarian society demanded another antidote to oppression, and that a prior one. It required the obliteration of the control exercised over the minds of the masses by the doctrines and institutions of religion. Only then could significant reforms be achieved and progress made toward the utilitarian utopia. In these terms, the established institutions of England – legal, political, ecclesiastical – were viewed by Bentham as all of a piece, an interdependent and mutually supporting network of influence designed to keep the Many subject to the Few.

In the *Constitutional Code* (parts edited by Richard Doane and published in 1831) Bentham provides us with his most extensive and detailed plans regarding the institutional make-up of his ideal state. In this vast text (662 double-columned small-print pages in the ill-fashioned and incomplete version in the Bowring edition of the *Works*) he mentions religion hardly at all, and when he does it is to say why it is to be absent from the utilitarian utopia.[52] It is plain that Bentham's attitude to religion was much the same as his attitude to political and legal institutions: it was a public establishment that, because of the vested interest of its functionaries in sustaining it in a corrupt condition, was in need of a complete overhaul. What made Bentham's treatment of religion unique, however, was that whereas reformed political and legal institutions would remain essential features of the utilitarian society, Bentham came to believe that even if disestablished, religion would still be an enemy to human happiness, due to the doctrines and beliefs it expounded. It was not sufficient merely to blunt the harmful political effects of religion; so long as religious beliefs constituted an active spring of human action, the temporal pursuit of self-interest would be thwarted.

The secularization envisaged by Bentham thus involved more than the disentanglement of the religious and political spheres of social life, more than the usual separation of church and state characteristic of the modern secularized liberal society. Certainly the policy of disestablishment set out in *Church-of-Englandism* was designed to achieve this end. Ultimately, however, secularization meant for Bentham the elimination of religious beliefs as influential psychological factors operating on the human mind, and this was to be the task of the legislator. Thus, in the *Analysis of the Influence of Natural Religion* and in *Not Paul, but Jesus*, he attempted to argue religious beliefs out of existence by concentrating on their 'illusory' nature. Nevertheless, Bentham well knew that the most effective way of proceeding along these lines was through education.

In the *Chrestomathia* (1816-17), Bentham's treatise on utilitarian education, religion is banned entirely from the curriculum. There are no concessions to the use of the Bible as in the Lancasterian schools.[53] To those afraid that instruction repugnant to religion would be given in the

Chrestomathic Schools Bentham solemnly vowed that 'no instruction ... disrespectful to Religion in general, to the Christian Religion in particular, or to any one form of it, shall ever be administered'.[54] While he was so heartily involved in his critique of the established church and its doctrines, however, such avowals could hardly be taken seriously. On the other hand, what *was* to be taught in the Chrestomathic Schools was a syllabus containing a large dose of the natural sciences, and Bentham was in no doubt as to the consequences for religion of a thorough-going education of this kind. His perception of the relation between human error and religion, and of the solvent provided by physical science, received remarkable expression in the pages of the *Chrestomathia*: 'In knowledge in general, and in knowledge belonging to the physical department in particular, will the vast mass of mischief, of which perverted religion is the source, find its preventive remedy'.[55] The reference to 'perverted' religion is a sop to the more sensitive of Bentham's readers. Ultimately, the remedy for all the mischiefs perpetrated by religion was to be found in physical science. Though prone to error, man need not accept anything that cannot be supported by experiment and observation. For Bentham 'blind faith' could never provide an adequate substitute for 'hard' empirical facts. Far from being the sceptic who holds that we must tolerate because we can never be certain of anything, his position in politics, philosophy, jurisprudence and theology alike, was that whatsoever is known must be based on reasoned argument from a solid scientific foundation of acceptable evidence. Hence, if Bentham was an advocate of the voice of reason, it was only in so far as this meant confidence in the authority of science.

A paradoxical conclusion

Bentham's secular version of the doctrine of utility stands in conspicuous contrast to that of his religious counterpart. Paley's religious version of the doctrine demands that we give priority to future possibilities in a life to come, rather than expend valuable time on fleeting and inconsequential temporal objectives. Surveying the legal and political institutions of his day, he saw little reason to embark on reform; whether it was the constitution with its unique system of checks and balances, or the legal code with its inconsistent enforcement of the death penalty, he spoke highly of their splendours and damned the reformers who would meddle with such exquisite mechanisms. By comparison, Bentham's secularized, materialistic version of the doctrine focuses the attention squarely on the temporal. Christianity stands condemned as a diversion from the benefits that men can actually experience in this life, and in so far as religion and other institutions

143

prevent the maximization of temporal happiness they are legitimate targets for reform. If Paley's world can be described as conservative and theocratic, then Bentham's was the universe of radical secularization. The language of utility, pleasure, happiness, and interest is common to both positions but, given Bentham's metaphysical nominalism and descriptive theory of language, the meaning of such terms is decidedly different in each case. How Paley and Bentham understood 'utility' and its related terms was largely dependent upon the metaphysical and moral presuppositions they held. And it was the very different nature of these presuppositions which led them to give voice to contrasting social and political philosophies.

The assumption, therefore, that in the era in question the 'greatest happiness' principle was necessarily an axiom of radical change is manifestly mistaken. As an organizing principle of moral and political philosophy it does not possess an inflexible logic; its status is that of a dependent variable. It is, therefore, the contingent nature of its relationship with other beliefs and principles which dictates the kind of politics that follow. But perhaps we can say more.

Paley's emphasis on the moral judgement and the good of the individual differentiates his doctrine, perhaps surprisingly it may seem, from the general legislative character of Bentham's social science. So much so that it may not be trivial to suggest that for Bentham, though not for Paley, the science of morality is largely irrelevant to the legislator's task of maximizing happiness. Indeed, it could be argued that Bentham's social science does not provide a moral theory at all, but really a legislative science built on a psychology of human behaviour. 'The art of the legislator', he once remarked,

> teaches how a multitude of men, composing a community, may be disposed to pursue that course which upon the whole is the most conducive to the happiness of the whole community, by means of motives to be applied by the legislator.[56]

Bentham seems to have imbibed and harnessed to practice the aphorism found in Helvétius' *De L'Esprit*, that 'the science of morality is nothing more than the science of the legislature [*sic*]'.[57] Certainly Bentham did not think that this is what he was doing; he believed that his was a *bona fide* theory of moral conduct. The truth of the matter, however, is that while he began with the maxim that the individual is the 'best' judge of personal interest,[58] he never subscribed to the tenet that each person is the 'sole' judge of what is in his or her interest.[59] As he wrote on one occasion in the context of political economy:

That the uncoerced and unenlightened propensities and powers of individuals are not adequate to the end [of happiness] without the control and guidance of the legislator is a matter of fact of which the evidence of history, the nature of man, and the existence of political society are so many proofs.[60]

In Bentham's legislative science the element of choice (individuals judging for themselves) is diminished. For the most part it is the legislator who decides what is for the good of the individual and of the society at large, and he has at his disposal the means, direct and indirect (coercion, education and the manipulation of public approbation and disapprobation), to determine what individuals will in fact do. Right-thinking utilitarian calculators can be left alone to 'judge' for themselves, for their choices conform to the official calculus. But all others are subject to 'control and guidance'. Individual autonomy is eroded. Rousseau's dictum is thus given a new twist: individuals are not forced to be free but (in ways prescribed by the legislator) forced to be happy.[61]

Naturally, this cuts across the grain of the position taken by those who view Bentham as a 'liberal',[62] and suggests that there is much more to the contrast between religious and secular modes of utilitarian thought than at first meets the eye. The Oxford-educated Bentham betrays a marked tendency toward paternalism while, paradoxically, it is the Cambridge-educated Paley who more comfortably fits the libertarian tradition after all. Despite his efforts to be theologically and politically conservative, Paley's doctrine preserves the element of individual autonomy, without which moral choices are rendered nugatory. Here there are sanctions (fear of Hell and hope of Heaven) which will no doubt influence us to 'be good', as Paley says, but there is no necessary relationship between these sanctions and the actions of individuals. We are placed in this world to prove our worth in the sight of God, but this would be meaningless without moral agency. Each of us is to fathom God's will (the general good of mankind) and fulfil it whenever we can; in this manner we aspire to true happiness. But this, the Anglican Divine Thomas Gisborne argued, is precisely the flaw in Paley's reasoning. Paley stresses the ability of individuals to discover what is best judged to maximize the happiness of others, yet their faculties are simply inadequate for the task. So much so, in fact, that Paley's doctrine is just as likely to provide a sanction for conduct contrary to Christian teaching as it is to promote God's will. It is for this reason, Gisborne admonished his fellow theologue, that revelation should not be relegated from its position as the cardinal dictate in settling questions of morality; men need a surer guide to conduct than utility.[63] Within the camp of the faithful, however, Gisborne's was one of few dissenting voices.

Indeed, in an age when religion had not yet vacated its seat at the centre of social and political life, the emerging secular form of moral thought, despite the Herculean efforts of Bentham, would find it difficult to displace Paley's individualistic, providential and prudential ethics. Even when Bentham finally brought himself to publish his *Introduction* in 1789, its very restricted circulation attracted little attention.[64] In fact it was well into the nineteenth century before the truly radical character of Bentham's thought was appreciated outside the tight band of disciples that gathered about him. Only from the middle of the 1830s onward was Paley no longer considered the central figure in philosophical discussions of utilitarianism.[65] Thomas Brown in his *Lectures on the Philosophy of the Human Mind* (1820) denounced the 'Paleyans' not the 'Benthamites'.[66] And when Coleridge flung out his anti-utilitarian barbs it was Paley rather than Bentham who was uppermost in his mind. Paley's doctrine he found 'neither tenable in reason nor safe in practice'.[67] Even those Unitarian dissenters most closely associated with the radicals in the movement for social and political reforms saw Paley and not Bentham as the fountainhead of the utilitarian doctrine. The moral thought of Thomas Belsham, William Jevons, and W. J. Fox represents a deliberate effort by the dissenters within the ranks of the radicals to retain the Christian dimension of utilitarian theory.[68] It is also notable that the deeply religious John Austin, commonly supposed to be a devoted disciple of Bentham, evidently drew inspiration in the philosophical part of his law lectures (of 1828) – reproduced in *The Province of Jurisprudence Determined* (1832) – from Paley's *Principles* rather than from Bentham's *Introduction*.[69] Yet it is indicative of an influential but frustrating misreading of the history of the development of utilitarian thought that Leslie Stephen should claim that Austin's utilitarianism was of 'the most rigid [Benthamite] orthodoxy'.[70] Only if Paley were also allowed into the ranks of the 'orthodox' could this be true. Finally, the 'religion of humanity' developed (under the influence of Auguste Comte) by John Stuart Mill, Bentham's self-styled spiritual grandchild, stands as a remarkable testimony to the perceived need to synthesize utilitarian principles and religious ideals. But this, in part at least, is the subject of Professor Vernon's essay and I have no wish to poach in territory where I know little of the terrain.

Acknowledgement

For their helpful comments on an earlier draft of this essay I should like to thank Douglas G. Long and A. M. C. Waterman.

Notes

1 A view most recently reiterated by A. Horowitz and G. Horowitz, *Everywhere they are in Chains: Political Theory from Rousseau to Marx*, Scarborough, Ontario, Nelson, 1988, pp. 117, 143–4. But see also E. Halévy, *The Growth of Philosophic Radicalism*, Eng. trans. M. Morris (1928), Clifton, NJ, Augustus M. Kelley, 1972, Introduction, p. xxvii; A. V. Dicey, *Lectures on the Relation between Law and Public Opinion in England during the Nineteenth Century*, 2nd edn, London, Macmillan, 1962, pp. 303–10; and W. H. Greenleaf, *The British Political Tradition*, 3 vols, London, Methuen, 1983–7, vol. 1, p. 248.

2 See J. E. Crimmins, 'John Brown and the theological tradition of utilitarian ethics', *History of Political Thought*, 1983, vol. 4, no. 3, pp. 523–50.

3 J. M. Keynes, *Essays in Biography*, London, Macmillan, 1961, p. 108 note. Paley's *Principles* became a text-book at Cambridge within a year of its publication in 1785 and remained on the syllabus well into the following century, providing an education in ethics and political economy for several generations of university graduates.

4 George Wilson wrote to Bentham (24 September 1786) during his sojourn in Russia informing him of Paley's advocacy of utility and of the public acclaim it had received. *The Correspondence of Jeremy Bentham*, vol. 3, ed. I. R. Christie, London, Athlone Press, 1971, pp. 490–1.

5 Bentham to Wilson (19–30 December 1786), ibid., pp. 513–14.

6 Bentham MSS, 'Law versus arbitrary power, or a hatchet for Paley's Net', 1809, University College London Library, Bentham MSS, UC 107/214; and 'Jury analyzed – analysis necessary, Paley', 1809, UC 35/309.

7 J. Bentham, *Supply Without Burthen* (1795), in *Jeremy Bentham's Economic Writings*, 3 vols, ed. W. Stark, London, George Allen and Unwin, 1952–4, vol. 1, p. 336; *A Table of the Springs of Action* (1817), in *Deontology*, ed. A. Goldworth, Oxford, Clarendon Press, 1983, p. 52; and Bentham MSS, UC 10/129. Paley is also praised by Bentham for certain observations on legislative assemblies in *An Essay on Political Tactics* (1791), in *The Works of Jeremy Bentham*, 11 vols, ed. J. Bowring, Edinburgh, 1838–43, vol. 2, p. 312, and in a collection of manuscripts on the 'Church' in 1812 he is cited as a fellow critic of Church patronage, Bentham MSS, UC 6/67.

8 See J. E. Crimmins, '"A Hatchet for Paley's Net": Bentham on capital punishment and judicial discretion', *Canadian Journal of Law and Jurisprudence*, 1988, vol. 1, no. 1, pp. 63–74. An earlier version appeared in *The Bentham Newsletter*, 1987, no. 11, pp. 23–34.

9 Bentham MSS, UC 107/193–277; 35/63–76; 35/297–316; 6/132–3; and J. Bentham, *Church-of-Englandism and its Catechism Examined*, London, 1818, p. 380.

10 [J. Bentham], *An Analysis of the Influence of Natural Religion on the Temporal Happiness of Mankind*, by Philip Beauchamp [pseud], London, 1822, and *Not Paul, but Jesus*, by Gamaliel Smith, Esq. [pseud], London, 1823.

11 See, for example, W. Whewell, 'Bentham', from *Lectures on the History of*

Moral Philosophy (1862), in B. Parekh (ed.), *Jeremy Bentham: Ten Critical Essays*, London, Frank Cass, 1974, p. 41; L. Stephen, *History of English Thought in the Eighteenth Century* (1902), 2 vols, London, Rupert Hart-Davis, 1962, vol. 2, p. 125; E. Albee, *A History of English Utilitarianism*, London, Allen and Unwin, 1901, pp. 165, 168, 190; J. Plamenatz, *The English Utilitarians*, Oxford, Basil Blackwell, 1958, p. 51; and D. Baumgardt, *Bentham and the Ethics of Today*, New York, Princeton University Press, 1966, pp. 314, 316.

12 See Bentham, *Article on Utilitarianism*, in *Deontology*, p. 328.

13 J. Viner, *The Role of Providence in the Social Order: An Essay in Intellectual History*, Princeton, NJ, Princeton University Press, 1972, p. 55.

14 Halévy's explication of the term 'philosophic radicalism' does not go nearly far enough toward explaining the philosophical character of Bentham's utilitarianism. This is done far better in R. Harrison, *Bentham*, London, Routledge and Kegan Paul, 1983.

15 For the relationship between the principles of Bentham's social science and his views on religion see J. E. Crimmins, 'Bentham's metaphysics and the science of divinity', *Harvard Theological Review*, 1986, vol. 79, no. 4, pp. 387–411.

16 For an exposition of Paley's ethics, especially his discussion of general rules see T. P. Schofield, 'A comparison of the moral theories of William Paley and Jeremy Bentham', *The Bentham Newsletter*, 1987, no. 11, pp. 4–22. In several respects the present essay begins where Schofield's leaves off.

17 W. Paley, *The Principles of Moral and Political Philosophy* (1785), in *The Complete Works of William Paley, D.D.*, 4 vols, London, 1825, vol. 2, bk. I, ch. VII, p. 38. Paley's definition is taken word for word from E. Law, 'On Morality and Religion', prefixed to Law's translation of W. King, *Essay on the Origin of Evil*, 5th edn, London, 1781, p. liv.

18 Paley, *Principles*, bk. I, ch. VI, p. 34.

19 See esp. Paley, *Sermons on Several Subjects*, XXVII, XXVIII, XXXIV, and XXXV, and *Sermons on Public Occasions*, VI, in *Complete Works*, vol. 4, pp. 199–210, 248–58, 329–40.

20 G. W. Meadley, *Memoirs of the Life of William Paley*, Edinburgh, 1810, *passim*; Halévy, *The Growth of Philosophic Radicalism*, p. 80; and E. Barker, *Traditions of Civility*, Cambridge, Cambridge University Press, 1948, pp. 193, 252. For a corrective to this view see M. L. Clarke, *Paley: Evidences for the Man*, Toronto, University of Toronto Press, 1974; and D. L. LeMahieu, *The Mind of William Paley: A Philosopher and his Age*, Lincoln and London, University of Nebraska Press, 1976.

21 Even in his own day the reputation Paley acquired as a critic of contemporary social arrangements rested in part on a misreading of his infamous parable of the pigeons, Paley, *Principles*, bk. III, part I, ch. I, p. 74. Of this one contemporary remarked: 'we defy any man to produce a passage from the works of either Paine or Thelwall, more truly mischievous', *The Anti-Jacobin Review and Magazine* (April 1802), p. 529. But what appears to be the basis for an argument reminiscent of Rousseau's *Discourse on Inequality*, is merely employed by Paley prefatory to a justification for the inequality of property, ibid., ch. II, pp. 75–7.

22 For Paley's views on subscription see *A Defence of the Considerations on the Propriety of Requiring a Subscription to Articles of Faith* (1774), in *Complete Works*, vol. 2, and *Principles*, bk. III, part I, ch. XXII, pp. 134–5; for his views on the slave trade, see Meadley, *Memoirs*, Appendix G, and *Principles*, bk. III, part II, ch. III, pp. 144–6; and for his argument that the established religion of a country ought to be that held by the majority of the population see *Principles*, bk. VI, ch. X, pp. 403–6.

23 Interestingly enough, Anthony Waterman also discerns a similar development in Paley's political inclinations, from a rather uncritical whiggery to a careful defence of the established order. See A. M. C. Waterman, 'A Cambridge *via media* in late Georgian Anglicanism', *Journal of the History of Ideas*, forthcoming.

24 A sermon preached in the Castle-Chapel, at the consecration of John Law, D.D., Lord Bishop of Clonfert and Kilmacduagh, on 21 September 1782, in *Complete Works*, vol. 4, pp. 283–94.

25 Paley, *Principles*, bk. VI, ch. VII pp. 326–7.

26 ibid., p. 327.

27 ibid., bk. III, part I and bk. VI, *passim*.

28 Paley, *Reasons for Contentment, addressed to the Labouring Part of the British Public*, in *Complete Works*, vol. 1, p. 438. LeMahieu is incorrect in styling this work as a reply to Paine's *Rights of Man* (1791, 1792), see *The Mind of William Paley*, p. 25. Originally given as a sermon at Paley's Cumberland parish in 1790, it is possible that the appearance of Paine's work influenced his decision to publish it.

29 Paley, *Reasons for Contentment*, p. 437.

30 *The Notebooks of Samuel Taylor Coleridge*, 3 vols, ed. K. Coburn, New York, Pantheon Books, 1957, vol. 1, p. 75.

31 W. Warburton, *The Alliance between Church and State* (1736), in *The Works of the Right Reverend William Warburton*, 12 vols, London, 1811, vol. 7, bk. II, ch. I.

32 The church-historian L. E. Elliott-Binns offers a different perspective in *Religion in the Victorian Era*, London, Lutterworth Press, 1964, p. 47: Paley, he writes, 'regarded the Church itself as a kind of government department; and organized religion as chiefly useful for preserving morals and supporting venerable institutions, as in fact the cement of the whole social structure'.

33 Paley, *Principles*, bk. VI, ch. X, p. 412.

34 In an ingenious but hardly persuasive dig at the advocates of universal suffrage, Paley writes that the right to vote, if it be a natural right, as it is claimed, 'no doubt it must be equal; and the right . . . of one sex, as well as of the other' – a *reductio ad absurdum* to Paley's mind. Every plan of representation, however, 'begins by excluding the votes of women; thus cutting off, at a single stroke, one half of the public from a right which is asserted to be inherent in all . . .', *Principles*, bk. VI, ch. VII, p. 340 note. Paley's *reductio* was widely used in sermons and pamphlets of the day.

35 For Bentham's discussion of the soul and of the nature of God see 'A fragment on ontology', in *Works*, vol. 8, p. 196 and note.

36 Bentham, *An Analysis of the Influence of Natural Religion*, pp. 19–20.

37 Bentham in his Commonplace Book of the years 1781–5, in *Works*, vol. 10, p. 143.
38 Two articles should, however, be mentioned as providing a starting point: J. H. Burns, 'Jeremy Bentham: from radical enlightenment to philosophic radicalism', *The Bentham Newsletter*, 1984, no. 8, pp. 4–14; and D. G. Long, 'Censorial jurisprudence and political radicalism: a reconsideration of the early Bentham', *The Bentham Newsletter*, 1988, no. 12, pp. 4–23.
39 J. R. Dinwiddy, 'Bentham's transition to political radicalism, 1809–1810', *Journal of the History of Ideas*, 1975, vol. 36, no. 4, pp. 683–700.
40 For a discussion of Bentham's 'philosophe-*ic*' 'Preparatory Principles' of the 1770s see D. G. Long, 'Bentham as revolutionary social scientist', *Man and Nature/L'Homme et la nature*, 1987, vol. 6, pp. 115–45. Around the same time Bentham toyed with the idea of publishing a critique of oaths and subscriptions to articles of faith. See Bentham MSS, UC 5/1–32 and 96/1–116 (*c*.1773), and J. E. Crimmins, 'Bentham's unpublished manuscripts on subscription to articles of faith', *British Journal for Eighteenth-Century Studies*, 1986, vol. 9, no. 1, pp. 33–44.
41 Bentham's essays on ontology, language and logic are contained in *Works*, vol. 8.
42 As part of his radical attack on the English political establishment in 1809, Bentham embarked on a study of the 'Church', Bentham MSS, UC 28/32, gradually expanding its scope over the next five years, UC 6/1–209, 5/94–316, 158/123–230, and 7/1–160.
43 See J. Bentham, *The Theory of Legislation*, ed. C. K. Ogden, London, Kegan Paul, Trench, Trubner and Co., 1931, pp. 435–7; and Bentham, *Church-of-Englandism*, Preface on Publication, and Introduction, part IV.
44 Bentham, *Works*, vol. 10, p. 226. For Bentham's correspondence relating his efforts and frustrations regarding the Panopticon enterprise see *The Correspondence of Jeremy Bentham*, vol. 5, ed. A. T. Milne, London, Athlone Press, 1981, *passim*.
45 Bentham, *Church-of-Englandism*, Preface on Publication.
46 See, for example, *Bentham's Handbook of Political Fallacies* (1824), ed. H. A. Larrabee, New York, Thomas Y. Crowell, 1971, pp. 215–16, 'Effect good government; obstacle represented as a cause, station of the bishops in the House of Lords'. Compare this with Paley, *Principles*, bk. VI, ch. VII, pp. 338–9.
47 Bentham, *Church-of-Englandism*, Preface on Publication, pp. x–xi.
48 Bentham MSS, UC 158/157.
49 Bentham, *Church-of-Englandism*, Introduction, pp. 93–4 note.
50 ibid., p. 99.
51 ibid., Appendix IV, pp. 193 ff.
52 The opening sentence of bk. I, ch. XIV states Bentham's position: 'No power of government ought to be employed in the endeavour to establish any system or article of belief on the subject of religion', *Constitutional Code*, in *Works*, vol. 9, p. 92. See also ibid., pp. 93, 452–3. In Rosen and Burns's new definitive edition of the first (so far the only) volume of the *Code*, religion is mentioned only once and then in an inconsequential fashion: there is no obligation for ministers to furnish information regarding

their personal opinions on religion, J. Bentham, *Constitutional Code*, vol. 1, ed. F. Rosen and J. H. Burns, Oxford, Clarendon Press, 1983, p. 292.

53 In the *Chrestomathia*, Bentham writes: 'if instruction in relation to controverted points of *Divinity*, were admitted, whatsoever were the tenets taught, a parent to whose notions those tenets were, to a certain degree repugnant, would not send his child to a school, which numbered among its objects and its promises, the impregnating with those tenets the minds of its scholars', *Works*, vol. 8, p. 40.

54 ibid., p. 42.

55 ibid., p. 13.

56 J. Bentham, *An Introduction to the Principles and Morals of Legislation*, ed. J. H. Burns and H. L. A. Hart, London, Athlone Press, 1970, ch. XVII, p. 293.

57 C. A. Helvétius, *De L'Esprit, or Essays on the Mind and its Several Faculties*, Eng. trans. (1810), New York, Burt Franklin, 1970, essay II, ch. XVII, p. 134.

58 Bentham, *Introduction*, ch. XVII, p. 290.

59 I am indebted to the late James Steintrager for this interpretation, 'Language and politics: Bentham on religion', *The Bentham Newsletter*, 1980, no. 4, p. 11.

60 J. Bentham, *Method and Leading Features of an Institute of Political Economy* (1801–4), in *Jeremy Bentham's Economic Writings*, vol. 3, p. 311.

61 That this undercuts a purely utilitarian justification for political obligation is the argument of E. J. Eisenach, 'The dimension of history in Bentham's theory of law', *The Bentham Newsletter*, 1981, no. 5, pp. 2–21. This article can also be found in *Eighteenth Century Studies*, 1983, vol. 16, no. 3, pp. 290–316. An alternative to my interpretation is argued in G. J. Postema, *Bentham and the Common Law Tradition*, Oxford, Clarendon Press, 1986, esp. pp. 314–17.

62 Most recently L. Campos Boralevi, *Bentham and the Oppressed*, Berlin, Walter de Gruyter, 1984.

63 T. Gisborne, *The Principles of Moral Philosophy*, 2nd edn, London, 1790, part I, ch. III, pp. 16–23, and ch. V, pp. 37–47. Paley's doctrine requires that individuals know the good to be sought, but his denial of a moral sense (also rejected by Bentham, *Introduction*, p. 26 note) leaves them incapable of so knowing. Later on the Anglican Whately seized on this objection to condemn all versions of utilitarian morality. See R. Whately, *Introductory Lectures in Political Economy*, London, 1831, pp. 21–4, 68.

64 No notices in periodical publications of the day have come to light. Bentham had this to say: 'the edition was very small, and half of that devoured by the rats', Bentham to Lord Wycombe (1 March 1789), *The Correspondence of Jeremy Bentham*, vol. 4, ed. A. T. Milne, London, Athlone Press, 1981, p. 34.

65 J. B. Schneewind, *Sidgwick's Ethics and Victorian Moral Philosophy*, Oxford, Clarendon Press, 1977, p. 151.

66 T. Brown, *Lectures on the Philosophy of the Human Mind*, London 1820, cited in Halévy, *The Growth of Philosophic Radicalism*, p. 23.

67 S. T. Coleridge, *The Friend*, 1809–10, vol. 1, in *The Collected Works of*

Samuel Taylor Coleridge, 16 vols, London, Routledge and Kegan Paul, 1971–81, vol. 4, sect. 1, essay XIV, p. 314. Coleridge rarely mentioned Bentham and did not show a close acquaintance with his work. There is, however, a copy of Bentham's *Not Paul, but Jesus* in the Library at University College London with copious annotations (which have neither been transcribed nor analysed) believed to be in the hand of Coleridge.

68 T. Belsham, *Elements of Philosophy of the Human Mind and of Moral Philosophy*, London, 1801; W. Jevons, *Systematic Morality, or a Treatise on the Theory and Practice of Human Duty, on the Grounds of Natural Religion*, 2 vols, London, 1827; and W. J. Fox, *Christian Morality*, London, 1833. Bentham is mentioned only in passing by Belsham and Jevons. However, there is a series of comments by Bentham on Jevons's work in Bentham MSS, UC 14/302, published as Appendix D to the *Deontology*, pp. 364–7.

69 For evidence of Austin's religious beliefs see *Letters of George Cornewall Lewis*, ed. G. E. Lewis, London, 1870, pp. 103–5.

70 L. Stephen, *The English Utilitarians*, 3 vols, London, London School of Economics and Political Science, 1950, vol. 3, p. 320.

Chapter seven

From God to man? F. D. Maurice and changing ideas of God and man

T. R. Sansom

The second half of the nineteenth century in England saw a tremendous increase in the concern of the middle class about the condition of the lower classes. This gave rise to an increase in individual philanthropic activity, the organization of innumerable philanthropic societies, and considerable successful agitation for government action through 'collectivist' legislation. According to Dicey, collectivism replaced individualism as the dominant force behind legislation.[1]

In her autobiography, *My Apprenticeship*, Beatrice Webb attributes some of these changes to changing beliefs about religion and science. She argues that, along with the growing belief that science would be able to solve all problems, there arose 'the consciousness of a new motive; the transference of the emotion of self-sacrificing service from God to man'.[2] She reiterates this more forcefully a few pages later: 'I suggest it was during the middle decades of the nineteenth century that, in England, the impulse of self-subordinating service was transferred, consciously and overtly, from God to man.'[3] Comte's religion of humanity and Owen's 'worship of the supremely good principle in human nature' gave man a new religion, one without God.[4] Christianity was dead, drowned in the rising tide of secular humanism. It is this, for Mrs Webb, that accounts for much of the effort towards the amelioration of the conditions of the lower classes.

This judgement, however, gives a distorted view of religious belief in the nineteenth century and its impact on social reform. It is true that some middle-class intellectuals, influenced by developments in science and historical criticism, abandoned completely not only Christianity but belief in a supreme being as well. They were by no means a majority. Furthermore, as Webb herself notes, many of those who gave up Christianity retained a belief in some kind of God. 'Practically we are all positivists; we all make the service of man the leading doctrine of our lives. But in order to serve humanity we need inspiration from a superhuman force towards which we are constantly striving.'[5]

A great many people (probably a majority of the middle class) retained their beliefs not only in a supreme being but in some form of Christianity as well. Some of these made the 'self-subordinating service to man' not a substitute for service to God but an essential part of it. Over the century the generally accepted ideas of God and man changed and, as they changed, the notion of service to God and service to man changed as well. These were probably the most important changes in religious beliefs during the nineteenth century, at least from the standpoint of explaining the extent to which religious motivations lay behind the attempts to improve the conditions of the lower classes.

One person who both exemplifies and contributed to these changes is F. D. Maurice, the theologian whose ideas were central to the Christian socialist movement.[6] Maurice was neither a great philanthropist nor primarily a social and political reformer. He accepted the existing social and political order, believed in hierarchy and opposed democracy. Unlike the great Evangelicals, Wilberforce and Shaftesbury, he was not actively trying to bring about specific social reforms. His main involvement in social activism – the Christian socialist attempt to establish working men's cooperatives between the years 1848 and 1854 – failed, and Maurice devoted his time afterwards to education for both working men and working women.[7] Maurice's importance lies in his theology, and it was theology not social reform that he considered to be his true vocation. In his often-quoted letter to Ludlow he explained:

> my business, because I am a theologian, and have no vocation except for theology, is not to build, but to dig, to show that economy and politics . . . must have a ground beneath themselves, that a society is not to be made anew by arrangements of ours, but is to be regenerated by finding the law and the ground of its order and harmony, the only secret of its existence in God . . .[8]

Maurice's aim was not to invent but to uncover what he saw as the essential truths of Christianity which had been buried by successive movements in various historical circumstances, so as to distinguish the central and permanent from the transitory. While often condemned as a heretic and criticized for his lack of clarity, he was by many revered as a saint and a prophet.[9] Horton Davies in 1961 wrote of him:

> In retrospect he, rather than Newman, seems the dominant figure of the Anglican Communion in the nineteenth century. . . . In him if anywhere, can be found the central meaning of churchmanship in the nineteenth-century Church of England. What is even more astonishing is that he alone combines a profound understanding of the Incarnation, the Church as the Divine Society, and the importance of

Sacramental life with a deep concern that these convictions and powers shall also be the levers to raise the level of the physical, spiritual, and social well-being of the poor . . .[10]

In this essay I want to sketch in elements of Maurice's thought against the background of Evangelicalism – the movement that dominated religious thought in the early part of the nineteenth century – in terms of three themes:

(i)   ideas about the nature of God, hell, and salvation;
(ii) ideas about the nature of man and of man in relation to God; and
(iii) ideas about the nature of man's relations with other men.

My purpose is to show that in Maurice's thought, at least, the idea of self-sacrificing service to man was an expression of, and not a substitute for, service to God. In Maurice's case, the route 'from God to man' was quite different from that outlined by Mrs Webb.

Of God, hell and salvation

At the beginning of the nineteenth century the prevailing idea of God in relation to man tended to dwell on the sinfulness of man and the vengeance of God against sinners. God was harsh, demanding and punitive. By the end of the century the concept increasingly emphasized was God's love and benevolence towards mankind as a whole.[11] Maurice's theology was based on and constantly appealed to the concept of the love of God for all of mankind.

Early nineteenth-century religious belief was dominated by Evangelicalism and, while Evangelicalism is a general movement and not a specific set of doctrines, the writings of those authors and preachers identified as Evangelicals would seem to indicate that certain ideas had a wide currency. While these people may have written of God as loving, just, merciful and benevolent, the relations of God to man that they preached hinged on the sinfulness of man and the awful punishments that God would inflict on the wicked and sinful. God's benevolence and love were reserved for the few who were to be saved.

Though the Evangelical revival of the eighteenth century was initially addressed to people with a sense of their own sinfulness,[12] Wesley and Whitefield attempted 'a balanced presentation of the judgement and mercy of God'.[13] Both believed they were presenting 'The fear and the love of God in the right proportion.'[14] Whitefield said, 'We must first shew people they are condemned, and then shew them how they must be saved.'[15] By the early nineteenth century, however, many Evangelicals preached mainly on the sinfulness of man and the awful punishments that God had reserved for sinners. Whatever the original intention of Wesley and Whitefield, Evangelicalism came to emphasize, at its extreme, the utter depravity of man and the awful power and vengeance of God. God was seen as loving and benevolent toward man but only if man did exactly what God commanded him to do. Geoffrey Rowell reports that 'Evangelical journals and tracts popularized a religion of petty providentialism, in which Divine judgement was executed on the perpetrators of "horrid wickedness" and the offenders against Evangelical etiquette alike'.[16] Tales of young girls who said 'damn' and immediately fell down dead were, according to Rowell, not uncommon in Evangelical magazines.[17] One of the milder examples of this view of God may be seen in a hymn for young children to sing quoted by Horton Davies:

> What if His dreadful anger burn
> While I refuse His offered Grace,
> And all His love to anger turn
> And strike me dead upon the place?
>
> 'Tis dangerous to provoke a God!
> His power and vengeance none can tell
> One stroke of his almighty rod
> Shall send young sinners straight to Hell.[18]

Hell was a place, and once there sinners, young or old, were there forever. While the idea of Hell as a place of everlasting punishment had declined during the eighteenth century and Whitefield had emphasized that the eternal fires of Hell were metaphorical (for Whitefield, Hell was 'the never-dying worm of a self-condemning conscience'),[19] many preachers in the nineteenth century talked of Hell as a place and dwelt lovingly on the terrible punishments that God would mete out to sinners for ever and ever.[20] On the extent to which mankind would be saved or damned Whitefield and Wesley disagreed. Wesley was an Arminian – a follower of Jonathan Arminius, a Dutch reformed Calvinist – who preached universal salvation. Whitefield, on the other hand, was closer to orthodox Calvinism and believed in the salvation of only the elect, a small proportion of the total numbers of mankind. Most early nineteenth-century Evangelicals, whether Anglicans or dissenters, appear to have followed Whitefield's views in this matter rather than Wesley's, and believed that most of mankind was destined to suffer everlasting punishment.

What distinguishes Maurice's views on God from those of most Evangelicals was his insistence that God was characterized by his love of humanity not his desire for vengeance. He did not deny the sinfulness of man, indeed he insisted on it quite as much as his Evangelical colleagues (though he may have conceived of sin differently than they did), but he denied that God's response to sin was vengeance and punishment. Redemption, not sin, was the centre-piece of Maurice's theology. In a letter to his son explaining his position he contrasted the Evangelical position and his own:

> I felt the worth of that direct appeal to the hearts and consciences of men which had distinguished the Evangelical preachers of the last century from the dry moralists, but I thought they had become weak, because they assumed sin, and not redemption, as the starting point.[21]

In 1853 Maurice published his *Theological Essays* in which among other things he put forward his idea of Hell. Already under attack in the religious press for his association with socialism,[22] he seemed to the Council of Kings College to be equally heretical and subversive in his ideas about Hell. In particular, they affected to believe that he was preaching universal salvation, a doctrine which, it was thought, was subversive not only of religion but of society as well. Without the threat of everlasting punishment in Hell, society, it was feared, would fly apart in an orgy of sinfulness.[23] If everyone could sin, then repent and be saved, there was nothing to stop people sinning as much as they liked. Despite several letters to the principal in which he explained his position in some detail, Maurice was tried by the Council and forced to resign.[24]

Maurice was innocent, though barely, of saying that all would be saved, but he was nevertheless closer to universalism than to the Calvinist doctrine of the elect. In almost every aspect, his conception of Hell appears to have been contrary to and much more optimistic than Evangelical orthodoxy. His ideas of the nature of Hell, of the punishments that sinners would receive, and of the numbers to be saved or damned, and above all his interpretation of the meaning of 'eternal', were all – as Maurice made clear in his essay 'On Eternal Life and Eternal Death' – contrary to the teachings of most early nineteenth-century Evangelicals.

While Maurice did not claim that all would be saved, he could not accept that God – whom he conceived of as a God of love – would allow the vast majority of human beings to be damned. He did not rule out universal salvation, but believed if ultimately some were to be damned it would be due to their own inability to accept God, not due to God's vengeance. If men were not saved it would be because they chose not to be.[25]

Further, Maurice's conception of the state of damnation was different from the Evangelical notion, though perhaps closer to Whitefield than to his nineteenth-century followers. For Maurice, Hell was not a place but a state: the soul's awareness of its separation from God. It did not consist of punishments imposed by God but seems rather to have been seen simply as a natural consequence or accompaniment of the condition of sin. Maurice argued that the Evangelicals had overemphasized punishment as the essence of man's relation to God. In the essay 'On Eternal Life and Eternal Death', he explicitly attacked the Evangelical Alliance, and those in the Church of England who supported them, for their preoccupation with punishment.[26] They had, he implied, carried on an earlier perversion of Christianity which Luther had fought against: 'the doctrine that the thing men have to dread is punishment and not sin, and the greatest reward . . . is the deliverance from punishment and not deliverance from sin'.[27] Against this view, Maurice contended that salvation or eternal life was the knowledge of God and that eternal death (Hell or damnation) was separation from or the loss of that knowledge.[28]

The interpretation of the word 'eternal' is the core of Maurice's argument and his conception of man's relation to God. He examined the uses of the word 'eternal' and the concept of eternal life and death in the Scriptures and traced their development in Christian theology. The modern interpretation of eternal as everlasting, he claimed, came not from the Scriptures or from theologians, but from Locke.[29] Maurice argued,

> I have come to the conclusion that the deepest and most essential part of the theology previous to the reformation, bore witness to the fact that eternal life is the knowledge of God who is Love, and eternal death the loss of that knowledge.[30]

Maurice did not deny the existence of a hereafter, or of the soul's progress from sin to salvation in that state (though he rejected the Catholic idea of purgatory). But he nevertheless insisted on eternal life and eternal death as experienced here and now as well as in the hereafter.

Maurice's notions of salvation and Hell, then, emphasized a God characterized by love, not vengeance and punishment, and, in so far as they dealt with the consequences of sin, focused as much on the present as on the hereafter. The direction of Maurice's theology is thus away from the Calvinist notion of 'God the Sovereign' and towards the notion of 'God the Father'. In this he both exemplifies and contributes to the movement in theology away from the harsher conception of a vengeful God and towards a more loving one.

There is, nevertheless, nothing in the concept of a loving God that necessarily leads one to stress man's relation with man or makes service to man a part of man's duty to God. More elements are needed. In

Maurice's theology some of these elements are to be found in his understanding of the nature of man, and of man's relation to God.

Human nature and the relation of man to God

Maurice's view of human nature was based on his interpretation of the Gospel, and was again much more optimistic and centred on this world than was the view of most Evangelicals. The tendency of the Evangelical movement was to focus on salvation in the life to come. This life, the physical life on earth, was unimportant. The distinction between man's animal nature and man's spiritual nature was sharply drawn, and the physical conditions of life in this world were often seen as irrelevant to spiritual life and salvation. Thus, the social conditions developing out of the dislocations caused by rapid industrialization and urbanization at the beginning of the nineteenth century were seen by most Evangelicals as unimportant. According to Desmond Bowen, Evangelicals

> seemed to make an unconscious division in their thought between matters of religion and matters of the world, even those of social reform. They had the mentality of Newman who confessed late in life that 'he had never considered social questions in their relation to faith'.[31]

The caricature that most often appears is that of the Evangelical giving tracts and sermons to the poor on how to improve their moral and spiritual life but with little concern for the physical conditions of that life. The Hammonds report that 'some Evangelicals reminded the starving labourers that they could have as much of the Gospel as they liked for nothing'.[32] The more devout may have genuinely believed in the irrelevance of social condition to individual salvation. The Evangelical belief in eternal punishment for the damned would tend to make physical suffering unimportant in the light of everlasting salvation and damnation.

Some Evangelicals tended to see 'catastrophes, famine and great social dislocation simply as acts of Divine Providence',[33] whereas others stressed the self-caused nature of poverty, either because of a religious belief in the sinfulness of man or a secular version of it: the essential laziness of man. Still others accepted the view that this world was a place of trial and suffering established by God to prepare those who would be saved for the life to come, and believed that pain and suffering were God's way of pushing a sinful and lazy man towards spiritual development. Many maintained the distinction between the deserving and undeserving poor and tended to assume that most of the poor were undeserving and that harsh measures were needed to prevent them living off the misguided philanthropy of the well to do. If God had designed the world to improve the spiritual development of the poor, then it was the duty of the rich to assist in God's plan, not to subvert it. With views like this about the service to God and man it is certainly easy to see how Beatrice Webb could see service to God and service to man as mutually exclusive categories.

In the early part of the century, only a small number of Evangelicals rejected the view that sin and immorality cause poverty, and were active in trying to change social conditions.[34] They held that, on the contrary, poverty and the conditions associated with it were a major contributing cause of the immorality of the poor. Ashley argued something like this in 1831: 'The condition of the dwellings of the people lies at the very root of one half of the social, physical, and moral mischiefs that beset our population.'[35]

Maurice's views are completely at odds with those held by the majority of Evangelicals and, while not inconsistent with the views of the minority group, appear to proceed from a different theological base.[36] The basis of Maurice's views is to be found in his account of the spiritual and the animal aspects of man's nature which, in turn, were derived from his beliefs about the incarnation.

'Men', he argued in a letter to Charles Kingsley, 'are not an animal plus a soul, . . . they are spirits with an animal nature'.[37] In his essay 'On the Incarnation' he argued not only that Christ came to save all of humanity, not just an elect, but also against the idea that Christ came 'from an ethereal world to save . . . souls from the pollution of the flesh'.[38] The physical world, he argued, is not treated by Christ as unimportant, nor are 'pain, suffering, and death . . . treated as portions of a divine scheme'. Christ was concerned, Maurice maintained, with the physical world and with the physical suffering of men. The Gospel tells us, he pointed out, that 'He heals their *bodies*.'[39] Thus, this world is not unimportant, nor is it God's providential design that people should suffer in this world so that they can be rewarded in the next. The world is not a place of trial and preparation for an afterlife. This world is an important part of man's existence. Just as eternal life or death is a state to be experienced in this life, so Maurice also insisted that the Kingdom of Christ exists here and now. The actual world is important, to be enjoyed and not merely endured. Christ is shown in the Gospels as being concerned to relieve physical suffering, with the physical state considered an aspect of man's spiritual state. He was concerned with bodies as well as souls. He 'proves man to be a spiritual being, not by scorning his animal nature and his animal wants, but by entering into them, bearing them, suffering from them, and then showing how all evils that affect man as an animal have a spiritual ground, how he must become a citizen of the Kingdom of Heaven, that everything on earth may be pure and blessed to him'.[40]

Human nature for Maurice was not something to be discovered simply by observing human behaviour. It could only be understood in relation to God. What was important was the view of man contained in the Gospel, for it showed in Christ 'the perfection to which man could be raised,' and provided a standard of human behaviour at which man could aim.[41] Because God became man, and showed the perfection of humanity in Jesus Christ, man can aspire to that perfection. Along with this view of the incarnation in relation to man, Maurice also argued that God was a part of man and immanent in him. Everyone, he believed, had Christ in them: 'The Gospel is, Christ is with you and in you and He is in me.'[42] 'We have the spirit of God within us!'[43] This is more than the assertion that we have it in us to be like Christ. It is meant to be taken literally – God or Christ is in all men – and provides further grounds for Maurice's optimism about the possibility of human salvation and the realization of the Kingdom of Christ and the human brotherhood which was a part of it.

The law of fellowship

Ideas about the relationship of man to God and man to man were, in the early years of the nineteenth century, dominated by the principle of individualism. A. V. Dicey has pointed out the parallels between the expression of individualism in the religious and in the secular spheres:

> The appeal of the Evangelicals to personal religion corresponds with the appeal of the Benthamite liberals to individual energy. Indifference to the authority of the church is the counterpart of indifference to ... the State. ... The theology, again, which insisted upon personal respons- ibility, and treated each man as himself bound to work out his own salvation, had an obvious affinity to the political philosophy which regards men almost exclusively as separate individuals.[44]

In religion, the Evangelicals, as we have seen, tended to separate the physical and the spiritual, to focus on the fear of punishment and on the hope of reward in the afterlife, and to be for the most part indifferent to the physical suffering of others. The emphasis was on personal salvation and on one's personal relation with God. Horton Davies argues that, 'in their revolt from the formalism of the day', Wesley and Whitefield, 'so emphasized a religion of the heart that converts became excessively introverted and individualistic'.[45] In economics, on the other hand, the emphasis was on self-interest and competition as the basis of material prosperity. Thus, in both religion and economics the tendency was for people to preach individual self-interest and to minimize cooperation and community. There were even attempts to fuse the two, as in some of the so-called Christian political economists who tended to see the competitive self-regulating economy and all of the suffering associated with it in that period as evidence of the design of a benevolent God.[46]

The main emphasis of Maurice's theology, in so far as it dealt with man's relation to man, was on fellowship. Opposed to individualism in both religion and society, he argued:

> The law under which we are placed is the law of fellowship; to be out of fellowship with God and man is to be in a wrong, disordered condition; the more we enter into it, the more we become the reasonable human beings we were meant to be.[47]

This law of fellowship was central to Maurice's thinking about both religion and society. Indeed, while he could separate the two conceptually, in practice the world was a unity. Society rested on human fellowship, and that fellowship rested on Christ. He believed that the nineteenth century required both a theological and a social revolution. In theology, he argues, 'certain truths need to be reasserted'. These are 'God's absolute Fatherly love . . . the incarnation . . . the sacrifice for all',[48] not just an elect few. 'Socially', what was required was

> the assertion on the ground of these truths of an actual living community under Christ in which no man has a right to call anything that he has his own but in which there is spiritual fellowship and practical co-operation.[49]

While Maurice does in part derive his notion of fellowship from the idea of the Fatherhood of God, with all human beings seen as, in a sense, the children of God and hence brothers and sisters, it is his ideas about Christ and the incarnation that form the basis of this fellowship. Maurice asserted in a letter to his son, 'I was sent into the world that I might persuade men to recognize Christ as the center of their fellowship.'[50] In another letter, explaining his book *The Kingdom of Christ*, he said:

> I have endeavoured in my tracts to prove that if Christ be really the head of everyman, and if He really have taken human flesh, there is ground for a universal fellowship among men (a fellowship that is itself the foundation of those particular fellowships of the nation and the family, which I also consider sacred). I have maintained that it is the business of the Church to assert this ground of universal fellowship; that it ought to make men understand and feel how

possible it is for men as men to fraternize in Christ; how impossible it is to fraternize, except in him.[51]

The two themes, the duty of the church 'to assert this ground of universal fellowship' (and to act on it as well) and the belief that there could be no fellowship except in Christ, were the basis for Maurice's involvement with Christian socialism, a label he adopted because it 'will commit us at once to the conflict we must engage in sooner or later with the unsocial Christians and the unchristian Socialists'.[52]

Maurice's fear was that Chartism and socialism, by focusing on political reforms, would be violent and disruptive of society and would not bring about the fellowship that such movements preached. For Maurice, such fellowship was impossible without Christ. He wanted to show the unchristian socialists that the church was concerned with them as brothers in Christ, not simply as brothers, and to show the unsocial Christians that a social duty was the essence of Christianity. Thus, in so far as political economy asserted that competition was the law of life, it was contrary to the Gospel which taught fellowship, and to reason and experience. 'Reason declares, the most painful experience proves, that if it does govern it is destructive of society – that it sets up every individual against his neighbour.'[53] The cooperative workshops that the group promoted were to be practical illustrations of cooperation in economic life. He did not, his son says, aim to Christian-socialize the universe, only to 'Christianize socialism'.[54]

Despite Maurice's often reactionary political opinions and the limited aim of his Christian socialism, he was seen by later Christian socialists, whose socialism was more in keeping with the modern definition, as their founder. In so far as this was true, it was not specifically because of his attempt to Christianize socialism, but rather his attempt to socialize Christianity, an attempt which, as we have seen, was central to his interpretation of the Gospel.

Ideas of God and man

Not only in Maurice, but in other writers of the nineteenth century, two themes become important in the interpretation of man's duty to God and man. First, Christ as a model for man to emulate was an important theme in the lives of many people: both those who stayed in the church and retained some version of Christianity and those who left organized religion completely. This is the theme of both W. H. White's *The Deliverance of Mark Rutherford* and Mrs Humphrey Ward's *Robert Elsmere*, and even of Seely's *Ecce Homo* which emphasized the purely human character of Christ. But it also was a theme for many who stayed in the Church, such as the 'ritualist slum priests' who combine the ideas of Maurice with those of the Oxford Movement.[55] It seems to have been something of a lowest common denominator acceptable across a wide range of theological views. Second, there is the emphasis on the incarnation, on the idea that God became man, thus raising man to a new dignity. This was used by some (for example, Gore) as the basis of a Christian socialism whose concern was to improve the social conditions of the poor to reflect that dignity, a theme that was carried on in the twentieth century by R. H. Tawney.

More generally, Maurice's interpretation of the Kingdom of Christ and of eternal life and eternal death as something actually present in this world helped to shift the attention of Christians from that exclusive preoccupation with an after-life which characterized many Evangelicals in the early part of the century. It was this shift, combined with Maurice's argument that Christ was concerned with men's bodies as well as their souls, which provided a theological basis for many in the later part of the century to work in the service of man. Very few people in the nineteenth century changed the object of self-sacrificing devotion from God to man. What changed, and what Maurice's theology both illustrates and contributed to, was the conception that people had of the nature of God and the nature of man.

Notes

1 A. V. Dicey, *Lectures on the Relation between Law and Public Opinion in England during the Nineteenth Century*, 2nd edn, London, Macmillan, 1962.

2 B. Webb, *My Apprenticeship*, London, Longmans, Green and Co., 1950, p. 112.

3 ibid., p. 123.

4 ibid.

5 ibid., p. 129, from MS diary, 15 March 1880.

6 The most detailed study of the Christian Socialist movement is to be found in T. Christensen, *The Origins and Development of the Christian Socialist Movement 1848–54*, Aarhus, Denmark, Universitetsforlaget I Aarhus, 1962. For a brief account, with specific essays on Maurice, Ludlow, Kingsley and Hughes and an excellent bibliography see E. Norman, *The Victorian Christian Socialists*, Cambridge, Cambridge University Press, 1987.

7 Maurice was a pioneer in arguing for the rights of women and in working for the education of women. For an evaluation of Maurice's efforts see F. McClain, 'Maurice on women', in F. McClain, R. Noris and J. Orens, *F. D. Maurice: A Study*, Cambridge, Mass., Cowley Publications, 1982. For an account of Christian Socialism and the development of the Working Men's College see J. F. C. Harrison, *A History of the Working Men's College 1854–1954*, London, Routledge and Kegan Paul, 1954.

8 F. D. Maurice, *Life of Frederick Denison Maurice Chiefly Told in his Own Letters*, 2 vols, ed. F. Maurice, New York, Charles Scribner and Sons, 1884,

vol. 2, p. 137.

9 The group centred on Maurice in the Christian Socialist movement referred to him sometimes as 'The Master', sometimes as 'The Prophet'.

10 H. Davies, *Worship and Theology in England: from Watts and Wesley to Maurice, 1690–1850*, Princeton, NJ, Princeton University Press, 1961, pp. 283–4.

11 S. Matthews, *The Growth of the Idea of God*, New York, Macmillan, 1931.

12 M. J. Crawford, 'Origins of the eighteenth-century Evangelical revival: England and New England compared', *Journal of British Studies*, 1987, vol. 44, pp. 361–97.

13 Davies, *Worship and Theology in England*, p. 152.

14 ibid.

15 G. Whitefield, 'The seed of women and the seed of the serpent', Sermon No. 1, cited by Davies, *Worship and Theology in England*, p. 152.

16 G. Rowell, *Hell and the Victorians*, Oxford, Clarendon Press, 1978, p. 1.

17 ibid., pp. 1–2.

18 Davies, *Worship and Theology in England*, p. 208.

19 G. Whitefield, 'The Eternity of Hell Torments', cited by Davies, *Worship and Theology in England*, p. 169.

20 Rowell, *Hell and the Victorians*, p. 297.

21 Maurice, *Life of Frederick Denison Maurice*, vol. 1, p. 236.

22 A. M. Ramsey, *F. D. Maurice and the Conflicts of Modern Theology*, Cambridge, Cambridge University Press, 1951.

23 Rowell, *Hell and the Victorians*, p. 297.

24 For the correspondence between Maurice and Dr Jeff, the principal of King's College, see Maurice, *Life of Frederick Denison Maurice*, vol. 2, ch. 6, *passim*.

25 F. D. Maurice, *Theological Essays*, London, James Clark and Co., 1957, p. 304.

26 ibid.

27 ibid., p. 311.

28 ibid., p. 308.

29 ibid., p. 317.

30 ibid., p. 314.

31 D. Bowen, *The Idea of the Victorian Church: A Study of the Church of England 1833–1889*, Montreal, McGill University Press, 1968, pp. 290–1.

32 J. L. Hammond and B. Hammond, *Lord Shaftesbury*, Harmondsworth, Penguin, 1939, p. 230.

33 J. D. Holladay, '19th century evangelical activism; from private charity to state intervention, 1830–50', *Historical Magazine of the Protestant Episcopal Church*, 1982, vol. 50, no. 1, p. 56.

34 The Minority not only included Wilberforce and Lord Ashley (later Shaftesbury), G. S. Bull, Michael Sadler and Richard Oastler, but also the Christian Influence Society and its newspaper, the *Churchman's Monthly Review*. See D. M. Lewis, *Lighten Their Darkness: The Evangelical Mission to Working-Class London, 1828–1860*, New York, Greenwood Press, 1986, pp. 151–75; and Holladay, '19th century evangelical activism', *passim*.

35 Cited by Holladay, '19th century evangelical activism', p. 262. Shaftesbury

made similar arguments when dealing with conditions in mines and factories. The theme appears again and again in the *Churchman's Monthly Review*, and later appears in the reports of those involved in the Scripture Reader's Association and the London City Museum.

36 Maurice was happy to work with Shaftesbury, but Shaftesbury did not like Maurice's theological views nor his association with socialism.

37 Maurice, *Life of Frederick Denison Maurice*, vol. 2, p. 272.

38 Maurice, *Theological Essays*, p. 91.

39 ibid.

40 ibid., p. 92.

41 ibid. That man should take Christ as a model and emulate Christ's treatment of others became an important theme in arguments for the service to man in the later part of the century.

42 Maurice, *Life of Frederick Denison Maurice*, vol. 1, p. 310.

43 ibid., vol. 2, p. 246.

44 Dicey, *Law and Public Opinion in England*, p. 402.

45 Davies, *Worship and Theology in England*, p. 182.

46 See A. M. C. Waterman, 'The ideological alliance of political economy and Christian theology, 1798–1833', *Journal of Ecclesiastical History*, 1983, vol. 34, no. 2, pp. 231–44.

47 Maurice, *Life of Frederick Denison Maurice*, vol. 2, p. 621.

48 ibid., p. 9.

49 ibid., p. 10.

50 ibid., vol. 1, p. 240.

51 ibid., p. 258.

52 ibid., vol. 2, p. 35.

53 ibid., p. 47.

54 ibid., p. 41.

55 See Bowen, *The Idea of the Victorian Church*, ch. 6, pp. 285–310.

Chapter eight

J. S. Mill and the religion of humanity

Richard Vernon

Mill's most sustained discussion of religion is offered in the essays on 'Nature', 'The Utility of Religion' and 'Theism', written separately but collected together as the *Three Essays on Religion*.[1] Among the many large issues posed by these essays is one of definition. The last essay, 'Theism', concerns religious belief in the conventional sense. It is a painstaking account, from an agnostic point of view, of the possibility of rational belief in God. Its tone is one that is typical of Mill, and is best described as judiciously lugubrious. If we consider rationally the respective quantities of good and bad things in life, Mill says, then a cheerful disposition should count as a mental disorder, just as melancholia does. But cheerfulness, unlike melancholia, does no harm, and if one chooses to 'dwell chiefly on the brighter side' one is free to do so.[2] One may hope that there is a God, and an after-life. But we must also remember that if we correctly weigh the arguments for God's existence, the most we can claim to find is an absence of decisive disproof. Moreover, what is the God whose existence cannot be decisively disproved? A being of only limited power and limited benevolence, who, if he intended to make us happy, has been so far an ignominious failure. But all the same, Mill says, hope if you want to.

The essay on 'Theism' concerns the traditional topics of natural theology and revelation, and tries to give them what is their due, even if Mill's message is somewhat less than inspirational. But the earlier essay on 'The Utility of Religion' had concerned religious belief in a non-traditional sense. Mill speaks of the human need for consolation, and of the importance of 'elevated feelings' to human life, but then wonders whether, 'in order to obtain this good, it is necessary to travel beyond the boundaries of the world which we inhabit'.[3] He decides that it is not, that feelings of consolation and enthusiastic devotion can be inspired by the common good of humanity itself:

> To call these sentiments by the name morality, exclusively of any other title, is claiming too little for them. They are a real religion. ... The essence of religion is the strong and earnest direction of the

emotions and desires towards an ideal object, recognized as of the highest excellence, and as rightfully paramount over all selfish objects of desire. This condition is fulfilled by the Religion of Humanity in as eminent a degree, and in as high a sense, as by the supernatural religions even in their best manifestations, and far more so than in any of their others.[4]

By the religion of humanity Mill means 'the cultivation of a high conception of what [our earthly life] may be made', a conception whose realization constitutes our 'grand duty' in life, the fulfilment of which, in turn, binds us together as fellow-participants in a common pursuit.[5] And when Mill returns to the religion of humanity at the very end of the essay on 'Theism', then and only then does enthusiasm enter his voice: that one can do something, however small, to aid in the progressive improvement of human life, 'is the most animating and invigorating thought which can inspire a human creature; and that it is destined . . . to be the religion of the Future I cannot entertain a doubt'.[6] Belief in God is quite consistent with the religion of humanity, provided that God is imagined as a benevolent being who, however, needs our assistance in realizing his benevolent intentions; but the religion of humanity is capable of standing 'with or without supernatural sanctions'.

This separation of the idea of religion from any essential link with theological belief is clearly an important step. It takes us half way but not all the way towards the thoroughly reductionist view to be developed at the end of the century, by Durkheim especially.[7] In that later view, religion was defined sociologically, as a set of beliefs or values to which a society attaches particular authority. But the mid-nineteenth-century view found in Mill, and before him in the Saint-Simonians and in Auguste Comte, does not make religion into a mere social fact. It is crucial that reference to personal experience is retained, for something is defined as religious not because many people think it important but because, for however many individuals, it expresses a sense of reverence subjectively similar to that experienced in theistic religion. It is a bit misleading to say, as George Eliot did, that the religion of humanity expresses 'religious yearning without a religious object',[8] for both Mill and Comte believed that supplying a new religious object, that is, humanity, was essential. But Eliot's remark displays well the subjective continuity that was demanded.

A human truth disguised in theological form

How one thinks of religion has much to do with how one may think of secularization. Let us distinguish between three models, each of which captures one of three broad tendencies in nineteenth-century thought.[9]

The most straightforward model, at first sight, is that of the elimination of religious belief in the traditional sense. A secularized society is an atheistic society. This is the view advanced, in Mill's own day, by theorists such as Pierre-Joseph Proudhon and Mikhail Bakunin. The idea of God is to be eliminated, typically, because it is seen either as the source or as the paradigm of authority itself. Fathers or priests or kings are God's shadows, and when God goes secular authority goes too, as it must if there is to be freedom. As a version of secularism, this view has the odd property of depending on a theological belief, that is, the belief in the non-existence of God; in that sense, although apparently radical, it is the version of secularism that remains most securely tied to the theistic past. It is clear that this is not Mill's view. He assigns the question of belief or unbelief to the realm of personal hopes or doubts, and denies that anything political hinges on it.[10] Once perhaps it did, when political reform required an attack on both state and church at once; but things have changed, and it is an implication of Mill's view that radicals like Proudhon and Bakunin are still fighting the battles of the eighteenth century.

A second familiar model is that of separation. A secular state is not one that is militantly atheistic but, on the contrary, one that disclaims any religious intention or capability. It distinguishes between political and religious objectives, and separates political and religious institutions. It goes without saying that a secular state in this sense may be proposed for religious reasons, as well as for political ones, and that it is wholly compatible with many kinds of religious belief.

The third model, however, again involves a theological claim. This is the model of transference: really perhaps a cluster of models, but with a common theme. Theistic beliefs are false; nevertheless they contain a kind of truth, a human truth disguised in theological form. In the past it was for one reason or another necessary that this truth be disguised, but now it can be laid bare. So while the idea of God is dispensed with, religion need not or must not go; it is revealed for what it is, a set of practices responding to secular needs. This is the model developed above all by Auguste Comte, who coined the term 'religion of humanity'.

In Mill's long essay on Comte, and elsewhere, his warm admiration for this feature of Comte's philosophy is expressed. 'The power which may be acquired over the mind by the idea of the general interest of the human race,' Mill writes,

> both as a source of emotion and as a motive to conduct, many have perceived; but we know not if any one, before M. Comte, realized so fully as he has done, all the majesty of which that idea is susceptible. It ascends into the unknown recesses of the past, embraces the

manifold present, and descends into the indefinite and unforeseeable future. Forming a collective Existence without assignable beginning or end, it appeals to that feeling of the Infinite, which is deeply rooted in human nature, and which seems necessary to the imposingness of all our highest conceptions.[11]

In *Utilitarianism,* when Mill tries to explain how the 'general interest' can eventually become an object of inspiration, he says that he can do no better than refer the reader to Comte.[12]

Mill's admiration is, of course, tempered with criticism. He will have nothing to do with the more bizarre ('ineffably ludicrous') aspects of Comte's proposed religion, or with his tiresomely literal-minded efforts to provide exact secular equivalents for baptism, prayer, catechism, excommunication, saints' days, the sign of the cross, and, excelling himself, for immaculate conception, which, he predicts, will become the normal mode of generation as morality improves. These are things which most people find funny in Comte, but which Mill, being Mill, finds sad. His rejection of them, however, only demonstrates how consistently he held to Comte's own model of transference. Comte, Mill's critique implies, failed to think through the implications of the model. If human life itself has come to provide the experiences that supernatural religions once provided, why labour to preserve all these bits and pieces of Catholic ritual? The episodes of ordinary life are to comprise religious experience, and it is the fulfilment of ordinary tasks that constitutes religious observance. To insist on the relics of older forms of observance is to fall between two stools.[13]

This view of Mill's, however, casts intriguing light on the nature of his liberalism. For liberalism is conventionally (and with good reason) associated strongly, perhaps even identified, with secularization in the second of the above senses, not with the third. Liberals have wished to separate religious and political institutions and religious and political authorities, because they have wished to distinguish between private and public realms. Religious belief belongs to the private realm because by its very nature it is a matter of personal reflection and choice. It should not, because it cannot, be authoritatively enforced. That is not of course to say that religious belief should have no political influence. But having political influence is one thing, being publicly institutionalized is another, and one could argue, as Tocqueville did in the book that Mill so admired, that it is when religious belief is disestablished that it has its strongest and most beneficent influence; that is why a society that is secularized in the second sense is not secularized in the first sense. But how are we to match this familiar liberal theme with the message of Mill's religion of humanity – Comtean not Tocquevillean – that there is no private life, that all of one's life including the most ordinary duties is a realm of public service? In the essay on Comte, Mill finds 'great beauty and grandeur' in Comte's notion that each should envisage himself (but not herself) as a 'public functionary',[14] thus referring to the very passage in Comte's *Système* in which the idea of division between private and public realms is denounced. What sort of liberalism is it that dispenses with the private realm? Can there even be such a liberalism, or do we have here, rather, another demonstration of the 'Two Mills' thesis of Himmelfarb: that the doctrine of *On Liberty* is best seen as a sort of escapade, and that the real Mill is a more conservative and authoritarian figure than liberals today would like to believe?[15]

The religious context of political thought

To the above question I shall state at once what I take the answer to be. We have seen that, in the kind of limited reductionism practised by Comte and Mill, the moral psychology of religion plays a key part, for religion is subjectively defined. Mill's conclusions differ from Comte's because he views the moral psychology of religion in a different way, and in a way that is governed by a different background tradition. If Comte is best described as a sort of Catholic atheist, then Mill may be seen as a Calvinist agnostic. They are led to opposite political conclusions because although they share a religion of humanity they do not share the same assumptions about what a religion is. In this way, I want to suggest, differences in religious culture continue to mould political beliefs, even after the religions in question have been abandoned.

The point is perhaps more obvious in the case of Comte, of whom it is a commonplace to say that he wanted Catholicism without God.[16] God he could do without, but not the magic of First Communion. Remarkably, he could not grasp that Catholic ritual and liturgy had a determinate and hence contingent historical origin. In a way that may cast doubt on the coherence of his whole historical theory,[17] he attributes to the inventors of Catholic ritual profound 'wisdom' and insight into the permanent needs of human moral life. One is reminded, somewhat, of the famous claim, in a Victorian text-book of grammar, that in English sentences the order of words is the order natural to the human mind. For Comte, Catholicism is the religion natural to the human mind, and in reproducing all its features the religion of humanity is merely recovering basic psychological insights that owe nothing essential to their theistic context.

What Comte develops in particular is a notion of religion that stresses the dependence of faith on institutional support, and does not stress at all the element of personal consent. Comte is driven to this notion because he does not believe there are such things as persons. What is called the person is a disparate and conflictual bundle of impulses, drives and faculties. If it is to achieve order it can do so only through religion, *religio*, which 'binds' together dispersed or warring things and makes them into one, through repeated exercises in public and private ceremony.[18] Religious practices thus precede and constitute the self, and religious experience is something worked upon the self, for it cannot be something that the self has chosen. It is true that, since the age of Enlightenment, the principle of consent must be recognized, and the religion of humanity can be imposed only by the free renunciation of scepticism and the voluntary acceptance of a new dogma. But plainly, given Comte's psychology, such consent must be given before one knows what one is assenting to. The parallel with Pascal's account of acquiring faith is exact.[19] Reason's last act is to renounce itself, and it renounces itself in favour of something it cannot understand.

For Mill, however, personal consent is related in a far more essential way to religious belief, for he explicitly attributes to the self the power not merely to submit itself to influences, but to form its own character.[20] For Comte, consent is no more than a political necessity in an age in which people have become unaccustomed to obey, so that they will have to consent to the process that will make them accustomed to obey again. Needless to say, their initial consent to this process adds nothing at all either to the force or to the value of the outcome. Consent merely solves a transition problem. Mill, however, conceives of full personal consent as an essential part of the authenticity of belief. In the essay on 'The Spirit of the Age', he refers to 'writers on religion' who have developed the notion of 'practical infidelity', to which notion Mill gives an interestingly stressed interpretation.[21] He takes it to mean a state in which one espouses, but does not understand, true belief. It is evidently something strongly parallel to this, in a secular context, that Mill foresees with some alarm in *On Liberty*. As knowledge advances, the number of disputed questions must diminish, and in some distant future nothing will remain to be questioned. This prospect affects Mill in rather the same way as his depressive fear, reported in the *Autobiography*, that one day every possible musical melody will have been written.[22] It must of course be good that everything will be known, for liberty has been justified, after all, precisely on the grounds that only liberty enables us to know things; but at this point in Mill's discussion the argument from knowledge suddenly gives way to an argument from authenticity. What is important is the way in which beliefs are held; that they are true is pointless if they are held merely as second-hand opinions, and not vividly understood.[23]

Mill goes on to say that this condition is 'exemplified' in the case of Christianity, or at least in the case of 'the majority of believers' for whom the maxims and precepts of Christ are held as 'dead beliefs, without being ever realized in the imagination, the feelings or the understanding'.[24] One wonders, though, whether Christianity might not provide more than simply an example, for Mill's concerns are vividly and precisely anticipated in a trend of Protestant writing to which the themes of *On Liberty* are obviously close. Thus Milton, in *Areopagitica*, wrote that if a man believes 'things only because his Pastor says so, or the assembly so determine, without knowing other reason, though his belief be true, yet the very truth he holds becomes his heresy'.[25] Locke, in the *Letter Concerning Toleration*, wrote:

> All the Life and Power of true Religion consists in the inward and full perswasion of the mind; and Faith is not Faith without believing. Whatever Profession we make, to whatever outward Worship we conform, if we are not fully satisfied in our own mind that the one is true, and the other well pleasing unto God, such Profession and such Practice, far from being any furtherance, are indeed great Obstacles to our Salvation.[26]

The argument of *On Liberty* has more in common with the ideas of Protestant theists than it does with Comte, despite the fact that Mill's views about God are very much closer to Comte's than to any theist's. That, no doubt, is why Mill seizes every opportunity to defend the Reformation against Comte's withering attacks upon it, as the beginning of scepticism or doubt and hence disorder.[27]

It may be possible to trace a more specific source or model for Mill's notion of belief. In his essay, 'The Spirit of the Age', Mill offers the following picture of a religious community:

> Every head of a family, even of the lowest rank, in Scotland, is a theologian; he discusses points of doctrine with his neighbours, and expounds the Scripture to his family. He defers, indeed, though with no slavish deference, to the opinion of his minister; but in what capacity? Only as a man whom his understanding owns as being at least as well versed in the particular subject – as being probably a wiser, and possibly, a better man than himself. This is not the influence of an interpreter of religion, as such; it is that of a purer heart, and a more cultivated intelligence. It is not the ascendancy of a priest: it is the combined authority of a professor of religion, and an esteemed private friend.[28]

Much the same description appears thirty-four years later in 'Auguste Comte and Positivism', although then, presumably as a result of Mill's having read Tocqueville on America, it is applied not only to Scotland but to communities in the New England states.[29] How might this long-standing picture of an ideal community illuminate the social ideal depicted in *On Liberty*? It suggests a precedent for Mill's clear distinction between 'neighbours', with whom one 'discusses', and children, to whom one 'expounds'. It shares with *On Liberty* a primary stress on the virtues of criticism. It also shares with *On Liberty* a distinction between acceptable and unacceptable modes of authority, between authority based on reasoned opinion and authority based on the silencing of reason. It helps explain the interesting fact that as an example of 'truth put down by persecution', Mill, *an agnostic*, should at once write: 'The Reformation broke out at least twenty times before Luther, and was put down.'[30] Above all, it draws attention to a neglected feature of *On Liberty:* its attempt to create a culture of mutuality. It would be a misunderstanding, he says, to suppose that he is arguing for indifference, or proposing that people should not take an interest in others' lives:

> Instead of any diminution, there is need of a great increase of disinterested exertion to promote the good of others. . . . Human beings owe to each other help to distinguish the better from the worse, and encouragement to choose the former and avoid the latter. They should be forever stimulating each other to increased exercise of their higher faculties and increased direction of their feelings and aims towards wise instead of foolish, elevating instead of degrading objects and contemplations.[31]

But, one may object, is it not just this that brings into play the Himmelfarbian critique? If Mill's intention is to impose on Victorian England a deep model of the Scottish Kirk, what has happened to his liberalism?

The character of Mill's liberalism

Political texts require to be understood in terms of their authors' fears. If we ask what Mill feared when he wrote *On Liberty*, the answer is clear enough: an 'insipid society', as he puts it in the *Autobiography*,[32] in which no one feels free to say what they think, and in which all are constantly under pressure to adjust their behaviour, or at least the impression that their behaviour is likely to produce, to the assumed expectations of others. If we bear this fear in mind, it is by no means implausible that Mill should have connected the defence of liberty with the creation of a moral community or secular religion; only the freedom to speak one's mind enables one to take part in the ceremonies of mutual improvement which constitute the religion of humanity. If we cannot say what we think, we have no chance of improving either ourselves or others. And mutual criticism is elevated to a religious duty because Mill's fear of complacency is so intense – intense to a degree that, one feels, could be attained only by the son of a man who was licensed to preach in the Scottish Church.

What gets in the way of seeing this, or what makes it seem anomalous when it is seen, is a quite misleading assumption of homogeneity in liberal thought. A liberal political theory is assumed to be composed of such things as belief in an open society, a doctrine of negative freedom, and a rejection of legal moralism as the ground of policy. But these things arise from Karl Popper's fears about Plato and Marx, Isaiah Berlin's fears about Rousseau, and H. L. A. Hart's fears about Lord Devlin; they have nothing to do with Mill's specific fears at all.

Mill's religion of humanity identifies the good society with a set of collective beliefs which, he predicts, will increasingly become universal, and to which is attached, he says, the most powerful moral sanction ever known in human history. These are beliefs of the most earnest and far-reaching kind, which no less than Auguste Comte's impose upon individuals extraordinarily demanding life-tasks, failure in which will be met by the criticism that others as a matter of duty must offer. This is not, indeed, an open society, and Popper's claim that anything in *On Liberty* resembles *The Open Society and Its Enemies* can only be regarded as far-fetched. But Mill does not claim to be anything but a closed-society theorist. In the essay on Coleridge, Mill writes that it is necessary

> that there be in the constitution of the State *something* which is settled, something permanent, and not to be called into question, – something which, by general agreement, has a right to be where it is, and to be secure against disturbance, whatever else may change.[33]

He goes on to call this something that is 'sacred'. Now Mill believes that this closure of political society is compatible with liberty because what may fill the role of collective belief can be precisely belief in liberty itself. How convincing that is may be open to question. But what is important is that, in finding that way out of the dilemma, Mill puts the belief in liberty on the same footing as belief in 'a common god' ('as among the Jews'), or belief in kingship by divine right. The liberal state is given no sort of special status or privilege by virtue of any claim to neutrality or any epistemic doctrine of fallibility. Mill's line of justification is frankly perfectionist, and is governed by a conception of human life rather than by a morally neutral account of the conditions of knowledge.

As for the notion of negative freedom, we must distinguish between two things at least: the definition of freedom, and the reasons for valuing it. There is no problem in seeing in Mill an appropriately 'negative' definition of freedom, as the absence of coercive restraint: *On Liberty* is concerned, after all, to set limits to the scope of coercive restraint. But there is no reason why the case for advocating negative freedom should not include its contribution to a positive conception of human virtue. Berlin's argument founders utterly when confronted with *On Liberty*. What Berlin wants to say, in his justly famous essay, is that perfectionists who have in mind an ideal of human character will glibly redefine freedom in terms of the attainment of their ideal, telling us that we are free while compelling us to do what they think we should. Perfectionists are snake-oil salesmen guilty of fraudulent labelling; liberals are plain dealers who give you a price up-front. But this whole equation comes apart when it touches a perfectionist liberal, an unhappy circumstance given that it just happens to be a perfectionist liberal who fills the role of liberal paragon. Mill simply does what Berlin, with such persuasive charm, says cannot be done. He defines freedom in a sensible way, and he defends it because he thinks it will lead to moral improvement, or at least is a necessary condition for moral improvement, since moral improvement cannot take place by means of legal compulsion. When Berlin tries to bring Mill into the ambit of his own theory, by claiming that, whatever Mill happened to say, he was really a pluralist or a sceptic, he simply ignores the historical Mill for the sake of saving the appearances.[34] Mill did not believe that the case for liberty rested on Berlinian pluralism any more than it rested on Popperian fallibilism.

The problem of legal moralism may be harder to surmount, not only because of its complexity, but also because it is Mill's own principle, the harm principle, that has been used as a wedge to force apart law and morality. What Mill's principle is taken to say is that the fact of something's immorality does not provide a warrant for its legal prohibition, and that legal prohibitions rest on grounds distinct from the grounds of moral condemnation. If this is indeed Mill's view, anyone who wants to impute to Mill a model of religious community has some explaining to do. We cannot simultaneously distinguish legal and political structures from morality, and view them as expressing a moral and religious vision. But surely a general explanation is not difficult to sketch. Mill's religion of humanity seeks to impose a comprehensive set of duties, but among these are some duties that entail coercion, and others that entail non-coercion. Coercion is required when an action damages or threatens to damage someone's right; non-coercion is required when an action is protected by someone's right. In both cases a morally determined action is required, but it so happens that in Mill's case, as opposed to Lord Devlin's, what one is morally required to do is to respect someone's freedom. To fail to do so, he says in *Utilitarianism*, is to hurt them, and hence to commit a moral offence.[35] He is different from Lord Devlin, not because he separates law from morality, but because he has a different morality, in which freedom is morally important. It is in fact so important that Mill equates the respecting of freedom with a religious observance, because some freedoms are essential to the well-being and development of humanity, in which we are to find our picture of an 'ideal object'.

It is quite true, then, that for Mill legal prohibitions of actions do not coincide with moral condemnations of actions, law and morality thus being distinct. But that is bound to be the case in any theory that gives a central place to rights. Rights protect an area of choice, but cannot determine what will be done with the choice, which may well be bad, if it is exercised at all. In protecting rights, then, law will protect some morally condemnable actions. Some 'experiments in living' would be better unmade, but to prohibit failed experiments would be the same as prohibiting all experiments, and that our concern for progress forbids us to do. But notice how different this position is from a position which establishes distinct criteria for public and private life. For Mill there is no private realm. There are realms which, for reasons of general utility, are excluded from legislative control; but they are excluded not because they are not the province of duty, but because they are provinces in which duties must be performed by means other than legislation. And that Mill took for granted the existence of 'other means' may perhaps suggest the residual place of churches, as opposed to states, in the structures of his thinking, while the vanishing of this residue in later thought may help to explain why Mill has not been understood. He has been seen as a theorist of a new kind of state, in isolation from his complementary project of creating a new kind of church. Mill could have said, with Milton: 'there were but little work left for preaching, if law and compulsion should grow so fast upon those things which heretofore were governed only by exhortation'.[36]

Re-interpreting Mill

Above I have suggested that *On Liberty* may be looked at in terms of background religious beliefs. It may be possible, however, to look at so complex a text in an indefinite number of ways, so perhaps one should try to do more. A final question that could usefully be opened is this: if we take the religion of humanity seriously, and look at *On Liberty* in the way proposed, does anything become clear that was not clear before? Can we do anything to smooth the furrowed brow of the Mill scholar? I do not think there is anything here (perhaps anywhere) to restore the

Mill scholar to perfect serenity; but perhaps one or two of his or her worries could be eased.

Let us begin by looking at some typical worries. Some well-known ones stem from Chapter Five of *On Liberty*, where Mill examines what his principles actually mean in terms of policy. The examples he discusses have long provoked concern; his conclusions generally seem less libertarian, and more interventionist, than some readings of his principles lead some people to expect. For example, he mentions two cases, that of a person about to cross an unsafe bridge, and that of public indecency, in which there is no prospect of causing harm to others, and yet he concludes in both cases that intervention is required. What has happened to the harm principle, if actions that do not harm others can and should be prevented? The alleged problem with the unsafe bridge example is that in failing to prevent someone from endangering their life one is not causing harm to them, one is only failing to prevent harm;[37] and if the harm principle is correspondingly revised to prohibit actions that fail to prevent harm, the political consequences are enormous. Instead of serving to restrict the scope of state activity, the principle could enlarge it; we are almost constantly guilty of failing to prevent harm, and a state that would compel us to protect each other from harm would look very different from the state that Mill apparently has in mind. The same sort of conclusion, some would think, follows from the prohibition of public indecency. For if the basis of prohibiting it is that people find it offensive, why should private indecencies not be prohibited if others find them offensive, as indeed they do?[38] What majorities or vocal minorities find offensive knows absolutely no bounds, and if they have a right to be protected against what offends them then the state knows absolutely no bounds either.

These difficulties have arisen, I believe, because attention has been paid to what Mill asserted at the expense of what he assumed. What he 'asserts' is of course 'a very simple principle', the harm principle, and in terms of that principle, baldly stated, it may be hard to see why we should lift a finger to save the hapless victims of flimsy bridges or why libertarianism should not flourish in public parks. But what Mill assumes is the context of a 'civilized community' with developed and complex moral relations within it. The harm principle assumes civilization as a background, and if we look at what Mill means by 'civilization', especially in the essay of that title, we find ourselves led directly to the central themes of the religion of humanity.

Following numerous eighteenth-century models, Mill defines civilization in terms of the division of social labour. Civilization is a matter of increasing interdependence, and hence of the loss of independence. As civilization advances, it is increasingly the case that individuals must take satisfaction from collective rather than personal projects. This leads them to take as their 'ideal object' the project of collective self-improvement. However, this process is accompanied by a frightening increase in personal vulnerability. In 'savage communities' (as Mill puts it) 'each person shifts for himself' and 'trusts to his own strength and cunning';[39] whereas in a civilized community we depend constantly on each other's self-restraint and conscientiousness. Hence the enormous weight that Mill places on personal security, against violations of which, he says, we must be in a state of 'constant protest'.

The concern for improvements in common human life, and the worry about individual fragility, are the two complementary aspects of Mill's religion of humanity. What that doctrine describes is not only the potential achievements of human organization but also a condition of shared vulnerability. We are of course vulnerable to direct and wilful or at least foreseeable injuries by others; hence the criminal law. But Mill is quite clear that civilized society depends on a more diffusely focused responsibility as well. In the most ordinary circumstances of life, and in work relationships, we rely constantly on each other's self-restraint and consideration. What Mill envisages as a 'civilized community' is not a community in the restricted sense of a face-to-face relationship; but it is crucial that it is not Adam Smith's substitute for face-to-face community either, that is, a 'great society' in which strangers are united not by mutual concern or benevolence but by reciprocal self-interest. What is distinctive is precisely that Mill's religion of humanity teaches and celebrates concern for strangers, on whose concern we likewise rely, and it is on this concern that a civilized as opposed to a savage community fundamentally depends.

When we fail to help the man on the unsafe bridge, we do indeed fail to prevent the harm that results to him from the bridge's collapse. But we also harm him directly, as a recent account has shown,[40] by failing to meet what, in a civilized community, is one of his expectations, and to disappoint reasonable expectations, Mill says elsewhere, is to inflict a 'real hurt'.[41] In a different way, the case of public indecency also involves the meeting of expectations. Mill does not in fact say public indecency is prohibited because it is offensive, he says it is an *offence*, and that it is an offence because it is 'a violation of good manners'. For whatever reasons, and rightly or wrongly, Mill evidently thinks of good manners as another set of mutual expectations whose maintenance arguably is important. Neither of these two cases can be understood if we insist on conceiving it as a two-person situation – a situation in which, simply, one person fails to preserve another from harm, or, simply, does something offensive to another person. They involve social institutions, and the obligation of one person to another is mediated by respect for social practices.

In John Locke's theological liberalism, the obligation of one person to another is mediated through God; individuals are beneficiaries of what we owe to God, not to them. In Mill's secular liberalism, individuals are beneficiaries of what we owe to humanity. In neither case is the grounding argument an individualist one, and attempts to understand classic liberal texts as successive versions of 'atomic' individualism are mistaken.[42]

That, then, is what the religion of humanity may help to make clear. It might help to explain why the conclusions of *On Liberty* should furrow no brow, for there is no reason to expect any other conclusions. What the text offers is an argument assuming the existence of a community – albeit not a face-to-face one – with shared ends, whose members face shared risks. The community imposes on its members various demands that stem from their shared situation, and it equates meeting these demands with acts of religious observance. In stressing the dangers and commitments of a shared quest, Mill's picture anticipates to a striking extent the picture of the virtuous community developed by Alasdair MacIntyre in his book *After Virtue*, despite the fact that this book is offered as a fiercely anti-liberal polemic. Conceivably, MacIntyre may feel he has done the liberals an injustice as far as Mill is concerned, for his list of exemplars of the virtuous life is as follows: St Benedict, St Francis, St Theresa, Frederick Engels, Eleanor Marx, Leon Trotsky and John Stuart Mill.[43] One feels that Mill would have preferred to be on a list with rather fewer Catholics on it.

Notes

1 J. S. Mill, *Three Essays on Religion*, New York, Henry Holt and Co., 1874. Citations below are from the *Collected Works of John Stuart Mill*: vol. 10, ed. J. M. Robson, Toronto, Toronto University Press, 1969, pp. 369–489. For an acute discussion of the essays on religion see K. W. Britton, 'John Stuart Mill on Christianity', in J. M. Robson and M. Laine (eds), *James and John Stuart Mill: Papers of the Centenary Conference*, Toronto, University of Toronto Press, 1976, pp. 21–34.

2 Mill, *Collected Works*, vol. 10, p. 484.

3 ibid., p. 420.

4 ibid., p. 422.

5 ibid., pp. 420, 421. For a discussion of Mill on the religion of humanity see T. R. Wright, *The Religion of Humanity: The Impact of Comtean Positivism on Victorian Britain*, Cambridge, Cambridge University Press, 1986, pp. 40–50.

6 Mill, *Collected Works*, vol. 10, pp. 488–9.

7 On the different meanings of 'secularization' see D. Martin, 'Towards eliminating the concept of secularization', in J. Gould (ed.), *Penguin Survey of the Social Sciences*, Harmondsworth, Penguin, 1965, pp. 169–82.

8 See U. C. Knoepflmacher, *Religious Humanism and the Victorian Novel*, Princeton, NJ, Princeton University Press, 1965, pp. 10–14.

9 See R. Vernon, 'The secular political culture: three views', *Review of Politics*, 1975, vol. 37, pp. 490–512.

10 Mill, *Collected Works*, vol. 10, p. 429.

11 J. S. Mill, 'Auguste Comte and Positivism', in *Collected Works*, vol. 10, p. 232.

12 Mill, *Collected Works*, vol. 10, p. 348.

13 On the significance of work for Mill see, for example, the Inaugural Address to St Andrews, in *Collected Works*, vol. 21, p. 255; 'Spirit of the Age', ibid., vol. 22(1), pp. 241–2; and 'Theism', ibid., vol. 10, pp. 488–9.

14 ibid., vol. 10, p. 348.

15 G. Himmelfarb, *On Liberty and Liberalism*, New York, Knopf, 1974. The religion of humanity is briefly discussed on pp. 90–1, where it is said to be entirely incompatible with belief in liberty.

16 See B. Willey, *Nineteenth Century Studies*, Harmondsworth, Penguin, 1964, pp. 205–6.

17 Or so I have argued in R. Vernon, 'Auguste Comte and development: a note', *History and Theory*, 1978, vol. 17, pp. 232–6. For a critique see W. Schmaus, 'A reappraisal of Comte's three-state law', *History and Theory*, 1982, vol. 21, pp. 248–66.

18 See, for example, A. Comte, *Catechism of the Positivist Religion*, Eng. trans. (1891), Clifton, NJ, Kelley, 1973, esp. Conversation VIII.

19 An excellent brief discussion is A. J. Krailsheimer, *Pascal*, Oxford, Oxford University Press, 1980.

20 See J. S. Mill, *A System of Logic Ratiocinative and Deductive*, in *Collected Works*, vol. 8, p. 837.

21 Mill, *Collected Works*, vol. 22(1), p. 293.

22 ibid., vol. 1, p. 148.

23 ibid., vol. 18(1), p. 251.

24 ibid., p. 248.

25 J. Milton, *Areopagitica*, in *The Student's Milton*, ed. F. A. Patterson, New York, Appleton-Century-Crofts, 1930, p. 746.

26 J. Locke, *A Letter Concerning Toleration*, ed. J. Tully, Indianapolis, Hackett, 1983, pp. 26–7.

27 Mill, *Collected Works*, vol. 1, pp. 219, 221.

28 ibid., vol. 22(1), pp. 312–13.

29 ibid., vol. 10, pp. 321–2.

30 ibid., vol. 18(1), p. 238.

31 ibid., p. 277.

32 ibid., vol. 1, p. 235.

33 ibid., vol. 10, pp. 133–4.

34 See I. Berlin, 'John Stuart Mill and the ends of life', in *Four Essays on Liberty*, London, Oxford University Press, 1969, pp. 173–206.

35 Mill, *Collected Works*, vol. 10, p. 241.

36 Milton, *Areopagitica*, p. 738.

37 For a careful discussion of this distinction see D. G. Brown, 'Mill on liberty and morality', *Philosophical Review*, 1972, vol. 81, pp. 133–58.

38 D. A. Conway, 'Law, liberty and indecency', *Philosophy*, 1974, vol. 49, pp. 135–47.

39 Mill, *Collected Works*, vol. 18(1), p. 120.

40 S. V. La Selva, '"A Single Truth": Mill on harm, paternalism and Good Samaritanism', *Political Studies*, 1988, vol. 36, pp. 486–96.

41 Mill, *Collected Works*, vol. 10, p. 256.

42 A vigorous example is C. Taylor, 'Atomism', in A. Kontos (ed.), *Powers, Possessions and Freedom*, Toronto, Toronto University Press, 1979, pp. 39–61. Frederick Dreyer has correctly pointed out to me that Mill is necessarily an individualist in some sense because, for a utilitarian, individual experience must be employed as a test. This is not, however, the sense of 'individualism' intended by communitarian critics of liberalism.

43 A. MacIntyre, *After Virtue*, Notre Dame, Ind., University of Notre Dame Press, 1981, p. 185.

Bibliography

Albee, E., *A History of English Utilitarianism*, London, Allen and Unwin, 1901

Ashcraft, R., *Locke's 'Two Treatises of Government'*, London, Allen and Unwin, 1987

Barfoot, M., 'James Gregory (1753–1821) and Scottish scientific metaphysics, 1750–1800', unpublished Ph.D. thesis, Edinburgh University, 1983

Barker, E., *Traditions of Civility*, Cambridge, Cambridge University Press, 1948

Barron, W., *History of the Colonization of the Free States of Antiquity*, London, 1777

Baumgardt, D., *Bentham and the Ethics of Today*, New York, Princeton University Press, 1966

Bellah, R. H., 'Civil religion in America', in J. F. Childress and D. B. Harned (eds), *Secularization and the Protestant Prospect*, Philadelphia, Westminster Press, 1970

Belsham, T., *Elements of Philosophy of the Human Mind and of Moral Philosophy*, London, 1801

Bentham, J., *Church-of-Englandism and its Catechism Examined*, London, 1818

—— *An Analysis of the Influence of Natural Religion on the Temporal Happiness of Mankind*, by Philip Beauchamp [pseud], London, 1822

—— *Not Paul, but Jesus*, by Gamaliel Smith, Esq. [pseud], London, 1823

—— *The Works of Jeremy Bentham*, 11 vols, ed. J. Bowring, Edinburgh, 1838–43

—— *The Theory of Legislation*, ed. C. K. Ogden, London, Kegan Paul, Trench, Trubner and Co., 1931

—— *Jeremy Bentham's Economic Writings*, 3 vols, ed. W. Stark, London, George Allen and Unwin, 1952–4

—— *An Introduction to the Principles of Morals and Legislation*, ed. J. H. Burns and H. L. A. Hart, London, Athlone Press, 1970

—— *Of Laws in General*, ed. H. L. A. Hart, London, Athlone Press, 1970

—— *Bentham's Handbook of Political Fallacies* (1824), ed. H. A. Larrabee, New York, Thomas Y. Crowell, 1971

—— *The Correspondence of Jeremy Bentham*, vols 1–2, ed. T. L. S. Sprigge,

London, Athlone Press, 1968; vol. 3, ed. I. R. Christie, London, Athlone Press, 1971; vols 4–5, ed. A. T. Milne, London, Athlone Press, 1981; vol. 6, ed. J. R. Dinwiddy, Oxford, Clarendon Press, 1984

—— *A Comment on the Commentaries and a Fragment on Government*, ed. J. H. Burns and H. L. A. Hart, London, Athlone Press, 1977

—— *Deontology together with a Table of the Springs of Action and the Article on Utilitarianism*, ed. A. Goldworth, Oxford, Clarendon Press, 1983

—— *Constitutional Code*, vol. 1, ed. F. Rosen and J. H. Burns, Oxford, Clarendon Press, 1983

Berlin, I., *Four Essays on Liberty*, London, Oxford University Press, 1969

Berman, D., 'Deism, immortality and the art of theological lying', in J. A. Leo Lemay (ed.), *Deism, Masonry and the Enlightenment: Essays Honoring Alfred Owen Aldridge*, Newark, University of Delaware Press, 1987

Blair, H., *Sermons* (1777), 5 vols, Edinburgh, 1802

—— *Lectures on Rhetoric and Belles Lettres* (1783), New York, 1817

Boswell, J., *Boswell's Life of Johnson*, 2 vols, London, Everyman's Library, 1960

Bowen, D., *The Idea of the Victorian Church: A Study of the Church of England 1833–1889*, Montreal, McGill University Press, 1968

Britton, K. W., 'John Stuart Mill on Christianity', in J. M. Robson and M. Laine (eds), *James and John Stuart Mill: Papers of the Centenary Conference*, Toronto, University of Toronto Press, 1976

Brown, D. G., 'Mill on liberty and morality', *Philosophical Review*, 1972, vol. 81, pp. 133–58

Brown, K. C., 'Hobbes's grounds for belief in a deity', *Philosophy*, 1962, vol. 37, pp. 336–44

Brown, T., *Lectures on the Philosophy of the Human Mind*, London, 1820

Burke, E., *The Works of the Right Honourable Edmund Burke*, 12 vols, London, 1887

—— *The Writings and Speeches of Edmund Burke*, 12 vols, Boston, Little, Brown and Co., 1901

—— *A Philosophical Enquiry into the Origin of our Ideas of the Sublime and Beautiful*, ed. J. T. Boulton, London, Routledge and Kegan Paul, 1958

—— *The Correspondence of Edmund Burke*, 10 vols, ed. T. W. Copeland, Cambridge, Cambridge University Press, 1958–78

—— *Selected Letters of Edmund Burke*, ed. H. C. Mansfield, Chicago, The University of Chicago Press, 1984

Burns, J. H., 'Jeremy Bentham: from radical enlightenment to philosophic radicalism', *The Bentham Newsletter*, 1984, no. 8, pp. 4–14

Burns, N., *Christian Mortalism from Tyndale to Milton*, Cambridge, Mass., Harvard University Press, 1972

Cameron, J., 'James Dalrymple, 1st Viscount of Stair', *Juridical Review*, 1981, vol. 26, pp. 102–9

Campbell, R. H., 'Stair's Scotland: the social and economic background', *Juridical Review*, 1981, vol. 26, pp. 110–27

Campos Boralevi, L., *Bentham and the Oppressed*, Berlin, Walter de Gruyter, 1984

Carroll, R. T., *The Common-Sense Philosophy of Bishop Edward Stillingfleet, 1635–1699, The Hague, Martinus Nijhoff, 1975*

Chadwick, O., *The Secularization of the European Mind in the Nineteenth Century*, Cambridge, Cambridge University Press, 1975

Chillingworth, W., *The Religion of Protestants*, Oxford, 1638

Christensen, T., *The Origins and Development of the Christian Socialist Movement 1848–54*, Aarhus, Denmark, Universitetsforlaget I Aarhus, 1962

Claeys, G., *Machinery, Money and the Millenium: From Moral Economy to Socialism, 1815–1860*, Princeton, N.J., Princeton University Press, 1987

Clark, J. C. D., *English Society 1688–1832: Ideology, Social Structure and Political Practice during the Ancien Régime*, Cambridge, Cambridge University Press, 1985

Clarke, M. L., *Paley: Evidences for the Man*, Toronto, University of Toronto Press, 1974

Coleridge, S. T., *The Collected Works of Samuel Taylor Coleridge*, 16 vols, London, Routledge and Kegan Paul, 1971–81

—— *The Notebooks of Samuel Taylor Coleridge*, 3 vols, ed. K. Coburn, New York, Pantheon Books, 1957

Colman, J., *John Locke's Moral Philosophy*, Edinburgh, Edinburgh University Press, 1983

Comte, A., *Catechism of the Positivist Religion*, Eng. trans. (1891), Clifton, NJ, Kelley, 1973

Conway, D. A., 'Law, liberty and indecency', *Philosophy*, 1974, vol. 49, pp. 135–47

Cox, R., *Locke on War and Peace*, Oxford, Oxford University Press, 1960

Craig, W. S., *History of the Royal College of Physicians of Edinburgh*, Oxford, Blackwell, 1976

Crawford, M. J., 'Origins of the eighteenth-century Evangelical revival: England and New England compared', *Journal of British Studies*, 1987, vol. 44, pp. 361–97

Crimmins, J. E., 'John Brown and the theological tradition of utilitarian ethics', *History of Political Thought*, 1983, vol. 4, no. 3, pp. 523–50

—— 'Bentham's unpublished manuscripts on subscription to articles of faith', *British Journal for Eighteenth-Century Studies*, 1986, vol. 9, no. 1, pp. 33–44

—— 'Bentham on religion: atheism and the secular society', *Journal of the History of Ideas*, 1986, vol. 67, no. 1, pp. 95–110

—— 'Bentham's metaphysics and the science of divinity', *Harvard Theological Review*, 1986, vol. 79, no. 4, pp. 387–411

—— '"A Hatchet for Paley's Net": Bentham on capital punishment and judicial discretion', *Canadian Journal of Law and Jurisprudence*, 1988, vol. 1, no. 1, pp. 63–74 (an earlier version appeared in *The Bentham Newsletter*, 1987, no. 11, pp. 23–34)

Cumberland, R., *A Treatise of the Laws of Nature*, trans. J. Maxwell, London, 1727

Cunningham, A., 'Sir Robert Sibbald and medical education, Edinburgh, 1706', *Clio Medica*, 1978, vol. 13, pp. 135–61

Davie, G. E., 'The Scottish Enlightenment', The Historical Association, Pamphlet G 99, 1981

Davies, H., *Worship and Theology in England: from Watts and Wesley to Maurice, 1690–1850*, Princeton, NJ, Princeton University Press, 1961

Bibliography

Dicey, A. V., *Lectures on the Relation between Law and Public Opinion in England during the Nineteenth Century*, 2nd edn, London, Macmillan, 1962

Dinwiddy, J. R., 'Bentham's transition to political radicalism, 1809–1810', *Journal of the History of Ideas*, 1975, vol. 36, no. 4, pp. 683–700

Donaldson, G., 'Stair's Scotland: the intellectual inheritance', *Juridical Review*, 1981, vol. 26, pp. 128–45

—— 'A lang pedigree: an essay to mark the centenary of the Scottish History Society, 1886-1986', *Scottish Historical Review*, 1986, vol. 65, pp. 1–16

Dunbar, J., *Essays on the History of Mankind in Rude and Cultivated Ages*, London, 1780

Dunn, J., *Locke*, Oxford, Oxford University Press, 1984

Dwyer, J., *Virtuous Discourse: Sensibility and Community in Late Eighteenth-Century Scotland*, Edinburgh, John Donald, 1987

Edwards, J., *Some Thoughts Concerning the Several Causes and Occasions of Atheism*, London, 1695

—— *Socinianism Unmask'd*, London, 1696

Eisenach, E. J., 'The dimension of history in Bentham's theory of law', *The Bentham Newsletter*, 1981, no. 5, pp. 2–21

Elliott-Binns, L. E., *Religion in the Victorian Era*, London, Lutterworth Press, 1964

Emerson, R. L., 'Conjectural history and Scottish philosophers', *Historical Papers 1984/Communications historiques*, Canadian Historical Association, pp. 63–90

—— 'Natural philosophy and the problem of the Scottish Enlightenment', *Studies on Voltaire and the Eighteenth Century*, 1986, vol. 242, pp. 243–91

—— 'Latitudinarianism and the English deists', in J. A. Leo Lemay (ed.), *Deism, Masonry and the Enlightenment: Essays Honoring Alfred Owen Aldridge*, Newark, University of Delaware Press, 1987

—— 'Sir Robert Sibbald, Kt., the Royal Society of Scotland and the origins of the Scottish Enlightenment', *Annals of Science*, 1988, vol. 45, pp. 41–72

—— 'Science and moral philosophy in the Scottish Enlightenment', in M. A. Stewart (ed.), *Oxford Studies in the History of Philosophy*, vol. 1, Oxford, Oxford University Press, 1989

Erskine J., *Discourses Preached on Several Occasions* (1798), 2nd edn, Edinburgh, 1801

Ferguson, A., *An Essay on the History of Civil Society* (1767), ed. D. Forbes, Edinburgh, Edinburgh University Press, 1966

—— *Principles of Morals and Political Science* (1792), 2 vols, Hildesheim and New York, Georg Olms Verlag, 1975

Ferguson, W., *Scotland 1689 to the Present*, Edinburgh, Oliver and Boyd, 1968

Firpo, M., 'John Locke e il socinianesimo', *Rivista storica italiana*, 1980, vol. 92, pp. 35–124

Fox, W. J., *Christian Morality*, London, 1833

Fox Bourne, H. R., *The Life of John Locke*, 2 vols, New York, 1876

Florida, R. E., 'British law and Socinianism in the seventeenth and eighteenth centuries', *Socinianism and its Role in the Culture of 16th to 18th Centuries*, Warsaw, PWN-Polish Scientific Publisher, 1983

Gauthier, D., *The Logic of Leviathan*, Oxford, Clarendon Press, 1969

Gay, P., *The Enlightenment: An Interpretation*, 2 vols, London, Norton, 1977

Gierke, O. von, *Natural Law and the Theory of Society*, Cambridge, Cambridge University Press, 1927

Gilson, E., *Reason and Revelation in the Middle Ages*, New York, Scribner and Sons, 1952

Gisborne, T., *The Principles of Moral Philosophy*, 2nd edn, London, 1790

Gough, J. W., *John Locke's Political Philosophy*, Oxford, Clarendon Press, 1950

—— 'James Tyrrell, Whig historian and friend of John Locke', *Historical Journal*, 1976, vol. 19, pp. 581–610

Grant, G., *Technology and Empire: Perspectives on North America*, Toronto, House of Anssi, 1969

Grant, R., *John Locke and Liberalism*, Chicago, Chicago University Press, 1987

Grave, S. A., *Locke and Burnet*, Perth, University of Western Australia, 1981

Green, V. H. H., *The Young Mr Wesley: A Study of John Wesley and Oxford*, London, Edward Arnold, 1961

Greenleaf, W. H., *The British Political Tradition*, 3 vols, London, Methuen, 1983-7

Grotius, H., *De Veritate Religionis Christianae*, Paris, 1640

—— *De Iure Belli et Pacis*, 3 vols, ed. and trans. W. Whewell, Cambridge, 1853

Guerrini, A., 'The Tory Newtonians: Gregory, Pitcairne and their circle', *Journal of British Studies*, 1986, vol. 25, pp. 288–311

Halévy, E., *The Growth of Philosophic Radicalism*, Eng. trans. M. Morris (1928), Clifton, NJ, Augustus M. Kelley, 1972

Halliday, R., Kenyon, T., and Reeve, A., 'Hobbes's belief in God', *Political Studies*, 1983, vol. 31, pp. 418–33

Halyburton, T., *Memoirs of Thomas Halyburton*, ed. J. W. Halyburton, Edinburgh, 1715

Hamilton, R., *The Progress of Society*, London, 1830

Hammond, J. L., and Hammond, B., *Lord Shaftesbury*, Harmondsworth, Penguin, 1939

Hamowy, R., 'The Scottish Enlightenment and the theory of spontaneous order', *Journal of the History of Philosophy*, Monograph Series, 1987

Harris, I., 'Locke on Justice', in M. A. Stewart (ed.), *Oxford Studies in the History of Philosophy*, vol. 2, Oxford, Oxford University Press, forthcoming

Harrison, J. F. C., *A History of the Working Men's College 1854-1954*, London, Routledge and Kegan Paul, 1954

Harrison, R., *Bentham*, London, Routledge and Kegan Paul, 1983

Hayek, F. A., *New Studies in Philosophy, Politics, Economics and the History of Ideas*, Chicago, University of Chicago Press, 1978

Helvétius, C. A., *De L'Esprit, or Essays on the Mind and its Several Faculties*, Eng. trans. (1810), New York, Burt Franklin, 1970

Henderson, G. D., *Mystics of the North East*, Aberdeen, Aberdeen University Press, 1934

Hepburn, R., 'Hobbes on the knowledge of God', in M. Cranston and R.

Peters (eds), *Hobbes and Rousseau*, New York, Anchor-Doubleday, 1972

Himmelfarb, G., *On Liberty and Liberalism*, New York, Knopf, 1974

Hobbes, T., *The English Works of Thomas Hobbes*, ed. W. Molesworth, 11 vols, London, John Bohn, 1889

—— *Leviathan*, ed. M. Oakeshott, London and New York, Collier-Macmillan, 1962

Holladay, J. D., '19th century evangelical activism; from private charity to state intervention, 1830-50', *Historical Magazine of the Protestant Episcopal Church*, 1982, vol. 50, no. 1, pp. 53–80

Hooker, R., *The Works of that Learned and Judicious Divine Mr. Richard Hooker with an Account of his Life and Death by Isaac Walton*, 3 vols, ed. J. Keble (revised Church and Paget), 7th edn, Oxford, Clarendon Press, 1889

Horowitz, A., and Horowitz, G., *Everywhere they are in Chains: Political Theory from Rousseau to Marx*, Scarborough, Ontario, Nelson, 1988

Hume, D., *A Treatise of Human Nature*, London, Pelican Classics, 1969

—— *A Treatise of Human Nature: Being an Attempt to Introduce the Experimental Method of Reasoning into Moral Subjects* (1888), 3 vols, ed. L. A. Selby-Bigge, Oxford, Clarendon Press, 1973

—— *The Natural History of Religion, and Dialogues concerning Natural Religion*, ed. A. W. Colver and J. V. Price, Oxford, Clarendon Press, 1976

—— *Essays Moral, Political, and Literary*, ed. E. F. Miller, Indianapolis, Liberty Classics, 1985

Jevons, W., *Systematic Morality, or a Treatise on the Theory and Practice of Human Duty, on the Grounds of Natural Religion*, 2 vols, London, 1827

Jolley, N., *Leibniz and Locke*, Oxford, Oxford University Press, 1984

Kato, T., 'The *Reasonableness* in the historical light of the *Essay*,' Locke Newsletter, 1981, no. 12, pp. 45-59

Keynes, J. M., *Essays in Biography*, London, Macmillan, 1961

King, Lord, *Life and Letters of John Locke,* London, 1858

King, W., *Essay on the Origin of Evil*, 5th edn, London, 1781

Knoepflmacher, U. C., *Religious Humanism and the Victorian Novel*, Princeton, NJ, Princeton University Press, 1965

Krailsheimer, A. J., *Pascal*, Oxford, Oxford University Press, 1980

Kramnick, I., *The Rage of Edmund Burke: Portrait of an Ambivalent Conservative*, New York, Basic Books, 1977

—— 'Religion and radicalism: English political theory in the age of revolution', *Political Theory*, 1977, vol. 5, no. 4, pp. 505–34

Kuhn, T., *The Structure of Scientific Revolutions*, Chicago, University of Chicago Press, 1970

Kurtz, P., *In Defense of Secular Humanism*, New York, Prometheus Books, 1983

La Selva, S. V., '"A Single Truth": Mill on harm, paternalism and Good Samaritanism', *Political Studies*, 1988, vol. 36, no. 486–96

Law, E., 'On Morality and Religion', prefixed to Law's translation of W. King, *Essay on the Origin of Evil*, 5th edn, London, 1781

Leighton, R., *The Works of Robert Leighton, D.D. . . . [with] A Life of the Author*, ed. J. Aikman, Edinburgh, 1839

LeMahieu, D. L., *The Mind of William Paley: A Philosopher and his Age*,

Lincoln and London, University of Nebraska Press, 1976

Lewis, D. M., *Lighten Their Darkness: The Evangelical Mission to Working-Class London, 1828–1860*, New York, Greenwood Press, 1986

Lewis, G. C., *Letters of George Cornewall Lewis*, ed. G. E. Lewis, London, 1870

Leyden, W. von, 'John Locke and natural law', *Philosophy*, 1956, vol. 21, pp. 23–35

Limborch, P. van, *Doctrina Christiana* (1686), Amsterdam, 1695

—— *A Compleat System, or Body of Divinity*, 2nd edn, London, 1703

Lochhead, M., *Episcopal Scotland in the Nineteenth Century*, London, John Murray, 1966

Locke, J., *The Works of John Locke*, 10 vols, London, 1823

—— *An Essay Concerning the Understanding, Knowledge, Opinion, and Assent*, ed. B. Rand, Cambridge, Mass., Harvard University Press, 1931

—— *An Early Draft of Locke's 'Essay'*, ed. R. I. Aaron and J. Gibb, Oxford, Clarendon Press, 1936

—— *The Second Treatise of Government*, New York, The Library of Liberal Arts, 1952

—— *Essays on the Law of Nature*, ed. W. von Leyden, Oxford, Clarendon Press, 1954

—— *Two Treatises of Government*, ed. P. Laslett, Cambridge, Cambridge University Press, 1960

—— *An Essay Concerning Human Understanding*, 2 vols, London, Everyman's Library, 1961

—— *Two Tracts on Government*, ed. P. Abrams, Cambridge, Cambridge University Press, 1967

—— *Essay Concerning Human Understanding*, ed. P. H. Nidditch, Oxford, Oxford University Press, 1975

—— *The Correspondence of John Locke*, 8 vols, ed. E. S. de Beer, Oxford, Clarendon Press, 1976–88

—— *A Letter Concerning Toleration*, ed. J. Tully, Indianapolis, Hackett, 1983

—— *A Paraphrase and Notes on the Epistles of St Paul*, 2 vols, ed. A. W. Wainwright, Oxford, Oxford University Press, 1987

Loen, A. E., *Secularization: Science without God?*, London, SCM Press, 1967

Long, D. G., *Bentham on Liberty: Jeremy Bentham's Idea of Liberty in Relation to his Utilitarianism*, Toronto, University of Toronto Press, 1977

—— 'Bentham as revolutionary social scientist', *Man and Nature/L'Homme et la nature*, 1987, vol. 6, pp. 115–45

—— 'Censorial jurisprudence and political radicalism: a reconsideration of the early Bentham', *The Bentham Newsletter*, 1988, no. 12, pp. 4–23

Love, W. D., 'Edmund Burke's idea of the body corporate: a study in imagery', *Review of Politics*, 1965, vol. 27, pp. 184–97

—— 'Meaning in the history of conflicting interpretations of Burke', *Burke Newsletter*, 1965–6, vol. 7, pp. 526–38

Lowde, J., *A Discourse Concerning the Nature of Man*, London, 1694

McClain, F., Noris, R., and Orens, J., *F. D. Maurice: A Study*, Cambridge, Mass., Cowley Publications, 1982

MacCormick, N., 'The rational discipline of the law', *Juridical Review*, 1981, vol. 26, pp. 146–60

—— 'Law and enlightenment', in R. H. Campbell and A. S. Skinner (eds), *The Origins and Nature of the Scottish Enlightenment*, Edinburgh, John Donald, 1982

MacIntyre, A., *Secularization and Moral Change*, London, London University Press, 1967

—— *After Virtue*, Notre Dame, Ind., University of Notre Dame Press, 1981

Mack, M. P., *Jeremy Bentham: An Odyssey of Ideas, 1748–92*, London, Heinemann, 1962

Mackenzie, R., *John Brown of Haddington* (1918), London, Banner of Truth Trust, 1964

McLachlan, H., *The Religious Opinions of Milton, Locke and Newton*, Manchester, Manchester University Press, 1941

MacLeod, J., *Scottish Theology in Relation to Church History since the Reformation*, 3rd edn, Edinburgh, Banner of Truth Trust, 1974

McNeilly, F., *The Anatomy of Leviathan*, London, Macmillan, 1968

Marshall, J., 'John Locke and Socinianism', in M. A. Stewart (ed.), *Oxford Studies in the History of Philosophy*, vol. 2, Oxford, Oxford University Press, forthcoming

Martin, D., 'Towards eliminating the concept of secularization', in J. Gould (ed.), *Penguin Survey of the Social Sciences*, Harmondsworth, Penguin, 1965

—— *The Religious and the Secular: Studies in Secularization*, Schocken Books, London, 1969

Matthews, S., *The Growth of the Idea of God*, New York, Macmillan, 1931

Maurice, F. D., *Life of Frederick Denison Maurice Chiefly Told in his Own Letters*, 2 vols, ed. F. Maurice, New York, Charles Scribner and Sons, 1884

—— *Theological Essays*, London, James Clark and Co., 1957

Meadley, G. W., *Memoirs of the Life of William Paley*, Edinburgh, 1810

Mill, J. S., *Three Essays on Religion*, New York, Henry Holt and Co., 1874

—— *Collected Works of John Stuart Mill*, ed. J. M. Robson, Toronto, Toronto University Press, 1969–

—— *Utilitarianism, On Liberty, and Considerations on Representative Government*, ed. H. B. Acton, London, Dent, 1972

Millar, J., *The Origin of the Distinction of Ranks*, London, 1771

—— *An Historical View of the English Government: From the Settlement of the Saxons in Britain to the Accession of the House of Stewart* (1787), 4 vols, London, 1803

Milton, J., *Areopagitica*, in *The Student's Milton*, ed. F. A. Patterson, New York, Appleton-Century-Crofts, 1930

Mintz, S., *The Hunting of Leviathan*, Cambridge, Cambridge University Press, 1962

Montuori, M., *John Locke: On Toleration and the Unity of God*, Amsterdam, J. C. Gieben, 1983

Moore, J., 'Natural sociability and natural rights in the moral philosophy of Gershom Carmichael', in V. Hope (ed.), *Philosophers of the Scottish Enlightenment . . . in Honour of George Davie*, Edinburgh, Edinburgh University Press, 1984

Moore, J., and Silverthorne, M., 'Gershom Carmichael and the natural jurisprudence tradition in eighteenth century Scotland', *Man and Nature/*

L'Homme et la nature, 1982, vol. 1, pp. 41–54

Namier, Sir L., and Brooke, J. (eds), *The House of Commons, 1754–1790*, The History of Parliament, London, Her Majesty's Stationery Office, 1964, vol. 2

Norman, E., *The Victorian Christian Socialists*, Cambridge, Cambridge University Press, 1987

Norton, D. F., *David Hume: Common-sense Moralist, Sceptical Metaphysician*, Princeton, NJ, Princeton University Press, 1982

Oakeshott, M., *Rationalism in Politics*, London, Methuen, 1962

O'Gorman, F., *Edmund Burke: His Political Philosophy*, Political Thinkers, London, Allen and Unwin, 1973

Olson, R., *Scottish Philosophy and British Physics, 1750–1880*, Princeton, NJ, Princeton University Press, 1975

Paley, W., *The Complete Works of William Paley, D.D.*, 4 vols, London, 1825

Parekh, B. (ed.), *Jeremy Bentham: Ten Critical Essays*, London, Frank Cass, 1974

Parker, S., *A Demonstration of the Divine Authority of the Law of Nature and of the Christian Religion*, London, 1681

Pintacuda de Michelis, F., *Socinianesimo e tolleranza nell'età del razionalismo*, Florence, La Nuova Italia, 1975

Plamenatz, J., 'Mr. Warrender's Hobbes', *Political Studies*, 1957, vol. 5, pp. 295–308

—— *The English Utilitarians*, Oxford, Basil Blackwell, 1958

Pocock, J. G. A., *The Machiavellian Moment*, Princeton, NJ, Princeton University Press, 1975

Popkin, R. H., 'Divine causality: Newton, the Newtonians, and Hume', in P. J. Korshin and R. R. Allen (eds), *Greene Centennial Studies: Essays Presented to Donald Greene in the Centennial Year of the University of Southern California*, Charlottesville, University Press of Virginia, 1984

Postema, G. J., *Bentham and the Common Law Tradition*, Oxford, Clarendon Press, 1986

Price, R., *A Discourse on the Love of our Country*, London, 1790

—— *Two Tracts on Civil Liberty*, New York, Da Capo Press, 1972

—— *A Review of the Principal Questions in Morals*, ed. D. D. Raphael, Oxford, Clarendon Press, 1974

Quinton, A., *The Politics of Imperfection: The Religious and Secular Traditions of Conservative Thought in England from Hooker to Oakeshott*, London, Faber and Faber, 1978

Ramsey, A. M., *F. D. Maurice and the Conflicts of Modern Theology*, Cambridge, Cambridge University Press, 1951

Reedy, G., *The Bible and Reason: Anglicans and Scripture in Late Seventeenth Century England*, Philadelphia, University of Pennsylvania Press, 1985

Robbins, C., *The Eighteenth Century Commonwealthmen*, Cambridge, Mass., Harvard University Press, 1961

Ross, I. S., *Lord Kames and the Scotland of his Day*, Oxford, Oxford University Press, 1972

Rowell, G., *Hell and the Victorians*, Oxford, Clarendon Press, 1978

Russell, J. L., 'Cosmological teaching in the seventeenth century Scottish universities,' parts I and II, *Journal of the History of Astronomy*, 1974, vol. 5, pp. 122–32, 145–54

Ryan, A., 'Hobbes, toleration and the inner life', in D. Miller and L. Siedentrop (eds), *The Nature of Political Theory*, Oxford, Oxford University Press, 1983

Sargentich, T., 'Locke and ethical theory: two MS pieces', *Locke Newsletter*, 1974, no. 5, pp. 24–31

Schmaus, W., 'A reappraisal of Comte's three-state law', *History and Theory*, 1982, vol. 21, pp. 248–66

Schneewind, J. B., *Sidgwick's Ethics and Victorian Moral Philosophy*, Oxford, Clarendon Press, 1977

Schofield, T. P., 'A comparison of the moral theories of William Paley and Jeremy Bentham', *The Bentham Newsletter*, 1987, no. 11, pp. 4–22

[Shaftesbury, Lord], *Several Letters Written by a Noble Lord to a Young Man at the University*, London, 1716

Shepherd, C. M., 'Philosophy and science in the arts curriculum of the Scottish universities in the seventeenth century', unpublished Ph.D. thesis, Edinburgh University, 1975

—— 'Newtonianism in Scottish universities in the seventeenth century', in H. Campbell and A. S. Skinner (eds), *The Origins and Nature of the Scottish Enlightenment*, Edinburgh, John Donald, 1982

——'The arts curriculum at Aberdeen at the beginning of the eighteenth century', in J. Carter and J. Pittock (eds), *Aberdeen and the Enlightenment*, Aberdeen, Aberdeen University Press, 1987

Sher, R., *Church and University in the Scottish Enlightenment: The Moderate Literati of Edinburgh*, Edinburgh, Princeton University Press, 1985

—— 'How moral was academic moral philosophy in eighteenth century Scotland?', in M. A. Stewart (ed.), *Oxford Studies in the History of Philosophy*, vol. 1, Oxford, Oxford University Press, 1989

Shiner, L., 'The meanings of secularization', in J. F. Childress and D. B. Harned (eds), *Secularization and the Protestant Prospect*, Philadelphia, Westminster Press, 1970

Skinner, A. S., *A System of Social Science: Papers Relating to Adam Smith*, Oxford, Clarendon Press, 1979

Skinner, Q., *The Foundations of Modern Political Thought*, 2 vols, Cambridge, Cambridge University Press, 1978

Smith, A., *The Theory of Moral Sentiments*, ed. A. L. Macfie and D. D. Raphael, Oxford, Oxford University Press, 1976

—— *An Inquiry into the Nature and Causes of the Wealth of Nations*, 2 vols, ed. R. H. Campbell, A. S. Skinner, and W. B. Todd, Oxford, Oxford University Press, 1976

—— *The Correspondence of Adam Smith*, ed. E. C. Mossner and I. S. Ross, Oxford, Clarendon Press, 1976

—— *Adam Smith: Essays on Philosophical Subjects*, ed. W. P. D. Wightman and J. C. Bryce, Oxford, Clarendon Press, 1980

Smout, T. C., *A History of the Scottish People, 1560–1830*, London, Collins, 1969

Spellman, W. M., *John Locke and the Problem of Depravity*, Oxford, Oxford Univerity Press, 1988

Steintrager, J., 'Morality and belief: the origins and purpose of Bentham's writings on religion', *The Mill News Letter*, 1971, vol. 6, no. 2, pp. 3–15
—— 'Language and politics: Bentham on religion', *The Bentham Newsletter*, 1980, no. 4, pp. 4–20
Stephen, L., *The English Utilitarians*, 3 vols, London, London School of Economics and Political Science, 1950
—— *History of English Thought in the Eighteenth Century* (1902), 2 vols, London, Rupert Hart-Davis, 1962
Stewart, M. A., 'Berkeley and the Rankenian Club', *Hermathena*, 1985, vol. 139, pp. 22–45
—— 'George Turnbull and educational reform', in J. Carter and J. Pittock (eds), *Aberdeen and the Enlightenment*, Aberdeen, Aberdeen University Press, 1987
Suarez, F., *Selections from Three Works*, ed. J. B. Scott, Classics of International Law, vol. 20, Oxford, Clarendon Press, 1927
Taylor, C., 'Atomism', in A. Kontos (ed.), *Powers, Possessions and Freedom*, Toronto, Toronto University Press, 1979
Tennant, R. C., 'The Anglican response to Locke's theory of personal identity', *Journal of the History of Ideas*, 1982, vol. 43, pp. 73–90
Thompson, E. P., *The Making of the English Working Class*, New York, Random House, 1966
[Trotter, C.], *A Defence of the Essay of Human Understanding*, London, 1702
Tuck, R., *Natural Rights Theories: Their Origin and Development*, Cambridge, Cambridge University Press, 1979
—— 'The "modern" theory of natural law', in A. Pagden (ed.), *The Languages of Political Thought in Early Modern Europe*, Cambridge, Cambridge University Press, 1987
Tully, J. H., *A Discourse on Property: John Locke and his Adversaries*, Cambridge, Cambridge University Press, 1980
—— 'Governing conduct', in E. Leites (ed.), *Conscience and Casuistry in Early Modern Europe*, Cambridge, Cambridge University Press, 1988
Tytler, A. F., *Plan and Outline of a Course of Lectures on Universal History*, Edinburgh, 1783
Unus de Multis, 'Modern Prophets', *Fraser's Magazine*, vol. 16, September 1877, pp. 273–92
VanLeeuwen, H. G., *The Problem of Certainty in English Thought, 1630-1690*, The Hague, Martinus Nijhoff, 1970
Vernon, R., 'The secular political culture: three views', *Review of Politics*, 1975, vol. 37, pp. 490–512
—— 'Auguste Comte and development: a note', *History and Theory*, 1978, vol. 17, pp. 232–6
Viner, J., *The Role of Providence in the Social Order: An Essay in Intellectual History*, Princeton, NJ, Princeton University Press, 1972
Voges, F., 'Moderate and evangelical thinking in the later eighteenth century: differences and shared attitudes', *Records of the Scottish Church History Society*, 1985, vol. 22, pp. 141–57
Walker, D. M., 'The importance of Stair's work for the modern lawyer', *Juridical Review*, 1981, vol. 26, pp. 161–76
Walker, J., *The Rev. Dr John Walker's Report on the Hebrides of 1764 and*

1771, ed. M. M. McKay, Edinburgh, John Donald, 1980

Wallace, D. D., 'Socinianism, justification by faith, and the sources of John Locke's *The Reasonableness of Christianity*', *Journal of the History of Ideas*, 1972, vol. 33, pp. 3–22

Warburton, W., *The Works of the Right Reverend William Warburton*, 12 vols, London, 1811

Waterman, A. M. C., 'The ideological alliance of political economy and Christian theology, 1798-1833', *Journal of Ecclesiastical History*, 1983, vol. 34, no. 2, pp. 231–44

—— 'A Cambridge *via media* in late Georgian Anglicanism', *Journal of the History of Ideas*, forthcoming

Watkins, J., *Hobbes's System of Ideas*, 2nd edn, London, Hutchinson, 1965

Webb, B., *My Apprenticeship*, London, Longmans, Green and Co., 1950

Weber, M., 'Science as a vocation', in *From Max Weber, Essays in Sociology*, ed. and trans. H. H. Gerth and C. W. Mills, Oxford, Oxford University Press, 1946

Weems, L. H., *The Gospel According to Wesley: A Summary of John Wesley's Message*, Nashville, Discipleship Resources, 1982

Wesley, J. (ed.), *Arminian Magazine*, vols. 5–7, London, 1782–4

—— *Minutes of the Methodist Conferences, From the First Held in London by the Late Rev. John Wesley A.M., in the Year 1744*, London, 1862

—— *The Journal of the Rev. John Wesley*, 8 vols, ed. N. Curnock, London, Robert Culley, 1909–16

—— *The Letters of the Rev. John Wesley, A.M.*, 8 vols, ed. J. Telford, London, The Epworth Press, 1931

—— *A Library of Protestant Thought*, ed. A. Outler, New York, Oxford University Press, 1964

—— *The Works of John Wesley*, 14 vols, ed. T. Jackson, Grand Rapids, Mich., Baker Book House, 1979

Whately, R., *Introductory Lectures in Political Economy*, London, 1831

Whewell, W., *Philosophy of the Inductive Sciences founded upon their History*, London, 1847

—— 'Bentham' (1862), in B. Parekh (ed.), *Jeremy Bentham: Ten Critical Essays*, London, Frank Cass, 1974

Whitehead, J. H. and Conlan, J., 'The establishment of the religion of secular humanism and its first amendment implications', *Texas Tech Law Review*, 1978–9, vol. 10, no. 1, pp. 1–66

Willey, B., *Nineteenth Century Studies*, Harmondsworth, Penguin, 1964

Williams, G. H. (ed.), *The Polish Brethren*, 2 vols, Missoula, Mon., Scholars Press, 1980

Witherspoon, J., *Ecclesiastical Characteristics: or the Arcana of Church Policy . . . the Character of a Moderate Man . . .* (1753), Edinburgh, 1843

Wodrow, R., *Analecta or Materials for a History of Remarkable Providences mostly relating to Scotch Ministers and Christians*, 4 vols, Edinburgh, 1842

Wood, P. B., 'Thomas Reid, natural philosopher: a study of science and philosophy in the Scottish Enlightenment', unpublished Ph.D. thesis, University of Leeds, 1984

—— 'Science and the pursuit of virtue in the Aberdeen Enlightenment', in M. A. Stewart (ed.), *Oxford Studies in the History of Philosophy*, vol. 1,

Oxford, Oxford University Press, 1989

Wootton, D., 'The fear of God in early modern political theory', *Historical Papers 1983/Communications Historiques*, Canadian Historical Association, pp. 56–80

Wright, T. R., *The Religion of Humanity: The Impact of Comtean Positivism on Victorian Britain*, Cambridge, Cambridge University Press, 1986

Yolton, J. W., *John Locke and the Way of Ideas*, Oxford, Oxford University Press, 1968

—— *Thinking Matter: Materialism in Eighteenth-Century Britain*, Minneapolis, University of Minnesota Press, 1983

Index

Abraham 28–9
absolutism, defence of (Locke) 42
Aikenhead, Thomas 70, 78
American revolution 111, 118
angels (Hobbes on) 34
Anglican National Schools Society 141
annihilation, as punishment for sin 45, 48
Apostle's Creed 47
Aristotle 32–3, 46, 70
Arminian Magazine 114
Arminianism 47, 156, 157
atheists 43, 45, 54, 55, 56, 60
atomism 70, 72
atonement 44, 45, 47, 48, 157
attributes of God 6, 50–2, 57, 59, 138

Bacon, Roger 19
Bacon, Francis 71, 72, 74, 80, 97
Bayle, Pierre 5, 51, 56, 61, 74, 79
— *Pensées Diversèes sur la Come* (1682) 56
Beccaria, Cesare 139
Bentham, Jeremy: anti-intuitive 91–2, 98–100, 103; atheistical works, suppression of 92; constructivist 95, 103, 106–7; education, views on 141, 142–3, 151n53; 'genius' and 101–3; Hume and 98–101; Helvétius and 98, 102–3, 139, 144; ideal state 142–3, 150n52; materialist 94, 99, 138–9; 'moral and legislative science' 92, 95, 97, 101–3, 106–7, 131, 138–9, 144–5; political establishment, attacks on 139–42; positivism 106; religion, attacks on 94–5, 132, 138–43, 150n52; science, views on 92, 94–7, 99, 106–7, 132, 143; utilitarianism 10, 97, 100–2, 106, 108n28, 131, 132–3, 138–44
— *An Analysis of the Influence of Natural Religion on the Temporal Happiness of Mankind* (1822) 132, 140, 142
— *Chrestomathia* (1816–17) 142, 143
— *Church-of-Englandism and its Catechism Examined* (1818) 132, 140, 141, 142
— *Constitutional Code* (1831) 142
— *Fragment on Government* (1776) 91
— *Introduction to the Principles of Morals and Legislation* (1789) 131, 139, 146
— *Not Paul, but Jesus* (1823) 132, 140, 142
— *Plan of Parlimentary Reform* (1817) 140
— *Supply without Burthen* (1795) 131
— *Swear Not at All* (1817) 140
— *A Table of the Springs of Action* (1817) 100, 131
Bible, as authority 25–7, 35, 71, 72, 73, 75, 76
Biddle, John 56

Boston, Thomas 78, 79
Boyle, Robert 69
Brown, John 10
Burke, Edmund: beauty and the
    senses 113–14; church 120–1;
    empiricism 113–14, 116; French
    Revolution 111, 115, 121–3;
    original contract 9, 122; Price and
    115–16; rights of man 111, 116;
    theory, rejection of 124–6
— *A Philosophical Enquiry into the
    Origin of our Ideas of the Sublime
    and Beautiful* (1756) 113, 118
— *Reflections on the Revolution in
    France* (1790) 111, 116, 121, 124,
    125
— *Sheriffs of Bristol* 116
Burnet, Gilbert 44, 49, 50, 51

Calvin, Jean 19
Calvinism 68, 77, 78, 79, 156, 157,
    158
Cambusland Work (1742) 78
Carmichael, Gershom 75, 76, 83
causal regression to a first mover 20,
    71
causality, Hume's theory of 96
Chartism 163
Chillingworth William 47, 71
— *The Religion of Protestants*
    (1638) 47
Christ, pre-existence of 45, 48
Christian socialist movement 154,
    163–4
church and state: alliance of 5, 137,
    141; distinction between 10,
    17–19, 29, 35, 46, 60, 120–1,
    136–7, 149n32
Cicero 56, 83
— *De Natura Deorum* 56
— *De Officiis* 83
'civilisation' (Mill) 178–9
Clarke, Samuel 7
clergy and laity, distinction of 48
coercion 176–8 *see also* sanctions
Coleridge, Samuel Taylor 137, 146,
    175
Comte, Auguste 12, 93, 146, 153,

    168, 169, 170, 171–2, 173, 175
Chadwick, Owen 3
conscience 6, 41–2, 44, 61, 100
contract, original: Bentham 101;
    Burke 9, 121–3; Locke 117–18;
    126; Wesley 9, 118 *see also*
    equality; liberty; rights of man
covenants, biblical 28–9, 31, 45
Crell, Samuel 46, 47, 56
Cumberland, Richard 42, 50, 51,
    65–35, 76

Davies, Horton 154, 156, 161
demonology 33
Descartes, René 52, 69
design, argument from 20, 71, 73,
    74, 132
doctrine, religious: authority of
    18–19, 27, 29, 30, 35; authority to
    prescribe 18–20, 27, 29–30, 31, 35
dreams (Hobbes on) 33, 37–65
Dryden, John 72
Durkheim, Emile 12

education 141–3, 151–53; of working
    classes 154, 164–7
Edwards, John 44, 47, 58
empiricism in natural and moral
    philosophy in Scotland
    1680–1800: 6–7, 72, 73, 74, 76,
    80–3
equality 61
Evangelicalism 10, 11, 78, 154,
    155–7, 158, 159–61, 164

Feathers Tavern petition (1772) 120,
    135
freedom of the will 61
French Enlightenment 96–7, 106
French National Assembly 121–3
French Revolution 9, 111, 115,
    121–3

Garden, Dr James 77
Gassendi, Pierre 69
'genius' 101–3
Gisbome, Thomas 145
God: attributes 6, 50–2, 57, 59, 138;

existence of 20, 50, 52, 71, 73, 74, 132

Grant, George 4, 12

Grotius, Hugo 43, 46, 47, 50, 76
— *De Iure Naturae* 43
— *De Veritate Religionis Christianae* (1640) 47

Halyburton, Thomas 70, 79

Hell 45, 48, 134, 155–8

Helvétius, Claude Adrien 97, 98, 101, 102, 103, 139, 144
— *De L'Esprit* (1758) 98, 101, 102, 144

Herbert, Edward 49, 50, 56
— *De Veritate* (1624) 49

historical writings, Scotland 1680-1800 70, 74–5, 80–1, 83–4

Hobbes, Thomas: authority in religion 5, 17–19, 27, 28, 29–30, 35; church and state 17–19, 29, 35; human nature 23, 26; 'kingdom' 26, 28–31, 35; natural law 5, 21–9, 31, 35, 40, 75; 'new science' 31–5; scriptural exegesis 5, 21, 26–35; sovereign's authority 5, 17–20, 27–31, 35; theology 4–5, 19–20, 31–5; visual perception 33, 34
— *de Cive* (1647) 22
— *Human Nature* 22
— *Leviathan* (1651) 5, 19, 23, 25, 26, 27, 28, 29, 30, 32, 44

Hobbism 40–3, 54–5, 59

Hume, David: causality, theory of 96; moral philosophy 101; obligations (moral duties) 101; religion 84, 93, 94–6; scepticism 8, 91, 93, 94–5; 'science of Man' 7, 97, 113; science, views on 7, 94–7, 103, 104, 106–7; utility 97, 101, 105, 108n28
— *Essays Moral, Political and Literary* 98
— *The Natural History of Religion* (1757) 84, 93, 94, 98
— *Treatise of Human Nature* 97, 98, 100, 101, 113

Hutcheson, Francis 7, 10, 76, 80, 100, 117

identity 44, 49, 52, 50, 66n41

immortality *see* soul, immortality of

infusion, divine 33–4

innate ideas, theory of 71, 114

Innes, Fr Thomas 74–5

'ipse-dixitism' 91–2, 100

Jews 18, 43, 45, 47, 48

Kames, Lord (Henry Home) 75, 76, 80, 81, 82

Kirk 77, 78, 79, 80

Lancasterian schools 140, 142

Latitudinarianism 46–7, 48, 57

Law, Edmund 10

laws, promulgation of 43, 50, 53–4, 59, 62–3, 66n47

Leibniz, Gottfried Wilhelm von 44, 49, 50, 116

Leighton, Robert 70, 71, 73, 75

liberty: Mill 175–7; Wesley 118 *see also* contract, original; equality; rights of man

Limborch, Philip van 46, 47, 48, 60
— *Theologia Christiana* (1686) 47, 48

Locke, John: changing views 40, 43, 48, 50–60; contract 117–18, 126; empiricism 112–16, 126; ethical hedonism 42, 43, 51, 54–6, 60, 61; exile 40, 56–7, 58; Hobbism 40–3, 54–5, 59; library of Socinian works 48, 56–7, 59, 60; natural law 6, 39, 41–3, 46, 49, 50–6, 58–9, 60, 61, 62–3, 117; possible interpretations 58–63; probability 52–3; promulgation 43, 50, 53–4, 59, 62–3, 66n47; secrecy 58, 60–1, 67n63; self-interest 42, 43, 51, 54–6, 60, 61; Socinianism 6, 39, 40, 43–4, 47–9, 50, 56–9, 60; theology 43–53, 56, 57, 59, 60, 61, 158, 173, 180
— *Essay Concerning Human*

Understanding (1689) 39, 40, 42, 44, 45, 48, 49, 50, 51, 52, 53, 54, 56, 57, 58, 59, 60, 61, 63, 112
— *Essays on Toleration* (1667) 57
— *Essays on the Law of Nature* (1663) 41, 42, 50, 55, 56
— *Ethica* (1692) 51
— 'Of Ethics in General' 53, 57, 58, 59, 60
— *A Letter Concerning Toleration* 18, 48, 60, 118, 173
— 'Morality' 54, 55
— *A Paraphrase and Notes on the Epistles of St. Paul* 42, 49, 50, 56, 57, 59, 60
— *The Reasonableness of Christianity* (1695) 39, 40, 43, 44, 45, 47, 48, 50, 54, 55, 56, 57, 58, 59, 60, 62
— 'Sacerdos' (1698) 56
— *Two Tracts on Government* 42
— *Two Treatises of Government* (1689) 39, 40, 42, 43, 50, 54, 55, 58, 59, 60, 63, 118
Loen, Arnold 3
Lucretius 69, 84
Luther, Martin 158, 174

MacIntyre, Alasdair 3
Maurice, Frederick Denison: Christian socialist movement 154, 163–4; eternity 158, 164; fellowship of man 162–3; nature of man 159–63; socialism and 154, 157, 162, 163–4, 164n7; theology 154–9, 163–4
— 'On eternal Life and Eternal Death' 157, 158
— *Theological Essays* (1853) 157
metempsychosis 49, 52, 53
Methodism 9, 112, 118–20, 123–4
Mill, John Stuart: 97; coercion 176–8; Comte 169–72; 'harm' principle 176–8; liberalism 170–1, 174–5, 180; liberty 175–7; 'personal consent' 172; 'practical infidelity' 172–3; religion of humanity 12, 146, 167–80;

theology 167–8, 172–3
— *On Liberty* (1859) 171–8 *passim*, 180
— *Utilitarianism* (1863) 170, 177
Millar, John 82, 97
Milton, John 173, 177
— *Areopagitica* 173
Molyneux, William 42, 44, 53
Montesquieu 76, 84, 94, 97
moral law: conscience 6, 41–2, 44, 61; legal moralism (Mill) 176–7; moral responsibility 44, 45, 61, 101; peace and 23–4; reason and 39, 42, 46, 50, 53, 54–5, 59, 60, 63, 76; revelation and 43, 50, 51, 56, 59, 61–2, 75; self-interest 42, 43, 51, 54–6, 60, 61 *see also* moral philosophy in Scotland; natural law
moral philosophy in Scotland 75–6, 82–3
moral responsibility 44, 45, 61
Morley, John 121
Morrow controversy 78
Moses 48, 75
Muslims 18, 47, 56

natural law: Hobbes 21–6, 28–9, 31, 35, 40; Locke 6, 39, 41–2, 43, 46, 49, 50–5, 58–9, 60, 61, 62, 117–18, 126; probability and 52–3 *see also* moral law
natural philosophy 7, 72–4, 81–2 *see also* science
natural religion 56
'new philosophy', impact of in Scotland 1680–1800 69–76
Newman, John Henry (Cardinal) 154, 159
Newton, Sir Isaac 53, 54, 73, 81, 96, 97
— *Optics* (1704) 81
— *Principia* 53
Nicole, Pierre 56, 61
Norris, John 114

opinion, public 41, 43, 55
ordination 48

original contract *see* contract, original
original sin 44, 45, 47, 48, 57, 60, 61
Owen, Robert 10–11, 153
Oxford Movement 163

Pagans 18, 47, 56
Paine, Thomas 120, 136
Paley, William: conservatism 131,
    134–8, 143; church and state
    136–7, 149n32; theology 135,
    137–8; unintended consequences,
    theory of 136; utilitarianism
    132–8, 143–6
— 'A Distinction of Orders in the
    Church, Defended upon Principles
    of Public Utility' (1783) 135
— *Evidences of Christianity* (1794)
    134
— *Natural Theology* (1802) 134
— *Principles of Moral and Political
    Philosophy* (1785) 131, 134, 135,
    136, 146
— *Reasons for Contentment* (1792)
    136
Parker, Samuel 42, 50
Pascal, Blaise 52, 53, 172
Pascal's wager 52–3
peace, as motivation for moral
    virtues 23
philanthropic activity in second half
    of nineteenth century 153–4, 164
Pitcairne, Archibald M.D. 72, 73, 74
'practical infidelity' 172–3
predestination 44, 45, 48
Price, Richard 115–16
— *A Discourse on the Love of our
    Country* (1790) 115
— *Observations on Civil Liberty* 115
— *A Review of the Principle
    Questions in Morals* 115
— *Two Tracts on Civil Liberty*
    (1778) 115
priesthood of all believers 48
probability and natural law 52–3
promulgation of laws 43, 50, 53–4,
    59, 62–3, 66n47
property 55, 136

Przypkowski 46, 56
public opinion 41, 43, 55
Pufendorf, Samuel von 75, 76, 83
punishment of wicked in Hell 45, 48,
    134, 155–8
Puritanism 112

Racovian Catechism 44, 56 *see also*
    Socinianism
reason, as basis for religious belief:
    Hobbes 19–21; Locke 47, 48, 49,
    54, 62; Scottish Enlightenment 69,
    70, 71, 73, 75, 76
redemption 44, 45, 47, 48, 157
reductionists 168
Reid, Thomas 74, 80, 81, 82, 100,
    114
reincarnation 49, 52, 53
resurrection: body of 44, 47, 49;
    Christ 45, 46, 47, 48, 54
revelation, as basis of religious
    belief: Hobbes 19–21, 23, 24–9,
    31, 35; Locke 41, 49, 50, 52–3,
    61–2; Scottish Enlightenment
    69–70, 71, 75, 85
rights of man: Burke 111, 116;
    Locke 6, 61, 62, 63; Mill 177 *see
    also* contract, original; equality;
    liberty
Rousseau, Jean-Jacques 145, 175

sanctions 18, 41, 42, 43, 49, 50, 51,
    52, 55, 56, 57, 62–3, 176–8
science: Bentham and 92, 94–7, 99,
    106–7, 143; Hobbes and 31–3, 35;
    religion and 7; *see also* natural
    philosophy
scientific enthusiasm, reaction
    against 92
'scientism' as term 92–6; atheistic 93
'scientist' as term 90–1, 95
Scotland 1680-1800: empiricism
    6–7, 72, 73, 74, 76, 80–3;
    historical writings 70, 74–5, 80–1,
    83–4; Kirk 77, 78, 79, 80; the
    Moderates 78–80; moral
    philosophy 75–6, 82–3; natural

philosophy 7, 72–4, 81–2; the new
philosophy 69–76; Scots law 75;
social sciences 82–3; theology and
religious practice 6–7, 68, 80, 84–5
Scots Law 75
Scottish Enlightenment 100–1, 105
'secular humanism' 12–13, 16n22
semantics 26, 31, 32, 34, 35
senses 112, 113–15
Shaftesbury, Third Earl of 10, 42,
76, 92
Shaftesbury, Seventh Earl of 154,
165n34
Sibbald, Sir Robert M.D. 72, 73, 74,
75, 83
slavery, negro 118, 135
Smith, Adam: religion 93–6;
scepticism 8, 91, 94–5; science,
views on 8, 94–7, 103–5, 106–7;
scientific method, theory of
103–4; utility 97, 104, 106,
108n28, 179
— *The History of Astronomy* 91, 94
— *An Inquiry into the Nature and
Causes of the Wealth of Nations*
105
— *The Theory of Moral Sentiments*
(1759) 94
social duty 155, 158–9, 163
social sciences: in Scotland 82–3 *see
also* Bentham, 'moral and
legislative science'
socialism 11, 157, 163; Christian
163; Owenite 10–11, 16n18
socialism (Owenite) 10–11, 16n18
Socinianism: beliefs 44–7, 65n24;
Locke and 6, 39, 40, 43–4, 47–9,
50, 56–9, 60; Scotland 73 *see also*
Racovian Catechism
Socinus 44, 46
soul: immortality of 44–53 *passim*,
55, 59, 60, 61, 134; material 44,
52; sleep of 44, 49, 52 *see also*
eternity concept; identity;
reincarnation
Spinoza, Baruch 68
Stair (James Dalrymple, First

Viscount of Stair) 75, 76, 86n16
state law 41, 55
Stephen, Leslie 121
Stillingfleet, Edward Bishop 44, 71
Suarez, Francisco 24

theology and religious practice in
Scotland 1680–1800: 6–7, 68–80,
84–5
Thirty-Nine Articles 120, 135, 136
Thompson, E.P. 112, 124
Tillotson, John, Archbishop 71, 77
Tocqueville, Alexis Clérel de 170,
173
Toland, John: *Christianity not
Mysterious* 44
toleration, religious 10, 18, 19, 42,
46, 57, 58, 77, 78, 134
Trinitarianism 47, 73, 135
Trinity, doctrine of 44, 45, 47, 48
Tyrrell, James 40, 41, 42, 49, 50, 51,
53, 59, 60

Unitarian Toleration Bill (1813) 140
Unitarians 48, 56
utilitarianism 132; Anglican
advocates eighteenth century 130;
Bentham 10, 97–8, 100–2, 106,
131, 132–3, 138–44; Hume 105;
Mill 97, 108n28; Paley 132–4,
135–8, 143–5, 146; Smith 97, 104,
106, 108n28

Voltaire 112, 113, 116
— *Candide* (1759) 113, 116
— *Micromégas* (1752) 113

Warburton, William 5, 10, 14, 93,
137
Webb, Beatrice 153, 155, 160
Wesley, John: American Revolution
111, 118; contract 9, 118–20;
empiricism 114–15; liberty 118;
Methodism 9, 112, 118–20,
123–4; senses 114–15; theology
111, 116–17, 155–6, 161; theory
and 123–6

Whewell, William 90, 91, 92, 94
Whitefield, George 155, 156, 157,
161

Wollaston, William 7

Zwingli, Ulrich 19